Vera Nünning, Jan Rupp, Gregor Ahn (Eds.)
Ritual and Narrative

Cultural and Media Studies

Vera Nünning, Jan Rupp, Gregor Ahn (eds.)
Ritual and Narrative
**Theoretical Explorations
and Historical Case Studies**

[transcript]

The publication of this book has been made possible by a generous grant from the DFG (German Research Foundation).

Bibliographic information published by the Deutsche Nationalbibliothek
The Deutsche Nationalbibliothek lists this publication in the Deutsche Nationalbibliografie; detailed bibliographic data are available in the Internet at http://dnb.d-nb.de

© 2013 transcript Verlag, Bielefeld

All rights reserved. No part of this book may be reprinted or reproduced or utilized in any form or by any electronic, mechanical, or other means, now known or hereafter invented, including photocopying and recording, or in any information storage or retrieval system, without permission in writing from the publisher.

Cover layout: Kordula Röckenhaus, Bielefeld
Cover picture: thokai / photocase.com
Proofread and Typeset by: Jan Rupp, Lea Marquart, Nina Schneider
Printed by: Majuskel Medienproduktion GmbH, Wetzlar
ISBN 978-3-8376-2532-5

Contents

Preface and Acknowledgments | vii

Ritual and Narrative: An Introduction
Vera Nünning & Jan Rupp | 1

I. THEORETICAL EXPLORATIONS: FORMS, FUNCTIONS, AND SOCIAL PRACTICE OF RITUAL AND NARRATIVE

Ritual Studies and Narratology:
What Can They Do For Each Other
Marie-Laure Ryan | 27

On the Narrativity of Rituals:
Interfaces between Narratives and Rituals
and Their Potential for Ritual Studies
Vera & Ansgar Nünning | 51

Obama's American Narrative:
A Narratological Approach to Complex Rituals
Roy Sommer | 77

II. HISTORICAL CASE STUDIES OF DIFFERENT MEDIA AND CULTURAL CONTEXTS: RITUAL AND NARRATIVE IN DEPTH

Depicting Sacrifice in Roman Asia Minor:
Narratives of Ritual in Classical Archaeology
Günther Schörner | 103

"He had just finished presenting the burnt offering ...":
Narrative and Ritual in the Context of Saul's Failure
(1 Sam 13-14)
Joachim Vette | 131

**Two Types of Magic in One Tradition?
A Cognitive-Historiographical Case Study
on the Interplay of Narratives and Rituals**
Dirk Johannsen | 165

**Ritual, Narrative, and Identity in
English Pageant Fictions of the Interwar Years**
Jan Rupp | 189

**Ritual and Narrative in the Intercultural British Novel
at the Turn of the 21st Century**
Scarlett Meyer | 217

**How to Commemorate a Fallen Soldier:
Ritual and Narrative in the Bundeswehr**
Stefanie Hammer | 237

Notes on Contributors | 267

Preface and Acknowledgments

Ritual and narrative feature prominently in the current discussion of cultural meaning-making. Even in the so-called secular West, we are witnessing a "return" or dynamic transformation of old rituals and the "design" of new ones, catering to what is arguably a timeless human need. Likewise, narrative and storytelling are now frequently seen as an anthropological constant, and they are revealed as a paramount social and cultural activity in a wide variety of areas of human life. This recent success story of ritual and narrative as academic topics and master tropes for engaging with the overarching cultural processes they shape makes it all the more surprising that there are only very few studies which have concerned themselves with the connections between ritual and narrative. And yet, these two forms of cultural expression have many features in common: stories frequently shape and appear in rituals, while rituals regularly become the subject of narratives. Moreover, there is often a ritualistic aspect to storytelling, narrative form, and genre.

Once we began to engage in a dialogue about the two phenomena and their fields of study, we soon got a sense of the close interconnection between ritual and narrative, of the manifold ways they feed into each other in cultural artifacts and activities, and of the intricate intellectual history they share. We therefore decided to initiate an interdisciplinary debate on the question of how models and categories from narrative theory might benefit the analysis of ritual, and, vice versa, of what we might gain from concepts of ritual studies in analysing narrative. At an international conference in Heidelberg in 2011, we were joined by colleagues from a wide range of disciplines including literary studies, archaeology, religious studies, and political science. We benefitted greatly from our discussions and their fruitful contributions, which are collected as theoretical explorations and historical case studies in this volume on the theory, history and media of ritual and narrative.

Our first and greatest thanks, therefore, goes to the contributors of this volume, and we are sorry it has taken longer for it to appear than we had hoped. We are also grateful to our colleagues at the Collaborative Research Centre on "Ritual Dynamics" at the University of Heidelberg, who generously shared their ideas and gave their support to this project in one way or another. The members of our working group were especially helpful, and the meetings with them were always as productive as they were pleasant. We are particularly grateful to Antony Pattathu, Carina Brankovič and Katharina Wetzel. We should like to single out for special thanks and praise Fletcher DuBois, whom we thank for pointing out international colleagues that might be interested in our project, for his generous hospitality and for his creative academic as well as musical contributions to our meetings. Anke Poppen at transcript publishers as well as our student assistants Lea Marquart, Nina Schneider, Jennifer Smith and Martin Zettersten were an invaluable help in preparing the manuscript for publication. Last but not least, we wish to thank the directorial board of the Collaborative Research Centre on "Ritual Dynamics" and the German Research Foundation (DFG) for generously covering the publication costs of this volume.

Vera Nünning, Jan Rupp & Gregor Ahn
Heidelberg, August 2013

Ritual and Narrative: An Introduction

VERA NÜNNING & JAN RUPP

Why bring together two phenomena which, at first sight, seem to be worlds apart? The odds seem to be overwhelming, especially since there is anything but agreement on what exactly "a ritual" is – not to mention the variety of approaches which provide definitions of narrative. And still it seems to be fruitful to bring together these two fields of study, which may turn out to have more in common than meets the eye. During several sessions of the collaborative research centre on "ritual dynamics" at Heidelberg University, it turned out that scholars concerned with the exploration of rituals often not only deal with, but are interested in narratives, just as a few narratologists have succumbed to the fascination of ritual studies. After all, both narratives and rituals provide structure and meaning to our lives, both appeal to the emotions, and both create worlds which have enchanted participants and readers for thousands of years. In spite of the apparent "uselessness" of rituals, which are neither necessary for survival in communities of hunters and gatherers, nor for life in complex modern societies, rituals have not lost their attractiveness. Indeed, in the contemporary world, old and new rituals seem to be more omnipresent than ever before, developing a wide range of forms and instances of "ritual design" even in the virtual world of the internet.[1]

---

1   For the concept and manifold phenomena of ritual design in present-day religious as well as secular contexts, see the volume *Ritualdesign. Zur kultur- und ritualwissenschaftlichen Analyse ‚neuer' Rituale* by Karolewski et al.

Moreover, in recent years, in which the functions and values of everything the humanities are concerned with have become subjected to scrutiny, narratologists have increasingly become aware of the ubiquity of narratives as well as the usefulness of narratological categories. Developed for a better understanding of literary works, the application of the "toolkit" of narratology to non-fictional texts has become one of the concerns of new developments in narratology. In this volume, we want to widen the existing scope of applications by extending it to ritual studies. In contrast to the (as yet rather small) number of books which use narratological categories in order to understand particular texts, such as the Bible, or particular images, we aim to establish a link between narratology and a whole field of studies, which includes the exploration of a wide range of different genres and images. After all, rituals are not only told and transmitted via verbal stories, they are also performed in various media; and the historical and geographical range covered in this volume reaches from rituals depicted in Mesopotamian friezes to those performed by German politicians in military contexts today.

In contrast to many (both productive and fruitful) attempts to use narratological categories as a "tool" in order to better understand non-fictional narratives in different media, in this volume we want to establish a dialogue between ritual studies and narratology. Instead of just extending the scope of applications of narrative theory, we have gathered specialists from various areas in order to explore the link between ritual studies and narratology. The contributions in this volume draw on perspectives from disciplines as varied as classical archaeology, religious studies, biblical hermeneutics and literary studies to scrutinize the nexus between ritual and narrative.

We proceed from the assumption that narrative structures and the telling of stories play an important role in rituals and ritual practice, just as ritual can be an important dimension of narrative. Storytelling often has an explicitly ritualistic character, especially where everyday stories are concerned. We indulge in telling and listening to stories to derive a tried-and-tested sense of meaning and aesthetic pleasure, similar to that which we glean from participating in a ritual. The same holds true for complex literary narratives, which have to refer to and repeat some kind of formula such as a genre even if they seek to subvert that script. As Wolfgang Braungart argues in *Ritual und Literatur*, ritual is a central aspect of literature as a symbolic practice: both ritual and literature can be viewed as forms of self-knowledge and cultural self-interpretation utilized by individuals and communities. This is evidenced in particular by popular literary forms such as occasional poetry, a kind of literature that has a fixed, ritualized place in the production and consumption not only by expert but also by ordinary writers and readers (see Braungart 24).

However, before we can go on to explore the links between rituals and narrative – and the value of exemplary interpretations of rituals in different media – it is necessary to at least briefly clarify what we understand by the terms "ritual" and "narrative," which, despite their ubiquity in everyday usage, are anything but simple or self-explanatory. Where definitions of ritual are concerned, one might as well start by acknowledging that "[d]efining the term 'rituals' is a notoriously problematic task. The number of definitions proposed is endless, and no one seems to like the definitions proposed by anyone else" (Snoek 3). It is not only the long history of debates about ritual, but also a certain scepticism and "general neglect of theory in ritual studies" (Kreinath et al. xv) which has produced a plethora of existing and often incompatible definitions. There is no shortage of "classic" and highly influential concepts of ritual, such as Victor Turner's formulation that "[b]y 'ritual' I mean prescribed formal behaviour for occasions not given over to technical routine, having reference to belief in mystical beings and powers" (Turner, *Forest* 19). However, this formulation is also a telling example of the waning currency and measure of disagreement besetting many definitions of ritual. The close connection drawn by Turner between ritual and religion, though true for many (and especially pre-modern) contexts and cultures of ritual, has (rightly) been criticized with a view to the widely mooted "return" of ritual in post-industrial Western societies, where many rituals or "ritual-like activities" (cf. Bell 138ff.) more often than not seem to lack a distinct religious character. Thus, religion is a case in point for the difficulty in deciding what the central characteristics of ritual are.[2]

This general difficulty (with any definition of anything) is exacerbated by the empirical approach in many projects of ritual studies, in the course of which scholars often have to realize that the "etic" (i.e. observer) perspective which they bring to a particular ritual is likely to be at odds with a

---

2   See Kreinath et al. xvi: "The scholarly concept of religion [...] came into being roughly simultaneously with the modern term 'ritual'. On the other hand, the inherently religious character of ritual can no longer be taken for granted, and this posits a challenge for theorizing both religion and ritual."

heterogeneous set of "emic" (participant) points of view. Some scholars then choose to stop defining their object of study altogether and focus on documenting the wide variety of emic "constructions" of ritual instead. This empirical approach often claims political or ethical motives for not wanting to impose an outside view on the self-understanding and experience of participants, but apart from this political (or politically correct) and sometimes overly self-congratulatory gesture the approach seems to be susceptible to positivistic relativism and conceptual defeatism. It is rather impracticable and academically limiting for anyone who wants to move beyond empirical research and tackle the theoretical work (deductive as much as inductive, normative as much as empirical) required to conceptualize the relationship between ritual and narrative, for example.

To get to grips with the "ritual" part of the equation explored in this volume, therefore, it bears repeating that "[a] theoretical discussion of ritual(s) can hardly avoid the tedious question of the definition of ritual" (Kreinath et al. xvii). Scholars of ritual have recently put forward a number of fruitful answers to this "tedious" question, which all share a belief that rituals cannot be identified by (and reduced to) a common set of essential characteristics. On the contrary, they have argued that rituals constitute a relatively open and flexible class of phenomena held together by Wittgensteinian "family resemblances." In this way, rituals are not seen as "monothetic," where a "(set of) characteristic(s) is present in all the members of the class," but as "polythetic": "Polythetic characteristics [...] are not present in all members of a polythetic class, but each occurs in a majority of them." (Snoek 5) Though no longer as a compulsory dimension as suggested by Turner, even religion can be part of such a polythetic definition of ritual again, because a polythetic class allows for rituals which are not defined by religion (though by other characteristics also shared by "religious" rituals).

To flesh out a polythetic definition of ritual which will have many points of contact and convergence with narrative "the task is no longer to search for a *few essential* characteristics of 'rituals', which unambiguously distinguish between them and everything else" (7; italics in the original). On the contrary, it is advisable to "sum up *as large as possible* a collection of characteristics which are typical for *most* rituals, or at least for those being considered in a particular project" (ibid.; italics in the original), such as conceptualizing the nexus between ritual and narrative. Such a collection may consist of a long list of characteristics, including the view of ritual as "culturally constructed," "marked off from the routine of everyday life," "structured; patterned; ordered; sequenced; rule-governed," or "formal(ized)" (11). It is obvious from these characteristics that there are some crucial points of departure here for juxtaposing and comparing ritual with major features of narrative (discussed in more detail below). For example, these points of departure include the cultural specificity or "situatedness" of narrative, or aspects of plot, narrative self-reflexivity, and genre.

While polythetic definitions may well cast their net wide and start by listing a large number of characteristics, it is pragmatic to then narrow down this list in order to arrive at a workable and more succinct definition. Thus, Catherine Bell makes out six key features by which rituals or ritual-like activities are characterized. These are "formalism," "traditionalism," "invariance," "rule-governance," "sacral symbolism," and "performance" (cf. Bell 138ff.). More specifically, "formalism" highlights the fact that ritual is different from informal or casual behaviour, and marked off by formalized speech, gestures, and movement. "Traditionalism" refers to the way in which rituals appeal to a long pre-history of ritual practice as a source of legitimization. "Invariance" indicates that rituals are based on an ideal of repetition and faithful re-enactment. "Rule-governance" requires that rituals follow prescribed rules which govern and facilitate interaction. "Sacral symbolism" is a dimension by which rituals use symbols to evoke a higher reality, either connected to religious life or to the sacred in a metaphorical sense, such as the collective, transcendent values of a group or nation. Finally, "performance" as a central element of rituals emphasizes the fact that rituals are based on immediate, bodily enactment or embodiment.

While some of these features are specific to ritual, such as (bodily) performance as opposed to verbal (narrative) representation, other characteristics are no doubt suggestive of similarities with narrative. For example, traditionalism and rule-governance in ritual seem to converge with the generic forms and conventional plot patterns that many narratives follow, even though narratives tend to make a point of deviating from as much as adhering to conventional patterns. In this respect, Bell's list of characteristics would need to be extended by the sense of transgression or "anti-structure" which scholars like Turner have claimed for ritual, and which aligns ritual with narrative (and its norm-breaking aspects) despite the measure of rule-governance they otherwise share.[3] Another item in Bell's list that is highly conducive to comparing ritual and specifically literary narrative is her emphasis on symbolism. The use of symbols and aesthetic elements more broadly is a central but also sometimes underestimated dimension of ritual.

Another useful definition of ritual has been put forward by Axel Michaels, who lists five key elements by which rituals are to be defined: "performance/embodiment," "formality," "framing," "transformation/efficacy," and "transcendence" (4f.). As can easily be seen, elements one, two and five clearly correspond with items in Bell's list ("transcendence" squaring with Bell's "sacral symbolism"). In addition, Michaels stresses framing as a key feature of ritual, i.e. a clear demarcation or stipulation of beginning and end. Framing in his view also requires an intentional act (a declaration of "*intentio solemnis*," 5) on the part of the ritual community, designating a given ritual as such. Michaels does not consider the aesthetic or symbolic dimension of ritual, but he in turn gives prominence to aspects of process, transformation, and change, which (though in different ways) are characteristics of narrative, too, both within and outside of the text.[4] Taken together, Bell and Michaels provide a good working definition and starting point to involve ritual in a dialogue with narrative. As recent perspectives and concepts of ritual dynamics and ritual design[5] generally make clear, ritual is culturally constructed as much as historically variable, rather like narrative, and far removed from stereotypical and obsolete views of ritual as a petrified and immutable cultural practice.

To explore and conceptualize the connection between ritual and narrative further, accounts of the former as discussed above now need to be complemented with a definition of the latter. Unsurprisingly, and as with

---

3   For the tripartite model of "structure – anti-structure – structure," which he reveals as the basic scheme of rituals, cf. Turner, *Ritual Process*.

4   For the shift in attention on aspects of "process" in ritual studies, see Kreinath et al. xix: "'process' has become a key-term in ritual theory. [...] Recent theorizing attaches greater importance to ludic elements in rituals and stresses the emergent qualities of rituals."

5   For the concept and definition of ritual design as a type of ritual dynamics characterized by intentional acts of transforming a given ritual and adapting it to a new situation, see Ahn, "Ritualdesign" and "Ritual Design."

ritual, definitions of narrative are much less straightforward than one might wish.

While more or less every child from age three or four is able to understand and construct stories of various forms – including excuses and stories which more or less subtly transfer the blame for the spilled milk to someone or something else – it is anything but easy to arrive at a precise definition of narrative. There is no doubt a wide variety of narratives. Moreover, media conventions frequently serve to heighten differences between a "paradigmatic" or "prototypical" story, like a coherent account of events told by a narrator in verbal form to a listener on the one hand, and "the story" of a drama or the narrative constructed jointly over the course of several weeks by a psychiatrist and his or her patient on the other. In order to cope with this wide variety of existing narratives, it has been suggested to define narrativity by way of "narratemes," in a term coined by Gerald Prince. Taking a cognitive approach to narrative, Prince views narrative as a macro-schema which is either triggered by the context in which we encounter narrative, e.g., literary works displayed under "fiction" in a bookshop, or by text-internal features (cf. Prince). These text-internal features, which include basic elements such as character or different types of action and chronological sequence, Prince calls narratemes, which can be further systematized into "content narratemes," "syntactic narratemes" and "qualitative narratemes," the latter referring to elements of narrative which evoke a certain kind of narrative experientiality (cf. Wolf). Adding up to a "morphology" of narrative, narratemes are the micro-frames which constitute a narrative work of art and which determine its grade of narrativity.[6]

This is certainly an ingenious way to solve the problem of ordering the wide field of narratives, but it is not sufficient in a context in which the relation between narratives and rituals is the focus of attention. We therefore want to suggest a number of features which can serve to define narratives. In the following account, we draw upon and integrate current conceptualizations, but it has to be admitted that there are any number of disagreements between narratologists, especially with regard to the weighting of the different features.[7]

---

6 See Schwanecke for a summary of the theoretical debate on narratemes.
7 The following brief overview, drawing on a number of narratological and psychological definitions of narrative, is a summary of (and partly quoted from)

First, narratives are characterized by the fact that they are addressed by a human being at a specific point in time with a particular cultural background to someone else.[8] This does not presuppose that every narrative must be told to someone who is able to personally listen to the teller. Indeed, stories are often used to make sense of situations by telling them to oneself. Moreover, narratives must "communicate something meaningful to the recipient," which also implies that narratives are placed in specific contexts, in cultures with shared values, beliefs, canons and story schemata, and in particular spatio-temporal settings (Ryan 8).[9] This situatedness in a cultural context informs the narrative world on many different levels: it influences the selection of what is depicted, the choice of register and style as well as genre conventions and patterns of causality.[10] Situatedness can also be considered a major aspect of ritual practice. Marriage rituals, for example, differ widely depending on the cultural setting in which they are performed, even if the same religious denomination is concerned. Contexts of migration and displacement often make it necessary to adapt the ritual, in a process of "ritual transfer" (cf. Langer, Motika, and Ursinus).

---

several texts in which Vera Nünning has put forth definitions of narrative; see Nünning, "Making of Fictional Worlds" as well as chapter two of *Fiction and Cognition* (in preparation). There is a host of definitions of narrative, which can be grouped into those which conceptualize it as a feature of texts, a rhetoric act or a cognitive pattern. Narratological definitions can also be distinguished by focus of attention: some concentrate on the plot (story/events), others on narrative transmission (discourse) or "experientiality."

8   Cf. Herman, "Narrative Ways" 74; McAdams 111.
9   Ryan's definition of narrative also includes many of the features which will be listed in the following (apart from embedded values, the perspectivization and the levels of narration; Ryan is concerned with narratives in different media). For a discussion of the importance of the addressee and the expectations of (sub)cultures see Nünning, "Erzählen und Identität."
10 In Bruner's account, this relation to the context is termed context sensitivity, and discussed together with the concept of negotiability (Bruner, "Narrative Construction" 16f.).

Just like rituals, narratives are cultural ways of world-making; they present a model of a world which changes.[11] This seemingly simple characteristic implies a number of aspects, which are often treated separately. On the one hand, readers must be able to construct a relatively coherent mental model of the narrative world; it is often stressed that there have to be characters that resemble human beings acting in a more or less defined space and time; there have to be agents with characteristics, intentions, thoughts and feelings. On the other hand, the occurrence of some kind of event is necessary, since the presence of a "plot" distinguishes narratives from descriptions or other forms of discourse. The transformation may be minimal or only take place in the consciousness of a character, but an event is necessary. Many theorists prefer an emphatic conception of an event, among them Tzvetan Todorov, Jerome Bruner and David Herman.[12] Bruner introduced the concept of "tellability" and the "breach of expectations" raised by a canonical story.[13]

Like stories, rituals also constitute a world of their own. Rituals are set off from the everyday world, often through a particular form of framing such as a ringing of bells, specific gestures or a formal announcement that the ritual begin (see Michaels 4). Like story worlds, ritual worlds are not static, but may change in the course of the ritual action. Importantly, rituals imply change and transformation not least for those participating in the ritual, as in initiation rituals, for example. In this latter sense, transformation has been described as one of the defining features of rituals.

In contrast to rituals, which frequently involve a large number of participants and in which different rites and events can occur in different spaces (for instance in processions, in which the pilgrims perform ritualistic acts in different places at the same time), narratives are linear; even events that happen simultaneously have to be brought into some kind of order.[14] Even

---

11 For the importance of Nelson Goodman's concept of "ways of world-making" see V. Nünning, A. Nünning, and Neumann, *Cultural Ways of Worldmaking*.
12 See the very good summary of the state of the discussion, which mentions a host of other scholars as well, Herman, *Basic Elements* 132-135.
13 Cf. Bruner, "Narrative Construction" 73f., and "Self-making."
14 In postmodern narratives, this feature of narratives was subjected to parodic plays as well: Bryan Stanley Johnson, in his novel *Albert Angelo* (1964), for in-

though the sequences chosen in most narratives do not conform strictly to the chronology of their story world – there are few stories without at least some flashbacks – this linearity also implies the construction of something only seemingly simple: the choice of a beginning, a middle and an end. These are of overall importance as far as our understanding of the respective event or development is concerned. In western societies, for instance, we tend to see narrative beginnings also as origins, as the "root" of what happened later. As Niels Buch Leander points out in a remarkable essay, "there can be no beginning independent of the particular narrative we bring to it" (Leander 19) – without a story, it remains a random date. We need beginnings as well as endings in order to make sense of our experience. In spite of the simultaneity of events in some rituals, sequentiality is a major concern of ritual studies, too. Because of their iterative character, rituals rely on recognizable sequences of ritual action almost by definition. These typical patterns of ritual action have been described as elementary building blocks of a "grammar" of ritual (see Gladigow).

Stories do not just relate events, but also experiences; they express a sense of "what it's like" for the characters involved in the events. Narrative representation "also conveys the *experience* of living through this story-world-in-flux, highlighting the pressure of events on real or imagined consciousness affected by the occurrences at issue" (Herman, "Narrative Ways" 73).[15] There are, of course, differences in degree, with modernist novels, for instance, featuring more "experientiality" than history books – but even stories which do not focus on the emotions or the consciousness of the characters imply them. Because of their construction of an alternative, ritual world, rituals have a strong experiential dimension, too. The degree of transformation that many rituals involve is frequently the product of a multi-sensory experience, involving mind and body.

Stories are always told by a narrator embodying a particular perspective; the narrative that is constructed of a particular event is always formed by the narrator's knowledge or beliefs, his or her values, dispositions, emotions and intentions: in a narrative, objectivity is not an option. Even in lit-

---

stance, occasionally uses two columns next to each other to indicate simultaneity.

15 The most important publication on the topic is Fludernik's *Towards a 'Natural' Narratology*.

erary works featuring an "authorial narrator," who is held to be omniscient and objective, there is no neutral description; the choice of "omniscience" also implies a particular standpoint, even though it often masks itself as "universal" and "neutral." In addition, narratives usually depict a number of points of view of various characters. These perspectives can converge, but more often they do not: "tellable" stories imply some breach of what is expected, and this is often connected to different points of view and the heterogeneous or even contradictory plans and goals of the characters involved in the event. The concept of the perspective of a story can also apply to a still higher level of abstraction; apart from the "perspectives" of characters and narrators it can refer to the story at large, for even the positioning of the different voices in a narrative implies a particular perspective upon it. In rituals, the concept of perspectivization on the one hand applies to the emic points of view of different participants – ranging from those seeking help to priests or healers. In narratives describing the events, on the other hand, the "etic" perspective of the storyteller or the observer of the ritual becomes important, too.

Like rituals, narratives are characterized by embedded values which are due to, for instance, the selection of what is told and what is left out; the weighting of the events; the establishment of relations between different characters (and their relative distance to the narrator). All of these aspects imply a moral positioning (see Lucius-Hoene and Deppermann 43, 234), even apart from the host of evaluative comments uttered by characters and/or narrators, which in everyday communication make up roughly 30% of the story. Narratives create a world with an inherent set of values and beliefs. Quite often, narratives confirm, popularize and disseminate cultural values, sometimes they modify or subvert them. Especially stories that are "tellable" in Bruner's sense – that is, stories that are interesting in that they do not only repeat well-known schemata – construct their own morality; they establish text-internal norms which supply the reference to which the behaviour of the characters and/or narrators is to be judged.

Values and norms are at the heart of ritual practice, too. Rituals frequently serve to express and legitimize a certain set of beliefs and views of the world (see Michaels 6). Just as communities are constituted as narrative communities (see Müller-Funk 14), informed not least by the values expressed and circulated through stories, the community-building nature of ritual has often been pointed out and frequently seems to rely on a dissemination of values, too. As public events, rituals are a popular and effective means of making visible and sustaining a given constellation of power.

Moreover, every story is formed not only by the specific situational context in which it is told, but also by the conventions of the genre which it pertains to. It makes a difference whether one tells an experience as an adventure story or as a didactic fable, as an anecdote or as a psychological novel. Many experiences can be expressed in different kinds of genres;[16] but the conventions of the genre which is chosen heavily influence the story: the selection of what is said and how it is said as well as the meaning we attribute to it differ widely according to the genre conventions that are adhered to. If one has chosen the frame of a comedy, for instance, it is very difficult to change it; when the frame of a comedy is chosen it is next to impossible to raise empathy or pity for the plight of those whose malheur has been the butt of the joke. The same journey can – without problems, but with great impact on the meaning of the story – be related as an adventure story, as a pilgrimage, as a *bildungsroman* depicting the development of intellectual and moral maturity of its hero or heroine, as a parable, and so on.[17] The degree of sophistication in producing and recognizing genres differs according to the education and socialization of readers, listeners or viewers. Perhaps there are nowadays more experts in the identification of media formats like "thriller," "soap," "costume drama," fantasy, "talk

---

16 Like the concept of "species" in biology, the term "genre" is extremely difficult to define; many scholars of literature and literary theory have spent much time on a host of explications of the concept (see, among others, Alastair Fowler, Klaus W. Hempfer, Tzvetan Todorov) or have come to use related terms like "generic frames." It is controversial, for example, whether genres can be determined on the basis of the features of a given body of texts which belong to a particular genre (which, however, would first of all have to be established) or whether we should base our explication on the concept of "ideal types." In spite of these difficulties, however, there seems to be widespread agreement that a knowledge of genres (which may be just as intuitive as our knowledge of what constitutes a narrative) is necessary for the production and understanding of texts.

17 It is important to remember, however, that genre conventions are dynamic – they change over time – and that they can be subverted; one can either write "within a genre against a genre" or develop new (sub)genres.

show" and others – which many viewers can recognize while zapping through the programmes – than the narratives which are mediated by language only. The relationship between story and genre is arguably similar to that between sequences of ritual action and the super-structures of larger ritual genres in which they appear. As elementary forms of ritual, typical patterns of ritual action will derive their meaning not least from the respective genre, such as different subtypes of initiation rituals, for example, in which they are employed.

Moreover, there are different levels of narration to be considered whenever a story is told by verbal means. How many levels there are, and which are the most important, however, is dependent on the specific media and genres; it is, moreover, a bone of contention between narratologists who have proposed quite different models for the structure of narratives and designations for the narrative levels they deem to be important.[18] In oral narratives which are told by one (or several) narrator(s) as well as in literary prose, there are arguably up to four layers involved: narrative worlds contain at least two layers or, in narratological terms, levels of existence. In every narration we distinguish between the story world, i.e. the world of the characters, and the level of discourse, i.e. the narrative mediation of the world of the characters, which is ascribed to a particular narrator and/or involves a specific form of mediation and perspectivization. In more complex stories, a third level is made up of the set of relations between those different levels, of the values which can be abstracted from textual features. As far as literary stories are concerned, the communication between the real "sender," author or teller of the tale, and the recipient who listens to or reads the story is only to be found on the fourth level. The actions and thoughts of characters are therefore embedded in a complex structure, which influences the meanings readers attribute to them.[19]

---

18 Many scholars only differentiate between two levels of "classical" narratives: that of the story and that of the discourse (or way of narration); the emphasis on either of these levels also characterizes different approaches to the study of narrative.

19 In other media and genres, such as plays or films, however, this is different.

Fig. 1: Communication model of different levels of narration

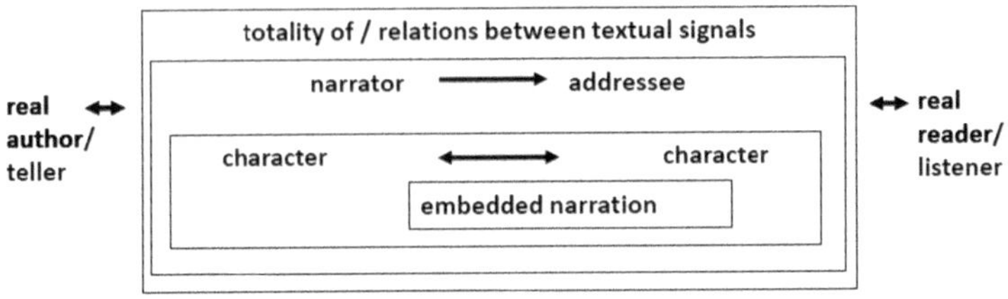

```
                    ┌─────────────────────────────────────────┐
                    │ totality of / relations between textual signals │
                    │   ┌─────────────────────────────────┐   │
real     ◄──►       │   │  narrator ──────► addressee    │   │       ◄──► real
author/             │   ├─────────────────────────────────┤   │           reader/
teller              │   │  character ◄──────► character  │   │           listener
                    │   │  ┌─────────────────────┐       │   │
                    │   │  │ embedded narration  │       │   │
                    │   │  └─────────────────────┘       │   │
                    │   └─────────────────────────────────┘   │
                    └─────────────────────────────────────────┘
```

Storytelling in rituals is also characterized by several layers or levels; for the dynamics of rituals, however, the level of "embedded narration" seems to be the most interesting or relevant one. It is on this level that characters who narrate a particular story – ritual experts such as priests, for example – can explain and justify changes within the plot or structure of the ritual. While in fictional and autobiographical stories the performative quality of narrative is situated on the level of the text-internal narrator, in rituals it is most pronounced on the level of characters.

The existence of several levels of narration and the relations between them also allow for self-reflexivity. The same motif, structure or value can be taken up on several levels of narration, allowing for them to be related to each other in multiple ways through mirroring and confirmation as well as through contrast and subversion. Apart from these implicit modes of self-reflexivity, narrators can refer to and reflect upon the attitudes, traits and values of characters as well as on their own characteristics and opinions, and the relations between the statements attributed to characters and narrators provide a web of meanings, allowing for ironic distancing between some elements.[20] A similar degree of self-reflexivity can also be achieved by storytelling in rituals, where self-reflexivity may arise from a tension between the level of (ritual) action and the embedded narratives told by those participating in the ritual.

---

20 The question of self-reflexivity is complex and has been explored by a host of scholars, some of whom focus on the lack of correspondence between events in a narrative and "real life," others on the importance of the language with which the story is told.

All of the features listed above shape the meaning that is attributed to narratives. Narratives generate meaning; they serve as a means to understand the world. There is no "objectivity" in a story; narrative forms purvey a specific, subjective interpretation of what has happened. An awareness of the features and importance of the form of narrative therefore enables us to understand and specify what Fredric Jameson has famously called the "ideology of form," emphasizing that "form is immanently and intrinsically an ideology in its own right" (Jameson 99).[21]

Both narratives and rituals thus create specific worlds; worlds which provide meaning as well as order. In a few studies, it has been argued that rituals and stories share a number of characteristics. For instance, both rituals and narratives can be understood as a complex form of mimesis: they not only represent a certain status quo which exists outside the ritual or narrative, but they envisage and enact what might seem to be possible and ethically desirable in relation to a given situation by engaging in symbolic communication (see Jameson 237ff.). Apart from the actual performance of ritual, there is an additional performative quality to both rituals and narratives, in the sense that they picture possible alternatives to the narrative's or ritual's referential context and thereby develop a transformative potential.

Another well-known debate linking ritual and narrative is the so-called myth and ritual school, and the longstanding question about whether myth developed out of ritual or the other way around (see Ackermann).[22] Different answers have been suggested to this question, both with good reasons, but what seems to be more interesting in our context is the close interrelationship between myth or narrative and ritual over time: whichever came first, there are countless instances which show that myths are adapted (and

---

21 See also Jameson 99: "What must now be stressed is that at this level 'form' is apprehended as content. The study of the ideology of form is no doubt grounded on a technical and formalistic analysis in the narrower sense, even though, unlike much traditional formal analysis, it seeks to reveal the active presence within the text of a number of discontinuous and heterogeneous formal processes. But at the level of analysis in question here, a dialectical reversal has taken place in which it has become possible to grasp such formal processes as sedimented content in their own right, as carrying ideological messages of their own, distinct from the ostensible or manifest content of the works."
22 For a critical perspective on the myth and ritual school, see Segal.

fulfil important explanatory functions) especially when rituals change. Vice versa, a change in myth will further influence the dynamics of ritual. In the words of Victor Turner, there is "a dynamic relation between social drama and expressive cultural genres" such as ritual and myth (Turner, "Social Dramas" 154). Myths are essentially a type of narrative, of course, and particularly powerful narratives at that. They frequently have a foundational quality similar to rituals, and the telling of myths often follows a ritual or ritualized pattern.

Another feature of the relationship between rituals and narratives has been spelled out by Langdon Elsbree in his *Ritual Passages and Narrative Structures*. Elsbree conceptualizes ritual and narrative from a neurobiological standpoint as activities which are characterized by a similar impulse of ordering and structuring experience. This fits well into the cognitive study of narrative, in which it is stressed that, by segmenting the flux of events into comprehendible units like "character," "situation," "action," and "episode," and then synthesizing those elements in a particular way narrations attribute meaning to events.[23] Highlighting structural similarities between narrative and ritual and applying concepts from ritual studies such as "social drama" (Turner) and "rites of passage" (van Gennep) to the study of literature, Elsbree and others persuasively identify and discuss these basic structures not only in real-life rituals, but also in the plot structures of fictional narratives. Moreover, ritual, just like narrative, has been described not only as (ritual) action, but also as a communicative act, using symbols as part of its aesthetic-expressive dimension (see Braungart 119).

Notwithstanding these productive and insightful studies, we argue that the nexus between ritual and narrative has not been sufficiently addressed so far. As yet, there is a lack of applications of current narrative and ritual theory in order to explore the similarities and relations between both fields. In responding to this research gap, the contributions in this volume try to shed light on the relationship between "ritual" and "narrative" and ask questions such as: where precisely do rituals and narratives intersect, what do they share? To what extent are rituals shaped by narrative structures? What are the stories that rituals tell, or that are told about them? Who does the story-telling in or about rituals, and to what end? In particular, the role

---

23 For a cognitive approach to narrative, see Herman, *Narrative Theory and Cognitive Sciences*.

of narrativity remains to be explored. What role does it play in rituals and in representations of ritual? What is the role of narrative strategies in media representations of rituals? To what extent do even non-fictional texts and other historical sources – documents which record and describe rituals – make use of narrative elements and strategies?

These questions constitute a broad thematic focus which accommodates theoretical or methodological reflections as well as in-depth case studies. Drawing on various disciplinary perspectives as well as new approaches in narratology, the present volume seeks to explore the manifold forms and functions of narrativity in (or of) rituals and in media representations of rituals. The first section of the book consists of a number of theoretical explorations of the various similarities and links between narratives and rituals. In the second section, scholars from various disciplines (ranging from classical archaeology, theology and political science to literary and religious studies) apply narratological concepts in order to analyse how rituals are received, experienced and perceived in terms of the senses, as well as how they are represented by narrative and media-specific means. A wide variety of experiential, cognitive, intermedial, transgeneric and other narratological approaches will be drawn on here, in an attempt to help research on rituals open up to a wide spectrum of media and genres in which rituals are represented.

Looking ahead to the individual chapters of this volume in more detail, much of its conceptual and theoretical backbone is provided by two thorough examinations. The chapters by Marie-Laure Ryan and by Vera and Ansgar Nünning bring rigorous narratological expertise to the study of ritual and ritual representations. They start from the observation that ritual and narrative stand to gain a lot from dialogue across disciplinary boundaries, though they have rarely engaged in it as yet. Against this background, Ryan asks in the title of her wide-ranging discussion, "Ritual Studies and Narratology: What Can They Do For Each Other"? This is a deliberately rhetorical question, as Ryan demonstrates a high degree of possible cross-fertilization. Her account is richly illustrated by forays into the history of ideas connecting the two fields, such as the myth and ritual debate. However, Ryan is also concerned not to collapse the two phenomena too easily. While pointing out many similarities she stresses that looking at ritual from a narrative point of view and vice versa will not only result in fruitful collaboration, but will also yield fresh insights into the distinctive (dissimilar) properties of each object of study and analytical perspective taken by itself. Ryan complements this argument on the disciplinary effects of interdisciplinary dialogue with a case study of the Escalade in Geneva, an annual re-enactment of founding events in the city's history. Based on various accounts and documents, this is an example of a story giving birth to a ritual, but the multiple performances of this story have also altered and "ritualized" it in turn. The various mechanisms of such feedback loops as analysed by Ryan provide ample illustration of the interrelationship between narrative and ritual.

Vera and Ansgar Nünning also explore theoretical territory in their chapter "On the Narrativity of Rituals: Interfaces between Narratives and Rituals and Their Potential for Ritual Studies." Mapping the field constituted by these interfaces, they list similarities and differences between rituals and narratives not only in terms of form but importantly also in terms of function. Moreover, by applying items from the analytical "toolkit" of narratology such as multiperspectivity to the study of ritual, they show which benefits these may have. For example, the extent to which rituals allow for a broad spectrum of agency despite their collectivizing impact can be demonstrated if one dissects the intricate network of individual points of view in rituals and representations of ritual with the help of narratological categories such as perspective structures. As Vera and Ansgar Nünning argue, narratology has a lot to offer when it comes to describing the formal level and indeed the narrativity of many rituals. They also demonstrate that while ritual studies may profit from the form-oriented endeavour of classical structuralist narratology, the social nature of ritual and the role of narrative in this sphere is a highly promising area of narrative study. Rituals and ritual culture here emerge as an expandable field of application in which to explore the manifold text-transcending and cultural (e.g. identity-forming) functions of narratives from the point of view of context-oriented postclassical narratology.

In the last chapter of the theoretical section, "Obama's American Narrative: A Narratological Approach to Complex Rituals," Roy Sommer starts by discussing the theoretical and methodological origins of ritual and narrative theory in structuralism. He identifies some crucial similarities between ritual and narrative; in particular drawing attention to the structuralist concern with "deep structures" and narrative grammar, which matches the ritualist interest in "deep structures" and the "morphology" of rituals. Acknowledging these commonalities bears the potential to explore ritual and narrative as related expressions of a shared cultural "DNA." In his case study, Sommer explores the uses of narrative in United States presidential elections. Analysing four speeches of President Obama from the 2008 election campaign, Sommer identifies five recurrent types of narrative (life stories, biographical stories, personal experience narratives, anecdotes, and micro-stories) that are designed to support political arguments and programmatic statements. Specifically, they tend to display a high level of experientiality in order to elicit an emotional or empathetic response on the part of the audience. Stories are manifestly a key element in the complex rituals of US presidential elections. Demonstrating this, Sommer highlights both the value of a narratological approach to ritual and the value of drawing on concepts from ritual studies when trying to gauge the cultural functions and purposes of storytelling as social practice.

With its rich illustration of theoretical aspects Sommer's analysis looks ahead to the emphasis on case studies in the second part of this volume. The chapters in the second part of our volume take some of the theoretical reflections in the first part as a springboard and explore the interfaces between narrative and ritual from different disciplinary perspectives. Far from already settling the debate over ritual and narrative, the case studies in the second section are meant to exemplify and illustrate the central concerns of this volume. The case studies are arranged in a roughly chronological order as far as their objects of study and related historical concepts of ritual and narrative are concerned. However, this chronological order is cut across by constantly combining historical and systematic concerns, as the various contributors bring "new" analytical categories to bear on "old" materials which often predate the modern development of narratology by far.

The first two case studies, "Depicting Sacrifice in Roman Asia Minor: Narratives of Ritual in Classical Archaeology" by Günther Schörner and "'He had just finished presenting the burnt offering ...': Narrative and Ritual in the Context of Saul's Failure (1 Sam 13-14)" by Joachim Vette, approach the nexus between ritual and narrative from classical archaeology and theology respectively. In combining ancient source materials and modern analytical methods, they both highlight the value and interdisciplinary promise of narratological categories for studying ritual and narrative in different media. Revisiting the Hierapolis Frieze in modern-day Turkey, Schörner draws on postclassical approaches to analysing pictorial narration.

The frieze dates back to Roman Asia minor and is the most detailed visual representation of animal sacrifice from this time. It is not a narrative proper, Schörner points out, but narratological distinctions make it possible to determine quite what degree of narrativity it does possess. They also allow for accommodating the performative, world-making and media-specific aspects of the frieze and the ritual it depicts, while at the same taking stock and extending the range and status quo of narrative analysis in classical archaeology. In a similar vein, Vette builds on the body of narrative scholarship of the Bible to trace the relationship of ritual and narrative in Old Testament Scripture. Vette carries out a close reading of the first book of Samuel 13-14, a text chosen for what he describes as the highest density of ritual action in any biblical narrative. Applying categories of a narrative poetics, he pays particular attention to the narrative function of these ritualized actions. Ritual actions in this text serve to propel forward, interpret and reflect on the narrative action, specifically pushing the ironic, satiric and tragic aspects of the story.

Moving forward in time and adding further disciplinary perspectives of religious and literary studies, the chapters by Dirk Johannsen, Jan Rupp and Scarlett Meyer look at more modern constellations of ritual and narrative in different national, literary and historiographical traditions. In his case study "Two Types of Magic in One Tradition? A Cognitive-Historiographical Case Study on the Interplay of Narratives and Rituals," Johannsen looks at the interaction between ritual forms of magic and narratives from a folk religious tradition in 19th-century Norway. Applying perspectives from narratology and the cognitive science of religion he shows how these rituals and their fictional representations in narrative texts mutually feed into each other as two types of magic sustaining a joint tradition. Contemporary images of magical experts were narratively constructed, Johannsen points out, while the appearance of these experts (and thus the intrusion of ritual) in fictional stories was marked by specific narrative techniques and devices.

In his chapter "Ritual, Narrative and Identity in English Pageant Fictions of the Interwar Years," Rupp looks at the crisis of collective identity and corresponding popularity of ritual in modernist pageant fictions of the 1930s. In the light of imperial decline and looming war, English pageant fictions responded to the early 20th-century boom of public ritual in the form of large-scale historical pageants. They are part of a literary reaction taking up and problematizing the twin phenomena of identity crisis and its containment through ritual. Rupp highlights the ways in which pageant fictions reflect on and rework narrative mechanisms of their ritual pretexts, developing alternative models to the national "rite of passage" from imperial Britishness to a more domestic Englishness as often staged in historical pageantry. As Meyer argues in her chapter "Rituals, Narrative and the Construction of Identity in the Intercultural British Novel at the Turn of the 21st Century," the intercultural novel in Britain is informed by a similar crisis or change of collective identity. For one thing, this degree of change is indicated by the depiction of immigrant rituals such as Indian marriage ceremonies and burials. Moreover, many intercultural novels use the *bildungsroman* genre, which resonates with the model of rites of passage. Like the fictional staging of intercultural rituals, the *bildungsroman* seems to transform notions of Englishness into a more inclusive sense of Britishness. Meyer points out the social resonance of fictional rites of passage, while also emphasizing the potential of literary narrative for critical engagement and self-reflexivity with regard to this ritual pattern.

The last case study by Stefanie Hammer, "How to Commemorate a Fallen Soldier: Ritual and Narrative in the Bundeswehr," turns to a non-fictional and highly topical context of ritual and narrative, i.e. the commemoration of fallen soldiers of the Bundeswehr in public ceremonies. Looking at the connection between ritual and narrative from the perspective of political science, Hammer analyses how narrative elements in speeches play an important part in the Bundeswehr commemoration services. Over time even slight alterations in the speeches have also transformed the overall ritual. Thus, the very term "fallen soldier" and rival terms conjure up competing historical narratives which configure the rituals discussed in and through narrative. Moreover, Hammer draws attention to changing public and media settings which further shape the relationship between ritual and narrative in the Bundeswehr. This case study gives ample evidence of the usefulness of applying new approaches of narratology in non-fictional contexts of ritual and public storytelling. Like the previous chapters, it casts an important spotlight on the ground to be covered and the connections to be drawn by further debate which we hope to inspire with this volume.

REFERENCES

Ackermann, Robert. *The Myth and Ritual School. J.G. Frazer and the Cambridge Ritualists.* New York: Routledge, 2002.

Ahn, Gregor. "Ritual Design – an Introduction." *Ritual Dynamics and the Science of Ritual.* Vol. IV Reflexivity, Media, and Visuality. Section IV: Ritual Design. Ed. Gregor Ahn. Wiesbaden: Harrassowitz, 2010. 601-606.

—. "‚Ritualdesign' – ein neuer Topos der Ritualtheorie?" *Ritualdesign. Zur kultur- und ritualwissenschaftlichen Analyse ‚neuer' Rituale.* Ed. Karolewski et al. Bielefeld: Transcript, 2012. 29-44.

Bell, Catherine M. *Ritual. Perspectives and Dimensions.* New York: Oxford UP, 1997.

Braungart, Wolfgang. *Ritual und Literatur.* Tübingen: Niemeyer, 1996.

Bruner, Jerome. "Self-making and World-making." *Journal of Aesthetic Education* 25.1 (1991): 67-78.

—. "The Narrative Construction of Reality." *Critical Enquiry* 18.1 (1991): 1-21.

Elsbree, Langdon. *Ritual Passages and Narrative Structures.* New York: Lang, 1991.

Fludernik, Monika. *Towards a 'Natural' Narratology.* London: Routledge, 1996.

Glasige, Burkhard. "Typische Ritensequenzen und die Ordnung der Rituale." *Zoroastrian Rituals in Context.* Ed. Michael Stausberg. Leiden: Brill, 2003.

Herman, David, ed. *Narrative Theory and the Cognitive Sciences.* Stanford: CLSI Publications, 2003.

—. *Basic Elements of Narrative.* Malden, MA: Wiley-Blackwell, 2009.

—. "Narrative Ways of Worldmaking." *Narratology in the Age of Cross-Disciplinary Narrative Research.* Eds. Sandra Heinen and Roy Sommer. Berlin: de Gruyter, 2009. 71-88.

Jameson, Fredric. *The Political Unconscious. Narrative as a Socially Symbolic Act.* Ithaca, NY: Cornell UP, 1981.

Karolewski, Janina, Nadja Miczek, and Christof Zotter. *Ritualdesign. Zur kultur- und ritualwissenschaftlichen Analyse ‚neuer' Rituale.* Bielefeld: transcript, 2012.

Kreinath, Jens, Jan Snoek, and Michael Stausberg. "Ritual Studies, Ritual Theory, Theorizing Rituals – An Introductory Essay." *Theorizing Rituals: Issues, Topics, Approaches, Concepts*. Eds. Kreinath et al. Leiden: Brill, 2006. xiii-xxv.

Langer, Robert, Raoul Motika, and Michael Ursinus, eds. *Migration und Ritualtransfer: Religiöse Praxis der Aleviten, Jesiden und Nusairier zwischen Vorderem Orient und Westeuropa*. Frankfurt a.M.: Lang, 2005.

Leander, Niels Buch. "To Begin with the Beginning: Birth, Origin and Narrative Inception." *Narrative Beginnings: Theories and Practices*. Ed. Brian Richardson. Lincoln, NB: U of Nebraska P, 2008. 15-28.

Lucius-Hoene, Gabriele, and Arnulf Deppermann. *Rekonstruktionen narrativer Identität. Ein Arbeitsbuch zur Analyse narrativer Interviews*. Opladen: Leske und Budrich, 2002.

McAdams, Dan P. "The Problem of Narrative Coherence." *Journal of Constructivist Psychology* 19 (2006): 109-25.

Michaels, Axel. "Zur Dynamik von Ritualkomplexen." *Forum Ritualdynamik* 3 (2003): 1-12.

Müller-Funk, Wolfgang. *Die Kultur und ihre Narrative. Eine Einführung*. Wien: Springer, 2008.

Nünning, Vera. "The Making of Fictional Worlds: Processes, Features and Functions." *Cultural Ways of Worldmaking. Media and Narratives*. Eds. Vera Nünning, Ansgar Nünning, and Birgit Neumann. Berlin: De Gruyter, 2010. 215-243.

—. "Erzählen und Identität: Die Bedeutung des Erzählens im Schnittfeld zwischen kulturwissenschaftlicher Narratologie und Psychologie." *Kultur – Wissen – Narration. Perspektiven transdisziplinärer Erzählforschung für die Kulturwissenschaften*. Ed. Alexandra Strohmeier. Bielefeld: Transcript (in print).

—. *Fiction and Cognition* (in preparation).

Nünning, Vera, Ansgar Nünning, and Birgit Neumann, eds. *Cultural Ways of Worldmaking. Media and Narratives*. Berlin: De Gruyter, 2010.

Prince, Gerald. "Remarks on Narrativity." *Perspectives on Narratology: Papers from the Stockholm Symposium on Narratology*. Ed. Claes Wahlin. Frankfurt a.M.: Lang, 1996. 95-106.

Ryan, Marie-Laure. *Avatars of Story*. Minneapolis, MN: U of Minnesota P, 2006.

Schwanecke, Christine. *Intermedial Storytelling: Thematization, Imitation and Incorporation of Photography in English and American Narrative Fiction at the Turn of the 21st Century*. Trier: WVT, 2012.

Segal, Robert A. "Myth and Ritual." *Theorizing Rituals: Issues, Topics, Approaches, Concepts*. Eds. Kreinath et al. Leiden: Brill, 2006. 101-121.

Turner, Victor. *The Forest of Symbols: Aspects of Ndembu Ritual*. Ithaca, NY: Cornell UP, 1967.

—. *The Ritual Process: Structure and Anti-Structure*. London: Routledge & Kegan Paul, 1969.

—. "Social Dramas and Stories about Them." *Critical Inquiry* 7.1 (1980): 141-168.

Van Gennep, Arnold. *The Rites of Passage*. London: Routledge, 1960.

Wolf, Werner. "Das Problem der Narrativität in Literatur, Bildender Kunst und Musik: Ein Beitrag zu einer Intermedialen Erzähltheorie." *Erzähltheorie Transgenerisch, Intermedial, Interdisziplinär*. Eds. Vera Nünning and Ansgar Nünning. Trier: WVT, 2002. 23-104.

I. Theoretical Explorations: Forms, Functions, and Social Practice of Ritual and Narrative

Ritual Studies and Narratology: What Can They Do For Each Other

MARIE-LAURE RYAN

1. INTRODUCTION

When scholars associate ritual with a form of expression, this form tends to be poetry rather than narrative (see Ryan). Baudelaire called poetry an "evocative magic" (*sorcellerie évocatoire*), and he requested for the words of the poet the rigorous exactness of the formula spoken by a magician casting a spell. Mallarmé conceived of his hermetic poetry as a secret ceremony accessible only to those who had been initiated into its mysteries. For Saint-John Perse, the purpose of poetry was to enact and celebrate a communion of mankind with cosmic forces, such as the wind, the sea and the earth. Art took a "primitivist turn" in the early 20th century (cf. Stravinsky's *Rite of Spring*, or the influence of African art on Cubist painting) that encouraged Surrealist associations of literary practices with magic, divination, the occult, and tribal customs. Nowadays we are more inclined to regard poets as skilled craftsmen than as oracles inspired by a supernatural presence, but the Romantic conception of the poet as a genius and visionary was a major force in these mystical visions. The analogy between poetry and ritual rests on three major points: both ritual and poetry deal with the sacred; both are supposed to lead to an event that deeply transforms the participants; in both cases, finally, the accomplishment of this event depends on the precise observance of formal requirements – gestures in the case of ritual, language in the case of poetry. The New Critics of the Fifties believed that one could not change a single word in a poem (which meant in a literary text, for poetry was regarded as the essence of literature) without changing its entire meaning; similarly, one cannot change any element in a ritual without depriving it of its efficiency.

Most of these analogies break down in the case of narrative. Novelists are keen observers of society rather than technicians of the sacred, and narrative is much less dependent than poetry on an exact choice of words, as the popularity of translation suggests. The two genres also differ in their tolerance of repetition, which forms the essence of ritual: we may re-read a poem many times, or recite it in our mind like an incantation, and fall every time under the spell of its language, but only children want to hear the same story over and over again. Despite these differences, however, I hope to show in this chapter that the relations between ritual and narrative are sufficiently rich and numerous to make their association productive. Let me start with a definition. Taking inspiration from the French ethnographer Jean Cazeneuve, I define ritual as a performance of actions and verbal utterances that fulfills three conditions:

Ritual must obey fixed rules. These rules specify that the actions must repeat other gestures or other words. The American ethnographer Roy Rappaport formulates this condition as follows: "I take the term 'ritual' to denote *the performance of more or less invariant sequences of formal acts and utterances not entirely encoded by the performers*" (Rappaport 24; italics original). Not entirely encoded by the performers means that the performance must at least to some degree conform to tradition, rather than being entirely the product of improvisation. This does not mean that rituals cannot change over the years; but as Rappaport observes, modifications, if they are to become a regular part of the ritual, rather than a unique occurrence, are typically introduced by individuals who claim to have been inspired in dreams or visions (33).

These gestures must be efficacious in a non-practical way. They must cause an event to happen through means that are symbolic rather than material. Yet the event is not merely a symbolic, but a literal transformation, and it can affect material objects. A prime example of an event that involves both the spiritual and the material is the transsubstantation that transforms the Eucharistic host of the Catholic Mass into the body and blood of Christ.

Rituals must be part of a "religious" vision of the world – a vision that rests on a dichotomy between two kinds of phenomena: on one hand, the visible, the everyday, the profane, on the other hand invisible forces that may be called the sacred, the numinous, or the supernatural. Ritual achieves its efficiency through a manipulation of these hidden forces; its goal is either to introduce them into daily life, or to keep them away.

If we insist on these three conditions, ritual is an endangered species. The hold of rituals on people's lives is much weaker in our increasingly secular cultures than in religious or tribal societies. But ritual behavior has not completely disappeared: think of the habit of singing the national anthem on certain occasions (for instance sports events), of the practice of hazing to be admitted in certain societies, or of the enduring celebration of Mardi Gras long after people gave up the habit of fasting before Easter. People also create private rituals, such as avoiding to step on lines on the sidewalk in order to avert bad luck. (There's a fine line between ritual and superstition.) These behaviors no longer reflect a world-view dominated by a division between the sacred and the profane, except when the sacred evolves into nationalism or belief in a certain political system. Similarly, if we want to regard as ritual the mating habits of animals, such as the dance of the fiddler crab or the display of the peacock's tail, we must regard condition 3 as optional. With the relaxation of condition 3, condition 2 is considerably weakened. If singing the national anthem leads to an "event," this event is not a physical transformation but the public testimony of belonging to a certain community. The efficiency of most, if not all, post-religious rituals lies in a psychological effect. If we allow condition 2 to be fulfilled by subjective mental events of which the participants may not be aware, this leaves only condition 1 as a hard and fast feature of ritual.

Yet not all repetitive and rule-governed behaviors qualify as ritual: for instance, games follow strict rules that confer a certain repetitiveness to the actions of the players; drama involves the oral performance of a written text that should not be substantially altered; and filing a tax report must be done annually and follows very specific regulations. How can we eliminate these activities from our definition of ritual? The case of the tax report is the easiest one to dismiss: it is not a ritual because it follows a logic of practical efficiency. Drama differs from ritual through its strict partition between performers and audience: in a ritual, the entire congregation participates in the performance. I find games the most difficult to distinguish from the secular form of rituals, and indeed many games are performed as part of a ritual, such as the Olympic Games in ancient Greece, and they have their share of ritual elements, such as spectators singing certain chants or wearing their team's colors. The main difference between games and rituals has been pointed by Lévi-Strauss: while games lead to victory and defeat, and therefore to a relation of inequality, ritual turns all participants into members of the same community, even if they came originally from different groups (Rappaport 45).

The weaker character of conditions 2 and 3, compared to condition 1, suggests that rituals form a fuzzy set tolerating various degrees of membership: according to this model, the Roman Catholic Mass, or human sacrifices in pre-Columbian civilizations achieve full ritual status because they fulfill all three conditions, and do so very strongly, while the mating dance of the fiddler crab, or the singing of the national anthem before a game of American football are marginal examples of ritual. This marginality does not mean however that they are rituals in a metaphorical way: they fulfill only one condition, but they fulfill it literally. Filing one's income tax, by contrast, can only be called a ritual in a figural way.

In recent years it has become fashionable for people to design their own weddings or funerals by writing their own vows, holding the ceremonies in unconventional places, or having their remains disposed of in a strange way: for instance, the journalist Hunter S. Thompson had his body shot through a cannon like a bullet, and the pop culture guru Timothy Leary had his ashes sent into space. These practices are expressions of individuality, and as such they are not meant to be repeated: it is their unique character that makes them important to their participants (or patient, in the case of funerals). Does this mean that condition 1 is no longer a defining feature of ritual? I will argue the opposite. If we are tempted to regard personalized weddings and funerals as rituals, it is because they signal a passage between stages of life, and such passages are almost universally marked by rituals (see van Gennep). We touch here on the difference between ceremony and ritual. It may be traditional (=ritualistic) to hold ceremonies on certain occasions, especially life transitions, but the exact form of the ceremony needs not be traditional. Ritual tolerates improvisation and variation as long they take place within a fixed frame – the frame that makes a certain event count as "wedding" or "funeral." Vows written by the couple to be married still fulfill the conditions of being vows (i.e. binding statements of intent); and strange disposal of remains still marks the end of a life, especially when it is publicly advertised.

Given the definition proposed above, how can we connect ritual to narrative? I see several ways of doing so. Some involve metaphorical relations, based on analogy, while others involve metonymic relations of part to whole: ritual can be an element of narrative, or narrative an element of ritual. The purpose of studying these resemblances, differences, and relations of containment is not to propose an ambitious general theory of the origins of myth and ritual, but more modestly to lead to a better understanding of each of these phenomena individually.

2. METAPHORICAL RELATIONS

2.1 Universality in Human Culture

If we look at narrative and ritual from an evolutionary point of view (see Boyd), the lack of material efficiency of ritual actions makes their existence as problematic as the existence of fictional stories. The answer to the question "Why would mankind waste its time performing rituals when people could solve problems through much more efficient practical actions" is closely tied to another question asked by evolutionary psychology about narrative: "Why do people enjoy so much stories about imaginary events, when they could use their time exchanging practical information about the real world – information that would play a much more obvious role in their survival." Despite their lack of practical efficiency, the practice of ritual and the creation of imaginary worlds through storytelling are both universal human activities and essential factors in what Roy Rappaport calls "the making of humanity." Both rituals and narrative make us human by building community: ritual coordinates activity into a collaborative event, while narrative requires joint attention to the words of the storyteller.

Another aspect of ritual and narrative that explains their cultural importance is captured by a formula often used by psychologists and cognitive narratologists: "Narrative is a way to make sense of the world" (see Herman). We can say the very same thing about ritual, and in fact the formula seems to apply much better to ritual than to narrative, especially if we conceive of "making sense of the world" as providing a feeling of belonging to a place or to a community. Many narratives only make sense of the world if "making sense" is understood as expressing an experience of alienation, of undergoing events that cannot be explained (think of Kafka's *Metamorphosis*). Still, if expressing existential anguish is a step toward making sense of life, one can say that both narrative and ritual represent ways of dealing with what is perhaps the most important source of anguish, namely the randomness of fate. But they do so in very different ways: ritual, by trying to eliminate this randomness from life, narrative, by turning it into a plot.

2.2 Need for Interpretation

Because the mode of operation of ritual is symbolic rather than practical, the purpose of ritual actions is not transparent to outside observers, as would be the purpose of actions with a material mode of operation. This means that rituals, like narratives, are "texts" that must be read and that provide a test for interpretive abilities.

2.3 Mode of Presentation

In its literary manifestations, narrative is a representation in the strict sense of the term: the audience imagines that the story concern events which took place independently of the act of narration. In the case of nonfictional narrative the report may or may not be accurate, and the hearer may or may not believe the story, but the very fact that she may not believe it means that she assumes the existence of an external referent. In fiction the events are produced by the discourse, but the audience pretends to believe that they have an autonomous existence. Another way to describe narration is to regard it as an act of assertion. Because what is asserted exists independently of the assertion, a distinction can be made between story – the represented events – and discourse – the act of representation. In ritual, by contrast, events are not narrated but enacted, except when the ritual includes the recitation of a myth. As a live performance, ritual is closer to drama than to verbal narrative, but according to the historian of religion Mircea Eliade it does not involve acting, which means the adoption by the performers of a foreign identity. In Eliade's account (1954), when a performer impersonates a mythical creature in the course of a ritual, he does not pretend to be somebody else for the entertainment of an audience, but rather experiences a mystical identification with this creature, and reintegrates the sacred time (*illud tempus*) during which the mythical events occurred. This account of ritual as a kind of time machine no longer holds true for the rituals of societies that have lost a sense of the sacred; nowadays many rituals tend to be mere commemorations of past events. The participants' awareness of the ontological difference between the commemorated events and their re-enactment means that ritual is closing the gap with narrative re-presentation. But when ritual retains its full force of manipulation of the sacred, it is not a game of make-believe, but something that happens here and now, something that happens "for real." Its mode of action is what speech act theory describes as a performative (and it is in fact no coincidence that most of the examples of performative speech act proposed by Austin and Searle are part of rituals: christening, marrying, swearing in). As a performative, ritual makes no distinction between events and representation. This means that it invalidates the narratological distinction between story and discourse.

2.4 Sequentiality

One feature that ritual and narrative have in common is sequentiality. In ritual, any tampering with the order of the actions would result in a loss of efficiency. The various parts of the ritual prepare each other and lead toward a denouement in a configuration which can be compared to the plot of a tragedy, even though the relation between the elements is not causal but largely conventional and symbolic. In narrative it is possible to tamper with chronological order on the level of discourse but not on the level of story. The events that make up a story are linked to each other by relations of causality, and these relations are fixed and unidirectional. Changing the order in which causally related events happen results in the best of cases in a different story, and in the worst cases in a logically incoherent sequence.

2.5 Eventfulness

Narrative typically consists of two types of events (see Hühn): repetitive events that describe the daily life of the characters and maintain the status quo; and unique events that introduce significant changes in the storyworld. It is the second type of events that guarantee the tellability of narrative: good stories do not concern the daily and the predictable, but the exceptional and newsworthy. When narrative reports a daily routine, for instance how Mr. Smith got out of bed, ate breakfast and started on his way to work, it is because this sequence will be interrupted by the events in which the tellability of the story is invested. We expect that on his way to work Mr. Smith will be hit by a car, abducted by space aliens, or that he will fall in love with a woman he meets on the subway. When narrative uses repetition, it is to highlight differences: for instance in a fairy tale the first son tries and fails, the second son tries and fails, but the youngest tries and succeeds. While narrative thrives on the unique and unpredictable, ritual represents mankind's way to exorcize it from life. In contrast to narrative, ritual offers no surprise: the congregation of a Catholic mass knows that the ceremony will end with the words *missa est* (at least if the mass is sung in Latin), and the fans of a football game know that it will begin with the national anthem. The only suspense occurs with rituals of healing or of control of the weather: the patient may or may be cured of the disease, rain may or may not fall, but these events are in a sense external to the ritual since they happen afterwards. All this makes the spirit of ritual profoundly alien to the spirit of narrative. Yet eventfulness is not absent from ritual, and while they differ in their tolerance of change on the level of the global world order, ritual and narrative have strong similarities in the domain of semantic structure.

2.6 Semantic Structure

To explain the semantic structure common to narrative and ritual I will rely on the model of plot proposed by Jurij Lotman. Lotman views the world of a story as structured by a system of relations between symbolic domains delimited by spatial boundaries. This system can be represented by a map, or by a Venn diagram. In a fairy tale, for instance, there is an opposition between "home," a realm of security, the forest, an area of danger and adventure, and "the castle," symbol of power and site of rewards. Myth may rely on an opposition between "the realm of the dead" and "the realm of the living," or between the habitat of the gods and the habitat of humans. In a novel, the segmentation may correspond to social classes: in an example provided by Lotman, there could be "main street," where rich people live, the suburbs, home to the working class, and "the tenements," where outcasts and immigrants reside (Lotman 237). The oppositions that structure the storyworld need not be anchored in space: the semantic map of a story may consist of purely conceptual categories, such as "the human" vs. "the non-human," or "the feminine" vs. "the masculine." Any opposition capable of being represented through a spatial diagram can form the background against which plot can be described. Lotman defines plot as the movement of an object – typically the hero – across a boundary between mutually incompatible categories. Plot, consequently, is the disruption of an established order, followed by either a new order, or the reestablishment of the old one. The narrative significance – which means, the eventfulness – of an event does not lie in its semantic definition, but in the resistance of the boundary that it violates, and in the importance of the boundary for the world order. In an example proposed by Lotman, "death" matters when it happens to the hero, and when it brings glory or shame, but not when its victims are anonymous soldiers: it is considered normal that many soldiers will die during a war (Lotman 236). Or to take another example: "marriage" becomes eventful when it takes place between people of different social classes, or between people of the same sex, but not when it respects established social rules.

This model is easy to transfer to ritual. Just as narrative divides the world into distinct symbolic domains, ritual relies on divisions in space, time, and society. The division of space operates both horizontally and vertically. Horizontal divisions single out certain places as different, as holy, such as sacred groves, sanctuaries, mountain tops, cultural houses, and menstrual huts, or they oppose public spaces to private ones. The crossing of these horizontal boundaries is experienced as a dangerous step – hence the importance in many cultures of the threshold and of the liminal, an area that belongs neither to the inside nor to the outside (see Turner) – and it is marked by rituals of purification, such as washing one's feet. These rituals suggest that the individual who steps over a threshold must become a different person. The horizontal structuring of space reflects a vertical division based on ontological differences: it is because they allow communication between humans and the gods and therefore break the boundary between the sacred and the profane that certain sites are marked as holy places. In addition to being delimited in space, the breaking of ontological boundaries may be delimited in time. Ritual structures time by instituting daily hours of prayer, weekly days of worship, or annual events such as celebrations of the solstice or equinox, harvest feasts, carnivals, and alternations between periods of fasting and rejoicing. While rituals based on natural phenomena presuppose a cyclical conception of time which brings a regular return of the same events, rituals that mark the different stages of human life rest on a linear conception, since these stages are irreversible. Rites of passage and of initiation follow a script that makes the crossing of temporal boundaries dependent on the crossing of spatial boundaries. In order to pass from boyhood to manhood, or to reach a higher status in a secret society, the candidate must undertake an initiatory journey consisting of three stages: separation from home; travel though a foreign territory, such as the land of the dead, where the candidate is subjected to various tests and undergoes a symbolic death and rebirth; and return home as a different person (see Vierne). These three stages form a script that fulfills Lotman's conception of narrative event as "the shifting of a persona across the border of a semantic field" (Lotman 233). Other examples of shift across boundaries in a ritual script are the transubstantiation of the Catholic mass, where the Eucharist host, a mere thing, passes from the realm of the material to the realm of the spiritual, and the ritual of the scapegoat, where the sins of a community are loaded upon an innocent victim, which is then expelled from the community, together with its load (see Girard).

Yet there is an important difference between the plots of narrative and ritual: in narrative the "eventfulness" of the narrated is valued for its own sake; it is, as I have suggested, an intrinsic source of tellability. Also, when a character or object crosses a boundary, the world order is changed; in order to restore its initial order the character must perform a second crossing of boundary, and this second crossing is a difficult task: think of the obstacles that Odysseus must overcome in order to return Ithaca to its original status. But in ritual, while the script enacts a crossing of boundary, this crossing is put in the service of the preservation of a global world order. There is no need to cross twice, to undo the event, in order to return to an original state. How can we explain this paradox of an event that both creates change and maintains the status quo?

The answer varies with the type of ritual. In the case of rites of passage, which rely on a linear conception of time, the eventfulness of the ritual affects an individual who must pass from one stage of life to another; but since every member of the community must cross the same boundary sooner or later, the change in the individual does not create changes in the community. In the case of rituals that rely on a cyclical pattern, such as the return of the seasons, the crossing of boundary marks the end of one cycle and the beginning of another. But why is it necessary to perform a ritual in order to initiate a new cycle, if periodicity is a natural part of cosmic order?

Time may not be cyclical after all, and the return of the same may not be guaranteed. If the same actions must be performed over and over again, it is because the order of the world is a fragile state in constant need of repair. By injecting the world and the community with a periodic dose of the sacred, ritual provides the nourishment necessary to maintain cosmic order. But the sacred must be held within spatial and temporal limits, for if it were allowed to spread across the entire world it would dissolve the distinctions on which order is based. This explanation may seem far-fetched for modern rituals, such as singing the national anthem or acting as a fool during carnival, but when the sense of the sacred disappears, as it tends to do in modern societies, ritual is still needed to refresh a social order which depends on the integration of the individual in a community.

3. METONYMIC RELATIONS

3.1 Representations of Ritual in Narrative

A first type of metonymic relation is illustrated by narrative fictions that make ritual part of their content. Here we can distinguish three cases.

First, stories can revolve around a ritual inspired by real world practices. An example of this situation is the tragedy *Antigone* by Sophocles: when the heroine disobeys the order of the king in order to give a proper burial to her brother Polynice, we can assume that she is performing an important ritual of ancient Greek society. As actions mandated by the gods, rituals belong to the domain of the obligatory; but the orders of the king create for his subjects another kind of obligation; burying Polynice is therefore an action both forbidden and obligatory. There cannot be a more striking example of dramatic conflict and of tragic situation. Another example of plot that relies on ritual comes from a totally different genre, the comic book Tintin. In *Prisoners of the Sun*, Tintin and his friends are captured by a group of descendants of the Incas who still practice human sacrifices. Our heroes are about to be sacrificed to the Sun god when Tintin, who knows that an eclipse is imminent, implores the god to veil its face in order to express his disapproval of the sacrifice. Presto, the sun is darkened, and the panicked natives free the would-be victims. Here we have a mockery of ritual as the barbarous practice of a primitive culture, while in *Antigone* ritual is presented from the point of view of the culture in which it is practiced, this is to say, as a sacred duty.

Rather than referring to existing rituals, narrative may concern private rituals invented by the characters. My example is the play by Jean Genet, *The Maids*. The play revolves around two maids, Claire and Solange, who feel oppressed by their mistress and by a class system that condemns them to a lower status. Everyday they perform a script of their invention in which Claire plays Solange, Solange plays Madame, their mistress (or vice versa), and Madame is murdered, but the maids never find the courage to complete the script. At the end of the play, however, the maids find themselves in a desperate situation – they are about to be caught for lying to their mistress – and they perform the ritual one last time. But this time they go all the way: Solange offers poisoned tea to Claire, who is playing Madame. The death of Claire, which counts ritually as the death of Madame (which means that it *is* this death, since ritual acts are not representations but performatives), acquires the significance of a human sacrifice that frees both maids from their inferior condition: one of them is dead, and the other will be sent to jail, a fate presented as preferable to the condition of a servant.

A third way for ritual to appear on the level of narrative content is through comparison between the experience of the hero and the script of a specific kind of ritual. The investigation of such analogies is the concern of an approach to literary criticism known as the "myth and ritual" school, which flourished in the Fifties and early Sixties and whose most prominent representative is the Canadian critic Northrop Frye. Under the influence of the psychoanalyst C.G. Jung, this school reads narrative texts as manifestations of archetypal patterns found all over the world. The most widely applicable of these patterns is the scenario of the rite of passage or initiation, which has been found in texts ranging from chivalric romance to *Bildungsroman* and from science-fiction to computer games (see Vierne). Another script that critics love to apply to literary works – for instance to Joyce, T.S. Eliot and D.H. Lawrence – is the cycle of the death and rebirth of nature, a cycle that forms the basis of many rituals around the world (Doty, chapter 6).

Ritual may also form the subject matter of non-fictional discourse, more particularly of ethnography. While this discourse is descriptive rather than narrative – it concerns repetitive habits rather than singular world-transforming events –, it can still be subjected to the methods of inquiry developed by narratology. Since description is an integral part of narrative, narratology has developed many concepts which can also be applied to globally descriptive texts. Ethnographic accounts of ritual could be studied in terms of such criteria as role of the observer, spatial point of view, use of omniscience, use of embedded discourse such as testimonies from the participants, and above all ideological stance.

3.2 Narrative Foundations of Ritual

While narrative can make ritual part of its content, in an inverse metonymic relation it is narrative that forms the content of ritual. Many rituals around the world involve a representation of events which are also narrated by a myth; the recitation of this myth may be an integral part of the ritual, or the participants in the ritual may impersonate the heroes of the myth in a dramatic enactment. In the late 19th century, the often observed connection between ritual and narrative inspired a school of thought known as the "myth and ritual" theory. This theory, first proposed by William Robertson Smith (1846-1894), then endorsed by Sir James Frazer (1854-1941), regards ritual as primary; people first performed rituals, and then justified their behavior by creating myths that recounted how the ritual had been given to mankind by supernatural creatures. For the proponents of this theory, the original ritual was a ceremony that marked the death and rebirth of nature at the end of the year and guaranteed the production of crops for the coming season. These practices, which supposedly involved putting a king to death, gave birth to myths telling of gods being dismembered and resurrected, of fertility goddesses spending part of the year in the underworld, and of supernatural beings giving crops to people and telling them how to practice agriculture. According to this theory, all of human culture can be derived from the foundational rite of renewal of the cosmos. Later scholars (for instance Mircea Eliade) turned the theory around, claiming that rituals are the enactment of myths. Critics of the theory, such as Clyde Kluckhohn, point out that certain cultures have a rich mythological tradition but relatively few rituals (the example is ancient Greece), while others, like ancient Rome, have lots of rituals but relatively few myths. (This may explain why the Romans had to borrow their mythology from Greece.) It may be ultimately impossible to verify a theory that presents a single, general answer to the chicken and egg question of whether ritual precedes myth or vice-versa, but the fact remains that myth and rituals present two complementary aspects of religious life: through myth, religion is defined as something that one believes, through ritual, as something that one practices. We don't need a grandiose unified theory of the origins of myth and ritual to study the multiple ways in which these two fundamental aspects of human culture interact with each other.

3.2.1 From Ritual to Narrative

As an example of narrative developed out of ritual, consider the modern legend of Santa Claus bringing presents to children on Christmas Day. The custom of Christmas gift-giving is a holdover of the so-called "gift economies" that preceded the advent of modern market economies. While in a market economy goods are exchanged for money, in a gift economy they are given for free, though the recipient may be placed under a social obligation to reciprocate. The pagan ritual of gift-giving became integrated into the Christmas celebration through association with the presents of gold, myrrh and incense brought to Jesus by the three wise men. In stories developed in many European countries, the donor was identified as a supernatural creature, such as the Christ Child (who went from recipient to donor), Father Frost, Père Noël, or St Nicholas, who became Santa Claus. The presents, rather than being an expression of pure generosity, soon became a way to control the behavior of children: while good children received toys, bad ones received coal, sticks (for their parents to spank them), or nothing at all. As the commercial dimension of Christmas began to overshadow its religious meaning, the story became more and more fleshed out, since it encourages consumerism: parents have to maintain the belief in Santa that they have implanted in their children, and the only way to maintain this belief is by purchasing toys. (The abbreviation to Santa shows that associations with St Nicholas have been largely forgotten.) Every child in the United States knows that Santa comes down the chimney, lives at the North Pole, where he manufactures the toys with the help of Mrs. Claus, and travels in a sleigh pulled by a dozen reindeer. One of these reindeer, a certain Rudolf, had been the butt of jokes because of his red nose, but when Santa chose him to lead the sleigh, the unsightly facial feature served as the guiding light for the whole expedition. I will spare my readers the summary of the countless spin-offs created every year by Hollywood just in time for

Christmas. But it is worth noting that as ritual gave birth to stories, the stories, in turn, generated their own rituals, such as placing cookies and milk for Santa on the fireplace mantle, hanging stockings above the hearth to be filled with presents, or having children (and nowadays even pets) photographed with Santa at the shopping mall.

The reverse situation – ritual growing out of narrative – will form the topic of a more detailed case study.

4. FROM NARRATIVE TO RITUAL: THE ESCALADE IN GENEVA

My example of narrative giving birth to ritual – a situation more frequent than ritual giving birth to narrative – is a celebration in the Swiss city of Geneva (until 1815 an independent Republic) that encapsulates for the citizens the identity of their city. This celebration is called *l'Escalade*, and it commemorates events which happened on the Winter Solstice of 1602, according to the Gregorian calendar; but since in 1602 Geneva still used the Julian calendar, the celebration takes place on December 11 and 12, a date that conveniently keeps it separate from Christmas. The Escalade differs from rituals based on pure myth through the historical nature of its foundational narrative. While rituals based on myth involve two layers, the story and the ritual, the Escalade presents three distinct layers: the historical events, the stories told about them, and the commemorative events.

4.1 The Events

According to the most reliable historical sources – such as the report of Sunday, December 12, 1602, in the Register of the City Council – the events unfolded as follows:

On December 11, 1602, the Duke of Savoy, Charles Emmanuel, chose the longest night of the year to launch a surprise attack on the Protestant city-state of Geneva, hoping to reclaim it for Catholicism and to expand his sphere of influence north of the Alps. His army consisted of about 300 mercenaries from Italy and Spain who were to conquer the city, with an additional 1,000 troops who were to occupy it. They marched silently on a moonless night to the gates of the city. There they set up ladders against the city walls and climbed inside the town (hence the name *l'Escalade*), but the first invaders stumbled upon a watchman who fired a gun and woke up the sleeping city. The citizens jumped out of bed, seized weapons, and managed to repel the invasion. A woman who was cooking soup for her husband, who worked a night shift, grabbed her cast iron pot and threw it on the head of an enemy soldier, instantly killing him. Another woman was so scared by the noise that she pushed a huge piece of furniture against the door to block it; the next day it took several strong men to remove the improvised barricade. 17 Genevans and 54 enemies were killed; 13 were taken prisoners and hung the next morning, in a blatant violation of the Geneva conventions (which of course did not exist at the time).

4.2 The Story

These basic events were soon celebrated in oral and written narratives that lie halfway between history and legend: they recount actual events, but they elevate these events to heroic status and they embellish them with many apocryphal details. The citizens of Geneva like to think of the Escalade as a major event in the history of modern Europe, but there is little or no mention of it in history books, except of course for those books that concern the history of Geneva. Had the attack succeeded, it is probable that the King of France, Henri IV, would not have tolerated the annexation of Geneva by his rival the Duke of Savoy. The Protestant Swiss cantons also had a vested interest in the freedom of the city. Nevertheless, the local narrative tradition builds the failed attack into an event with decisive consequences, not just for Geneva, but for the future of enlightened and progressive mankind (represented by the political and religious institutions of Geneva).

A song about the Escalade was penned around 1603 by an unknown author who must have been a direct witness. This song, known as *Cé Qué Laino* (the one who is up there), is written in a franco-provençal dialect as incomprehensible to speakers of standard French as Swiss German dialects are to speakers of High German. It consists of 64 strophes, 30 of which recount in grisly detail the execution of the prisoners. The failure of their Catholic prayers to the Virgin Mary to save them from the gallows is noted with rather sadistic pleasure. The text also describes executions that did not take place through a colorful counterfactual narrative devoted to the unpleasant fate that awaited the pastors of Geneva if the enemy had won: they would have been paraded through Rome in a triumph reminiscent of the customs of ancient Rome, a prelude to their being burned at the stake. The first three and the last strophe of *Cé Qué Laino*, which give credit to the Almighty for the victory, have become something like the national anthem of Geneva, and they are sung on several official occasions beside the Escalade, including the swearing in of the City Council. Because *Cé Qué Laino* is written in a dialect that few people understand, and because most people know only four of its strophes, the "official" version of the Escalade comes from a 19th-century song, *La Belle Escalade*, which is sung to the tune of *La Carmagnole*, the song of the French revolution of 1789, and is it widely distributed in the form of illustrated posters. Most children have it memorized. For the 400th anniversary of the Escalade in 2002 a comic-book version of the story, *Sauvez Genève*, appeared; this version tries to counter the political incorrectness of *Cé Qué Laino* by promoting tolerance of diversity. The story tells about a young Catholic boy who happens to be in Geneva on the night of the attack and fights bravely to save the city. In this version Geneva is not the Protestant Rome that it long prided itself to be, but a breeding ground of religious fanaticism.

For a narratologist, it is easy to see why the story of the Escalade has become something like a national epic of Geneva. The tale combines the excitement and tellability of fictional narrative with the informational appeal of stories based on historical facts. Its tellability lies in its simple dichotomy of "us" – the good guys, Genevans, representatives of religious freedom and political self-determination – versus "them," the bad guys, Catholicism, the Pope, mercenaries, oppression by foreign powers. It is also rich in comic episodes; for instance when the troops returned to the castle and the Duke of Savoy greeted his defeated commander, he used a scatological expression that delights schoolchildren: "Vous m'avez fait là une belle cacade." The story leads to the most satisfactory of denouements: the victory of the underdog over a much more powerful opponent (hints of David and Goliath), and it offers a valuable moral captured by the proverb "Aides-toi, le ciel t'aidera" ("God helps those who help themselves"). For the schoolteachers of Geneva, the story of the Escalade is a golden source of *edutainment*: it teaches about life in the old days and about the history of the city, it has its share of female heroines, and it presents a vivid spectacle to the imagination. It is used not only in history classes, but also in art projects (children are asked to illustrate it), in composition classes (children retell it from various perspectives), and in music education (through the teaching of the numerous songs inspired by the events).

4.3 The Ritual

According to tradition, the day after the Escalade – which was a Sunday – Théodore de Bèze, the successor of Calvin, led the population of Geneva to the Cathedral for a religious service, during which the congregation sang Psalm 124 of David, a Psalm that thanks God for liberating Israel from its enemies. Psalm 124 has become known as the Psalm of the Escalade, and it is sung every December 12 in a commemorative service in the Cathedral.

In the following years the commemoration of the Escalade quickly took the form of a carnival, a development which met with strong disapproval from the religious authorities. In Calvinist Geneva all religious celebrations had been banned, not just the celebrations linked to Catholic Saints, but also Christmas and Easter. The festivities of the Escalade provided a much needed occasion for rejoicing and merriment. Even the rather dour Jean-Jacques Rousseau, who spent most of his life in exile, made it a point to get together with other Genevans in Paris for the Escalade and to drink a couple of bottles of wine, for as he wrote, the Escalade should be celebrated with wine, not with milk (Genève, Département de l'Instruction Publique 17).

To this day two tendencies can be observed: an austere, patriotic, religious commemoration reminiscent of Thanksgiving in the U.S., and a wild, noisy, unbridled celebration reminiscent of Halloween. The spirit of Thanksgiving is maintained by the Company of 1602, a rather exclusive society consisting mainly of members of the Geneva aristocracy, who are the descendents of Huguenots and other refugees from the wars of religion. The company of 1602 parades across the Old Town of Geneva, dressed in historical costumes, and stops in various places to read the list of the 17 people who gave their life to defend the city. The pageant ends in front of the cathedral with a bonfire and the singing of *Cé Qué Laino*. It is all very orderly and respectful of the Calvinist heritage of the city. The spirit of Halloween and of the carnivalesque, on the other hand, manifests itself in the habit of holding costume parties. Originally people dressed as Savoyards, which means as peasants with a blue blouse, a red neck scarf and a straw hat. (This costume reflects a misidentification of the enemy, for the soldiers of the Duke were not peasants from Savoy but foreign mercenaries from Italy and Spain. In fact the people from neighboring Savoy were rather on the side of Geneva.) Nowadays we see a full range of costumes, especially scary ones inspired by Halloween. The highlight of Escalade parties is the breaking of a chocolate pot filled with marzipan vegetables in memory of the heroic feat of Mère Royaume, the woman who killed an enemy soldier with a pot of soup. This is done by the oldest and youngest people in attendance, and they must recite the traditional formula: "Ainsi périssent les ennemis de la République" ("So may perish the enemies of the Republic"). Children wearing costumes go from door to door, singing *Cé Qué Laino* and *La Belle Escalade*, and this being Switzerland, they are rewarded with money instead of candy. A more recent tradition is a foot-race that starts from the castle where the Savoyard army began its march, and ends in the old town. Everybody can participate in the foot-race, and all kinds of costumes are welcome, in contrast to the historical pageant, in which only members of the Company of 1602 can march. (In fact the Company was not too happy about the race, and they insisted on having it take place a week before their own show.)

Despite its religious façade, the Escalade has all the markings of a secular, modern-day ritual that fulfills only condition 1. As a commemoration of historical events, the celebration does not involve any existentially significant crossing of boundaries. Its time is linear, not cyclical: *pace* Mircea Eliade, the celebrants do not believe in an eternal return that transports them every December 12 into *illud tempus*, the sacred time of the foundation of a community by mythical creatures. Participants seek entertainment, not purification, spiritual renewal, or access to a higher status, and they do not act out of civil duty, since there is no obligation to attend the festivities. Does it mean that the Escalade is pure hedonistic gratification? We should remember that in the early 17th century it served the covert purpose of making the religious world order of Calvinist theocracy more bearable through a temporary suspension of rules similar to what takes place during the carnival in Catholic countries. Nowadays opportunities for entertainment have become so numerous that they no longer need a ritual justification. But insofar as it brings to its voluntary participants pride in their city, a sense of identity, and integration in a community, the fun of the Escalade still fulfills the fundamentally social function of ritual.

4.4 The Ritualization of the Story

The transformation of the story – or stories – of the Escalade into a public celebration rests on several operations:

Selection. Rather than reenacting the story in its totality, the ritual makes a choice of particularly "performable" elements. (Performability is to ritual what tellability is to narrative.) The celebration commemorates the killing of a soldier with a pot of soup, the death of 17 citizens, and more recently, with the staging of the foot-race, the march of the Savoyards from a nearby castle; but it leaves out the deed of the woman who pushed a heavy dresser against her door, the hanging of the prisoners (an episode that people would rather forget), or the climbing of the walls with ladders.

Transformation. The death of the defenders is not represented through simulated action but read as a list. The soup pot is no longer a metal container but, as one would expect in Switzerland, a chocolate confection. (The Escalade is used by the local chocolatiers as an opportunity to flaunt their skills.) In the original story the pot breaks the head of a soldier, but in the reenactment it is the pot that gets broken.

Expansion. There is a tendency to add new events every year. For instance, the smashing of the chocolate pot by the youngest and oldest member of the company is not part of the original story but an added symbol: the youngest and oldest stand for everybody whose age falls within the limits they embody – in other words, for the entire population of the Geneva. A more recent addition is the foot-race, which dates back to the seventies, when physical fitness, and particularly running became a fad. But introducing new elements is contrary to the spirit of ritual. As the Escalade expands into a popular feast, it tends to become a nondescript festival similar to the fairs and carnivals of other cities, and to lose sight of what makes it a unique expression of Genevan identity.

Blending of multiple stories and rituals. The narrative background of the Escalade weaves together internal and external stories. The internal stories include all the versions of the historical events, from the report found in the archives of the city to the songs and fictions that turn the facts into legend.

The most important of the external narratives is the story told in Psalm 124, which can be regarded as embedded within the internal narrative, since the singing of the psalm is something that the citizens of Geneva reportedly did on December 12, 1602. Its relation to the internal narrative is a matter of analogy between Israel and Geneva, both beneficiaries of divine protection. Since the Escalade took place on the longest night of the year, the festivities allude very indirectly to the myth of death and rebirth of the Winter Solstice, and the little marzipan vegetables in the chocolate pots suggest the widespread tradition of celebration of the harvest. But the richest source of external narratives resides in the costumes of the participants. Almost all costumes tell a story. When people dress as peasants from Savoy the reference is internal, but when they dress as Batman, Superman, Pirates of the Caribbean, cowboys and indians, Disney princesses, angels and witches, they bring in the full narrative spectrum of modern popular culture.

If we take "narrative" in a rather broad sense that makes it synonymous with "interpretation," or "explanation," we can say that the Escalade combines the external narratives of Thanksgiving and of Halloween. These two narratives present Genevan identity in sharply different ways: while the Thanksgiving type of commemoration equates Geneva with the chosen people of Israel and implicitly defines Genevan identity in opposition to foreigners and Catholics (even though Catholics are now in majority), the carnivalesque spirit of Halloween embraces the cultural diversity of present-day Geneva, a city that takes pride in its international institutions.

5. Conclusion

In this chapter I have outlined three ways in which the fields of narratology and ritual studies can enrich each other:

Comparison of narrative and ritual. This approach is based on the assumption that even though ritual and narrative are distinct phenomena, we will gain a better understanding of each of them taken individually through the study of their similarities and differences.

Contribution of ritual studies to narrative. Drawing on state-of-the art conceptions of ritual should lead to better informed interpretations of narrative when ritual is part of its content – either through direct mention, structural similarity, archetypal patterns, or invention by the characters of private rituals.

Contribution of narratology – or perhaps, more generally, of the concept of narrative – to ritual studies. This field of investigation focuses on the feed-back loop that connects narrative and ritual: how ritual is narrated; how ritual gives birth to stories; and conversely how narrative becomes ritual. The excavation of the rich narrative underground in which ritual grows its roots seems to me the most promising avenue for a collaboration of narrative and ritual studies.

REFERENCES

Austin, John L. *How To Do Things With Words*. Oxford: Oxford UP, 1962.
Bardet, Daniel and Rachid Nawa. *Sauvez Genève*. Nyon: Editions Glénat, 2002.
Boyd, Brian. *On the Origin of Stories: Evolution, Cognition, and Fiction*. Cambridge, MA: Belknap Press of Harvard UP, 2010.
Cazeneuve, Jean. *Les rites et la condition humaine*. Paris: Presses Universitaires de France, 1957.
Doty, William G. *Mythography: The Study of Myths and Rituals*. Tuscaloosa, AL: U of Alabama P, 1986.
Eliade, Mircea. *The Myth of the Eternal Return*. Trans. Willard R. Trask. New York: Pantheon, 1954.
—. "Myth and Reality." *The Myth and Ritual Theory*. Ed. Robert A. Segal. Oxford: Blackwell, 1998. 180-89.
Girard, René. *La violence et le sacré*. Paris: Grasset, 1972.
Guillot, Alexandre, with illustrations by Edouard Elzingre. *La nuit de l'escalade*. Genève: Editions Slatkine, 1998.
Herman, David. *Basic Elements of Narrative*. Malden, MA: Wiley-Blackwell, 2009.
Hühn, Peter. "Event and Eventfulness." *Handbook of Narratology*. Eds. Peter Hühn, John Pier, Wolf Schmid and Jörg Schönert. Berlin: De Gruyter, 2009. 80-97.
Kluckhohn, Clyde. "Myths and Rituals: A General Theory." *The Myth and Ritual Theory*. Ed. Robert A. Segal. Oxford: Blackwell, 1998. 313-40.

Lotman, Jurij M. *The Structure of the Artistic Text*. Trans. G. Lenhoff and R. Vroon. Ann Arbor, MC: U of Michigan P, 1977.

Rappaport, Roy. *Ritual and Religion in the Making of Humanity*. Cambridge: Cambridge UP, 1999.

Ronget, Pierre, Luc Wunderli and Anne Macheret, eds. *L'Escalade a 400 ans: 1602-2002*. Genève: Département de l'Instruction Publique, 2002

Ryan, Marie-Laure. *Rituel et poésie: une lecture de Saint-John Perse*. Berne: Peter Lang Verlag, 1977.

Searle, John. *Speech Acts*. London: Cambride UP, 1969.

Smith, William Robertson. "Lectures on the Religion of the Semites." *The Myth and Ritual Theory*. Ed. Robert A. Segal. Oxford: Blackwell, 1998. 17-34.

Turner, Victor. *The Ritual Process: Structure and Anti-Structure*. Chicago: Aldine, 1969.

Van Gennep, Arnold. *The Rites of Passage*. Trans. M.B. Vizedoma and G.L. Caffee. Chicago, IL: U of Chicago P, 1960.

Vierne, Simone. *Rite, roman, initiation*. Grenoble: Presses Universitaires de Grenoble, 1973.

On the Narrativity of Rituals: Interfaces between Narratives and Rituals and Their Potential for Ritual Studies

VERA & ANSGAR NÜNNING

PROLOGUE: ARE NARRATIVE THEORY AND RITUAL STUDIES STRANGE BED FELLOWS? INTRODUCTION TO THE OBJECTIVES AND THE STRUCTURE OF THE CHAPTER

Whoever attempts to address the question of how narrative theory and ritual studies are related must venture deep into new territory. That is to say, whoever wants to plunge into the research on what rituals have to do with narrative, what narration has to do with rituals, and how narrative theory and ritual studies are related, is likely to find themselves at a loss: when reviewing the vast multitude of publications on narrative theory, now burgeoning to the point that even the experts themselves can barely gain an overview of it, it is astounding to observe that while narrative studies has pursued interests in many subjects – one could almost say: in almost all subjects – it has, to date, hardly concerned itself at all with rituals or ritual-narration. When reading the latest handbooks, monographs and collections on the equally booming topic of ritual studies, however, one arrives at the sobering conclusion that narrativity and narration, though mentioned in passing, have themselves hardly ever been the object of systematic or theoretical reflections. Burckhard Dücker's excellent introductory monograph *Rituals: Forms – Functions – History*[1] or the wide-ranging two-volume anthology *Theorizing Rituals*, which of course provide an incomparably more comprehensive overview than we can offer here, can be taken as representative of many works in ritual studies in that they dedicate no separate chapter to either the narration or the narrativity of rituals. Attempts to find any such concepts from narrative theory in the index of this handbook or any other publication on ritual studies will, at present, be in vain. Until now, ritual studies and narrative theory have hardly even taken notice of one another.[2] Thus, one might – at first sight – arrive at the conclusion that narrative theory and ritual studies are strange bed fellows. Yet this first impression is deceptive. A closer look – this, at least, is our first thesis – reveals a close connection between narrative and rituals.[3] One can even go so far as to talk about the narrativity of rituals and the rituality of (at least certain) narratives.

Since making bold, sweeping statements is typical for programmatic contributions such as this, we would like to begin by introducing three deliberately exaggerated theses. The first thesis is that rituals and narratives are closely connected, as evidenced by a multitude of similarities, parallels and structural analogies. We will present these in an introductory overview of the interfaces of narratives and rituals, as well as of narrative theory and ritual theory, and, in doing so, identify and elaborate on the different levels and forms of these interfaces. Our second thesis is that the examination of both the narrative structure and the perspectivity of rituals and ritual narrations can be especially profitable from the point of view of narratology or literary narrative theory, as sections two and three will reveal. The third

---

1 All translations from German-language scholarship are by Simon Cooke, who also provided a draft translation of an earlier version of the manuscript. Moreover, thanks are due to Jan Rupp for valuable suggestions and to Martin Zettersten, who provided a number of stylistic improvements.
2 However, Dücker refers to the long-standing debate over the relationship between "myth and ritual, word and narrative on the one hand and action on the other" (76). For this debate over "myth and ritual theory" (76), see also Segal.
3 This connection is suggested yet not fully developed by the following studies: Elsbree, *Rituals of Life* and *Ritual Passages*. For a more general study of the relationship between literature and ritual, see Braungart.

thesis proposes that, above all, rituals and narratives display a number of formal equivalences, which we will try to outline in the last section – "Cultures as Communities of Narratives and Values" – from the point of view of both cultural studies and functional-historical narrative research.

As the above theses already make clear, this chapter tries to provide some theoretical underpinnings that linking concepts and categories from narrative theory and ritual theory can be profitable for both fields. The chapter also endorses a premise that has become controversial in ritual studies in recent years: though we are highly aware of the substantial differences between types of rituals and narratives, and even more aware of the heterogeneity of particular rituals and stories which are subsumed under a heading like "marriage ritual" or "*bildungsroman*," we still think it is profitable to try to abstract away from these divergences and construct a kind of "ideal type" of both ritual and narrative. It is quite obvious that almost every single instance does not entirely conform to these constructs – after all, there is no "narrative" as such, there are only particular narrations, marked by their genre-specific features, the particular cultural situation in which they are told, the particularities of their styles, character conception, perspectivization, embedded values and so on. Even a well-known and seemingly simple genre like the "*bildungsroman*," for instance, covers a broad spectrum of different – and contradictory – sub-genres, which depend on the cultural preferences, the (rejection of) teleology, as well as the particularities of the "female" *bildungsroman* or those of different generations of authors with a migration background. But aware as we are of these differences, we still think that much would be lost if scholars refrained from exploring the general features of narratives and rituals. After all, the concentration on particular ritual performances or texts shifts the focus away from the features they have in common with others, and can thus hide from view the elements in which a given ritual or story significantly undercuts and changes genre conventions.

In the following, we would like to focus on the question of the possible benefits that new concepts and developments in narrative research might have when applied in ritual studies. Therefore, we will start with a short review of the interfaces of narratives and rituals – the aforementioned narrativity of rituals and rituality of narratives.

1. NARRATIVITY OF RITUALS AND RITUALITY OF NARRATIVES: AN INTRODUCTORY OVERVIEW OF THE INTERFACES OF NARRATIVES AND RITUALS, AND NARRATIVE THEORY AND RITUAL THEORY

Rituals and narratives are so closely linked that it is actually quite astonishing that narrative theory and ritual theory have both largely ignored each other. On the one hand, since rituals themselves often possess a narrative structure, it is possible to talk about a narrativity of rituals. On the other hand, the second part of the chiasm – namely, the rituality of narratives – is meant to point out that many narratives and cultural plots contain features of rituals.[4] In addition to the narrative structure of rituals, the perspectivity of rituals and ritual narrations is another aspect that connects rituals and narrations. Finally, one needs to mention functional equivalences between narratives and rituals which are based on the respective performative qualities we will analyse in the final part of this chapter.

Since these parallels, structural similarities and functional equivalences will be presented in the following section in more detail, a short overview of the most important overlaps between narratives and rituals will suffice at this point. Without attempting or being able to claim completeness, one can distinguish at least twelve different forms or levels of these interfaces. The first three emanate from the definitions of narrativity currently used in narrative theory and are – though from a different perspective – briefly outlined in the introduction to this volume:

1. The situatedness of narratives and rituals: Both narratives and rituals are embedded in a particular cultural moment, and in a particular situation which is, among other aspects, influenced by the emotions, knowledge and intentions of the participants as well as by their social and personal relations to each other. This "situatedness" influences the form and design of the particular narrative as well as ritual performance.

---

4 Cf. Braungart 27, who points out that literary texts often feature ritual-like elements and follow a certain aesthetic of repetition, as a matter of generic conventions, for example.

2. The creation of a world which changes: Both narratives and rituals create a world of their own, a world apart from the ordinary context in which readers, viewers or participants find themselves. This world is peopled by agents who are human (or resemble human beings in significant ways, be they gods or talking animals) and is characterized by the fact that certain (although sometimes slight, psychological rather than physical) transformations occur within this world.
3. The narrative structure of narrations and rituals: Both narrations and rituals usually feature a certain sequencing. In addition to the beginning and the ending, one can distinguish a number of mandatory and optional sequences respectively.[5] While the sequencing of elements is, in some ritual types, relatively rigid, most narrative genres make it possible to loosely join a variety of scenes; even the chronological order of the depicted events is rarely adhered to. However, some genres feature a rather rigid structure; fairy tales or early forms of detective fiction are cases in point, as well as eye-witness accounts of traffic accidents or short narrative CVs handed in for job applications.
4. The perspectivity of narratives, rituals and ritual stories: A second interface is based on the fact that the narrative-theoretical category of perspective plays a role in both the investigation of rituals and in the analysis of narratives. In both fields, different levels of perspectivity have to be considered: in rituals, there are the perspectives of participants – with all the differences between them – to be distinguished from those of observers, who may be in a position to overlook the whole field and get a more or less holistic impression of the event, but also lose a certain understanding of the event or have a restricted viewpoint. Ritual stories are usually written from the perspective of one of the observers or participants; in order to get a more balanced account of the ritual in question, one has to take into account the different perspectives of several witnesses. But even though it is possible to take into account categories like the spatio-temporal position of the witness as well as aspects such as his or her beliefs, emotions, norms and values, it seems impossible to arrive at "the objective" story of the ritual. The perspectives of characters and narrators in stories resemble those in rituals, as they are

---

5   On this aspect of the sequencing or (narrative) structure of rituals, see Gladigow; Oppitz.

subject to the same restraints. In contrast to rituals (though not to stories about rituals), there probably are more levels of the embeddedness of perspectives to be considered with regard to narratives: the level of characters (who themselves may tell "embedded" stories), the level of narrators talking about those characters and positioning them in a meaningful structure, and the abstract level of the perspective that the story as a whole provides (which may include an ironic distance to the narrator). This abstract level of perspectivity, which results from the way the events are mediated by language and/or images and sounds, is thus lacking in rituals.

5. The experientiality of narratives, rituals and ritual stories: This aspect, which is sometimes held to be the defining characteristic of narrativity,[6] presents a parallel between narrations and rituals or ritual stories, too, for the latter also feature characters and participants who experience the ritual from a subjective point of view. While the experientiality of people engaged in performing or observing rituals is marked by fleeting perceptions and feelings as well as more lasting impressions, which are often made up of very heterogeneous, if not contradictory elements, the experiences of characters or narrators in stories are formed – and thus ascribed meaning – by the use of language and narrative. The experientiality made accessible by narratives is structured, ordered and interpreted.

6. Narrative as a part of rituals: Furthermore, rituals often involve narrations as one of their elements. This becomes especially apparent in marriage rituals, for example, in which short versions of the bride's and bridegroom's life-stories are told (often much to their chagrin). An example from the realm of politics is the use of certain cultural plots made in the nomination of a candidate for the American presidential elections – such as narrations of the *American Dream*.

7. The performative power of narrations and rituals: In terms of their potential functions and effects, another similarity between narratives and rituals consists in the fact that both possess a high degree of performativity. In ritual studies, the focus on individual performances has been strong from the beginning, whereas narratological studies have on-

---

6 Experientiality is a feature of most narratological definitions of narrative. See Fludernik; Herman.

ly recently concentrated on the "mimesis of narrating," exploring the ways in which the event of narrating is represented in tales which serve to highlight the performance of the narrator.

8. Closely connected to this performativity is the power of both narratives and rituals to create and change worlds. Both are privileged "ways of worldmaking" in Nelson Goodman's sense. While the functions of narratives and media as means of creating new worlds have been the focus of recent scholarship,[7] the changes that can be brought about via narratives within and about rituals have not received much attention – even though changes in ritual performances are often justified by means of narratives.[8]

9. Ritual narrations, narratives and narrative genres are some of the most important media for the transmission of rituals. For ritual studies, not only documentary text types like statements gathered via interviews or documentary videos, but also literary genres and travelogues prove to be important sources for collecting data.

10. The combination of rituals and narratives in ritual stories: Most rituals and ritual sites themselves have a story – the story of ritual performances (Dücker 213) – which features a narrative structure. What Aleida Assmann has written of memorial sites holds true for ritual sites as well: they also retain "material traces, which become narratives and with that points of reference for a new cultural memory" (309). Furthermore, rituals and their respective ritual histories should be of equal importance for the histories of institutions, enterprizes and nations.

11. The self-referentiality of rituals and narratives: Just as the self-referential dimension of ritual actions is based on every new ritual performance being related to the history of the respective ritual (cf. Dücker 53), the self-referentiality of cultural narratives is based on their being highly conventionalized and related to respective pretexts.[9] One can generally assume that, in being a part of them, narratives raise the self-

---

7 See A. Nünning, V. Nünning and Neumann, *Cultural Ways* and *Aesthetics and Politics*.

8 We owe this insight to Axel Michaels, who suggested this after a lecture we gave at the Collaborative Research Centre "Ritual Dynamics," University of Heidelberg.

9 On the aspect of intertextuality and "interrituality," see Gladigow; Michaels.

referential dimension of rituals in so far as they are often ritualized themselves and explicitly express a given ritual occasion.[10]
12. Both rituals and narratives are characterized by a structure of agency. In both cases agency can be distributed widely rather than lying with ritual experts or narrators alone. Thus, questions such as who acts or is given the possibility to act, and who has their story told or their perception represented are central to the study of rituals as well as narratives. Categories which indicate narrative agency, such as narrative transmission and perspective structure, might be productively applied to the analysis of rituals, just as, vice versa, concepts of ritual agency to the analysis of narratives.[11]

Thus, the first preliminary conclusion is that there are several overlaps between narratives and rituals on various levels. Furthermore, it is obvious that one of the primary assumptions of the collaborative research centre on "ritual dynamics" – namely that rituals constitute a special mode of human behaviour (cf. Michaels 3) and that "the activities we think of as 'ritual' can be found in many periods and places" (Bell ix)[12] – also holds true for narrations and narrative actions respectively: narrating is, likewise, an anthropologically basic human need, a special type of activity found universally, whereas the respective characteristics are, like rituals, dependent on culture and history.[13]

While it is inherent to our theme to emphasize the similarities and parallels between narratives and rituals, the differences between them should not be forgotten. Rituals are symbolic actions with a high degree of physical performativity, which, as a result of their performative and scene-like dimensions, can, as a rule, activate all channels of the human senses. Narratives, by contrast, are predominantly constituted of cognitive and emotional components – at least if one restricts the meaning of the term to writ-

---

10 On the aspect of ritual "self-referentiality," see Stausberg, "Reflexive Ritualisation" and "Reflexivity."
11 We owe this insight to Jan Rupp. Further on the aspect of ritual agency, see Sax.
12 For this "hypothesis that ritual activities are special types of activity which are found universally," see also Dücker 2.
13 On story-telling as a basic human need, see Sugiyama, "Origins of Narrative" and "Narrative Theory."

ten narratives. With regard to a wider definition of the term narrative, which includes stories told in drama, ballet, or pantomime (see Ryan, *Narrative*; Barthes 79), different aspects have to be considered: paintings, sculptures or friezes, for instance, also appeal to the eye, while films usually integrate sounds as well. Touch and olfactory signals, however, are – at the moment – largely confined to rituals, and the stories told in rituals. One important difference seems to remain, however, for while rituals are usually characterized by the tendency to be repetitive, affirmative and constructive (cf. Dücker 31), narrations in general and literary genres in particular can, to a greater degree, be innovative and function as a revisionist counter-discourse or a culture-critical meta-discourse (cf. Zapf). Thus, while the generally dominant features of rituals are the self-presentation of the prevailing order and the establishment, visualization and preservation of community- and consensus-creating value-orientations, this only holds true for certain, culturally dominant or collective narratives. But this difference, which was long held to be a given, fades if one takes into account the broad variety of individualized rituals. And even with regard to the contrast between eventfulness and repetition, the case is far more complex, as Marie-Laure Ryan points out in her brilliant contribution to this volume.

Despite these differences however, the multitude of overlaps between narratives and rituals, which can be found on various levels, indicates that a cooperation between narrative theory and ritual theory could be fruitful for both sides. The most obvious field of interdisciplinary cooperation would be the application of the narratological toolkit for the interpretation of narratives to the stories told in and about rituals. After all, most of the accounts of rituals are narratives – so why not take advantage of the highly differentiated tools for the analysis of stories developed in the field of narratology? At the same time, the question arises as to which aspects of rituals appear especially interesting from a narratological point of view. We would like to take a closer look at two of the overlaps mentioned above, namely the narrative structure of rituals and the perspectivity of rituals.

2. THE NARRATIVE STRUCTURE OF RITUALS AND RITUAL NARRATIONS: RITUALS AND RITUAL THEORIES FROM A NARRATOLOGICAL POINT OF VIEW

The most obvious parallel between narratives and rituals is surely that rituals themselves often have a narrative structure. "Because ritual acts follow a course from their beginnings to set destinations, they have a sense-making narrative structure" (Dücker 11; cf. 127).[14] According to most typologies that have been developed by ritual studies for the description of the forms of ritual actions, sequencing – which is a characteristic of narrativity – is a constitutive characteristic of rituals. Both formulaic narrative genres like folk tales and the ritual process are divided into certain sections or sequences which proceed according to a set order.

Initiation and transition rituals which facilitate transitions in life serve to exemplify the narrative structure of rituals. One example is Arnold van Gennep's three-phase model, which he developed in order to analyse the spatial, temporal and social transition processes. This model – which takes as its starting point the phase of the initial condition, followed by the liminal, intermediate phase during which the change takes place, which leads to the connection-phase – features distinctive temporal and narrative structures. Paraphrasing van Gennep's model, "[t]he three phases – separation, liminality, and incorporation – enact a powerful homology of our personal sense of beginnings, transitions, and endings in life and literature" (Elsbree, *Ritual Passages* 16). However, other cultural events such as the empowerment or disempowerment of rulers are not only strongly ritualized by strictly set procedure structures, but also possess a narrative structure as well.

As mentioned above, many rituals not only feature a narrative structure, they also often integrate narratives as elements of their ritual forms of action. When narratives become a part of rituals, they usually further emphasize their narrative structure by summarizing the life or development of the

---

14 Cf. also Elsbree, who describes "ritual and narrative structures as coexisting, ordering activities of the brain" (*Ritual Passages* 13). Similar to narrative, "ritual [is] a coherent set of symbolic actions that has a real, transformative effect on individuals and social groups" (Lincoln 6).

ritual's protagonist up until the present point in time in a narrative, and often highly conventionalized and ritualized, way. This is not only evident in the private domain in marriage rituals, but also in the field of academic honours and ceremonies at which the laudation, which usually has a narrative structure, is the central element. Just like any other narrative genre, the stories told – or read aloud – in rituals are subject to both cultural norms and historical change. As Stefanie Hammer's contribution to this volume shows, even within a relatively brief period of time, and in a very specific ritual like the burial ceremony of German soldiers, such embedded narratives do change within the space of only a few decades, thus expressing a new evaluation of both the role of the state and the status of soldiers.

Especially in the case of rituals which mark central transitions in life, the narrative structure of the ritual also shapes the respective life-story of the person participating in the ritual. Of course, the significance of the rituals for the biographies of those participating in them either as protagonists or as spectators is well known (cf. Großklaus). However, the formative power which narrative patterns of sense-making exert on the level of the ritual itself and on the level of retrospective sense-making deserves greater attention. Dücker rightly observes that rituals are, "in sum, action-sequences which one remembers because they are meaningful for one's own life-*history* and which have become a symbolic point of reference for a narrative context which generates meaning" (8). Thus, the close connection between rituals and stories or narrations is based on the fact that transition rituals such as school enrolment, graduation from school or university, and weddings mark especially important stages which play a central and structuring role for both the individual life-story and the family memory. It is also grounded in the importance of stories within one's own life, as a central element of constructing identity, especially in times of crises.[15]

From the point of view of narrative theory, this firstly raises the question of to what extent culture-specific patterns of narration or narrative genres have emerged for the telling of such ritually emphasized situations. This is especially pertinent since many narrative genres are themselves ritualized so strongly that one can speak of their "rituality." During the past couple of years the genres of biography and autobiography in particular have displayed a strong tendency towards self-reflexivity which has led to the de-

---

15 See, for instance, Eakin; Echterhoff and Straub.

velopment of innovative forms of fictional meta-(auto)biographies. In the same way as the practice of rituals usually includes criticism of rituals (cf. Dücker 13), self-reflexive meta-biographies, which continue the practice of the genre, often function as a medium of genre memory and genre criticism (cf. Nadj).

Secondly, the narrative structure of rituals raises a further question: to what extent do certain rituals correlate with certain narratives or culturally available plots? With the aid of categories developed in narrative theory for the analysis of event sequences and plots, ritual studies could describe more exactly the respective narrative structure of certain types of rituals.

Since narrations are often important parts of rituals, the third question to arise is of what functions narratives fulfil as elements of rituals. In the case of funerary and burial rituals, narrations can help to commemorate the deceased in an idealized or wished-for form, just as pictures turn absence into presence. Barack Obama's speeches, which frequently include biographical narrations, illustrate four further functions which narratives can serve in political rituals: they introduce the candidate as a representative and protagonist of the cultural plot of the *American Dream*; they integrate the event into the tradition and, in so doing, suggest continuity; they propagate the values and norms he represents by appealing to the emotions; and, thus, are meant to promote the reintegration of the nation.

The thesis of a structural and functional analogy between narratives and rituals is further supported by the extensive overlaps between the so-called "building blocks of narrative" and the useful matrix of characteristics developed by Burckhard Dücker and Dietrich Harth for "Ritual" as a frame- and framing-concept.[16] The categories of analysis from narrative theory can be useful for ritual studies as a means of examining the following dimensions of the narrative structure of rituals more closely:

- the time structure of rituals or the "ritual time-structure" (Dücker 39ff.),
- the structure and semantization of ritual sites (cf. 44ff.),
- the action-structure of rituals, ritual scripts and ritual narrations, and the sequence of obligatory and optional sequences,
- the event-relation (cf. 100),

---

16 Cf. Dücker 100-102. The concept of framing is, however, more difficult to apply to any given ritual than it appears at first sight; cf. Jungaberle and Weinhold.

- the ritual's participants, and the various roles played respectively by the protagonists, specialists, participants and onlookers, as well as their interrelations (cf. 48ff.).

Thus, the conclusion so far is that rituals and ritual narrations not only feature a narrative structure but often constitute important elements of rituals as well. Furthermore, aside from those embedded narrations, rituals feature other typical elements of narratives. Beyond that, individual life stories, family histories and the histories of institutions, enterprises and nations are strongly shaped by ritualized narratives.

3. THE MULTIPERSPECTIVITY OF RITUALS AND RITUAL NARRATIONS: RITUALS AND RITUAL NARRATIONS FROM THE POINT OF VIEW OF LITERARY STUDIES AND NARRATIVE THEORY

While the narrative structure of rituals is already widely known – even if, to the best of our knowledge, it has hardly ever been the subject of systematic or comparative cultural research – there is another narratologically interesting aspect of rituals that has as yet attracted relatively little interest: that is, the perspective from which ritual action-processes are observed and represented (cf. Dücker 63). Instead of just focusing on the level of the ritual action-sequences, it is important to systematically consider the perspectivity or multiperspectivity of rituals and ritual narrations as well.

Ritual studies has so far made a distinction between the interior or lifeworld perspective of the people participating in the ritual, i.e. the emic perspective, and the exterior or system-perspective of onlookers, the etic perspective. Even though this theoretical and methodological distinction between the interior perspective of the participants and the exterior perspective of the onlookers is without doubt fundamental and important, it only begins to reflect the perspectival complexity and multiperspectivity of many rituals and ritual narrations. Specialists and persons in charge of a ritual performance surely have a different perspective than other participants and onlookers, who are involved nonetheless. Moreover, the distinction according to the criterion of belonging vs. non-belonging (i.e. us vs. them; cf. Dücker 124) appears to be too crude to grasp the multitude of perspectives that must be taken into account if we are to analyse rituals and ritual narrations in a sophisticated way.

As is generally known, literary narrative theory has developed a broad spectrum of competing models for the description of the possible ways in which an event or an action sequence can be narratively and perspectivally mediated. Though constraints of space do not allow for a separate, detailed presentation of these models,[17] we would at least like to point out that these models can also be profitable for the analysis of the perspectivity or multi-perspectivity of rituals and ritual narrations.

On the one hand, the models from literary narrative theory offer analytical categories for defining the respective forms of perspectivization and changes of perspective in narrative sources on which ritual studies rely for the collection of data. In doing so, it becomes clear which perspective is privileged in a certain culture or epoch. This is closely related to questions of authority: which perspectives (in particular with regard to social/religious status or role as well as moral and religious values) are given a voice or privileged against other, "peripheral" subjects? It is also linked to formal and structural issues, such as the choice of genre or the creation of the "persona" of a narrator within a text.

On the other hand, the analytical categories which we have developed for forms and functions of multi-perspective narrations in literary narrative texts (cf. Nünning and Nünning, *Multiperspektivisches Erzählen*) can profitably be adapted for the study of multi-perspectivity in rituals and ritual narrations. Furthermore, literary narrative theory has developed differentiated categories for resolving the question of the credibility, or the degree of (un-)reliability – especially relevant for travelogues – which might prove beneficial for the analysis of ritual narrations.

---

17 See, for instance, the discussion about the concept of "point of view," "perspective" and "focalization," which are conceptualized in different ways by any number of theorists, among them Gerard Genette, Seymour Chapman, Dorrit Cohn, James Phelan and a host of others. For a brief introduction to categories for the analysis of narratives see Neumann and Nünning; a good overview of the main concepts and areas of research is provided by Herman, Jahn and Ryan.

4. CULTURES AS COMMUNITIES OF NARRATIVES AND VALUES, OR: THE NARRATIVE-PERFORMATIVE CONSTRUCTION OF CULTURAL MEMORY, SOCIAL NORMS AND COLLECTIVE IDENTITY: RITUAL AND RITUAL-NARRATION FROM THE POINT OF VIEW OF CULTURAL-HISTORICAL AND FUNCTIONAL-HISTORICAL NARRATIVE RESEARCH

In this penultimate section we aim to shed some light on the question of the functions which narrations and ritual performances can fulfil for their respective cultural formations. Both have a broad spectrum of different functions which, at the same time, they are never fully absorbed into (cf. Wulf 190). Moreover, it is always controversial which functions can be held to be most important and even differentiated from other ones. Particularly with regard to functions, any kind of typology is bound to be as arbitrary as it is – hopefully – useful for an understanding of the features narratives and rituals have in common.

From the point of view of cultural-historical and functional-historical narrative research, the most important parallels between narratives and rituals consist in some extensive functional equivalences which both of them feature. Even if it is obvious that different kinds of narrations or rituals also fulfil a host of different functions respectively, it seems fruitful to theoretically distinguish a number of functions which can emerge together in narrative or ritual practice with respective variations, of course, in their dominant relations:

1. Narrations and rituals have an ordering and structuring function which shapes chaotic events into certain action sequences and, in doing so, arranges and structures both individual and social life (cf. Michaels 5-6; Herman, "Stories").[18] This function of ordering and structuring relates to the overarching time-structure of a culture. Through narratives and

---

18 Cf. also Elsbree, *Ritual Passages* 1: "As two ongoing, homologically related activities, ritual and narrative are among the primary means we employ to structure ourselves and our societies and to generate the semantic systems which go beyond both self and society."

rituals, the endless flow of experiences which marks our waking moments becomes meaningful; they make it possible to construct units like episodes and turning points such as the decision to marry or the marriage ritual.

2. By establishing order and structure, narratives and rituals secondly contribute to the reduction of complexity. In doing so, they open up possibilities for coping with contingencies and crises for both the individual and the collective (cf. Wulf 193f.; Herman, "Stories" 179). Both rituals and cultural narratives provide reliable patterns of action which offer relief by telling us what is expected in given situations, or what to do when there is a "breach of the canonical" (cf. Bruner, "Narrative Construction" and *Making Stories 28).*

3. Thirdly, both narrations and rituals fulfil an important community-building and consensus-making function: narratives and rituals support the coherence and the continuity of cultural formations and can therefore function as media of internal integration.[19] However, this community-building function is dependent on the position of the individual within the community; it only works as far as those belonging to that particular community are concerned. Rituals as well as narratives work "integratively towards the inside, exclusively and hierarchically towards the outside" (Böhme 61).

4. This, fourthly, is linked to a differentiating function which narratives and rituals fulfil as media which mark the borders with other cultural formations. What Dücker remarks concerning rituals in this respect is equally true for many cultural narratives: "In this way integration and differentiation are among the central functions of ritual and ritualized action forms." (31) Differentiation also includes highlighting borders and excluding those who do not belong.

---

19 See Bruner, *Making Stories* 25: "[T]he sharing of common stories creates an interpretive community, a matter of great moment ... for promoting cultural cohesion." For the community-building function of ritual, see Durkheim 43: "The really religious beliefs are always common to a determined group, which makes profession of adhering to them and of practicing the rites connected with them. They are not merely received individually by all members of this group; they are something belonging to the group, and they make its unity."

5. Fifthly, narrations and rituals fulfil normative functions: both narratives and rituals serve as a means of constituting and passing on norms and values. Whereas rituals make a spectacle of those value-orientations in a performative way through symbolic actions, narrations usually vividly exemplify values and norms through the description of individual fates. In doing so, narratives make an equally important contribution as rituals to both the stabilization of social orders and to the preservation or change of social values and norms. Just as rituals do, narratives mediate between what is expected and what can be tolerated: they "define the range of canonical characters, the settings in which they operate, the actions that are permissible and comprehensible" (Bruner, "Transactional Self" 93). However, the "tellability" of stories depends on the "breach of the canonical." Expectations are not only raised but disappointed, otherwise there would be no point in telling the story at all.[20] The performance of routine actions is uninteresting from the narrative point of view, they only are mentioned if they are new, somehow broken, or related to another issue within the story.
6. Sixthly, narrations, just like rituals, are "central sites of social knowledge-transfer" (Dücker 3) that stage "collectively shared knowledge and collectively shared action-practices" (Wulf 189). By mediating cultural orientational knowledge, they serve as a means of providing and justifying culturally accepted patterns of actions at the same time.
7. The seventh function, which we have termed the "cultural-memory function," relates to narratives and rituals as important media of cultural remembrance as well as of the construction and modification of existing cultural memory. This includes the creation of "counter-narratives," which aim at criticizing, delegitimizing or even superseding existing memories. Rituals belong to the "privileged objects of memory politics" (Dücker 12) in just about every culture. This can be seen in the way they are preferably remembered – or thematized and staged – in their respective culture-specific narratives (cf. Birk).

---

20 Among the scholars favouring an emphatic definition of event and tellability are Tzvetan Todorov, Jerome Bruner and David Herman. See the very good summary of the state of the discussion, which mentions a host of other scholars as well in Herman, *Basic Elements* 132-135.

8. Whereas the cultural-memory function is related to the past and to ritual narration, the future-shaping function of narratives and rituals consists in the fact that they contribute to both the mediation of schemata and scripts and to the dispositions for sequential actions (cf. Dücker 34). Thus, the history-forming function (9) of narratives and rituals is based on the fact that both narratives and rituals "legitimize future everyday actions beyond the ritual performance" or that they "create institutionally ensured behavioural dispositions" (9). Hence, if Christoph Wulf is right to speak of "ritual as memory and projection" (192), his formulation characterizes equally well an important function of narratives: because of their role as a medium of memory both rituals and narrative participate in what Daniel Schacter et al. think of as the most important function of memory: to imagine and plan future actions (cf. Schacter, Addis and Buckner).
9. Ninthly, the identity-generating (or identity-changing as well as identity-destroying) function, which narratives and rituals fulfil as media for the construction of collective identity, is based on the interaction of the functions which have previously been separated for analytical purposes. It has to be remembered, of course, that such memories of events which serve to construct collective identities are always sites of contest – contests which can even lead to the persecution and destruction of those who happen to belong to the group losing the fight (cf. V. Nünning).
10. Finally, the performative or worldmaking function might best be considered as the result of the interaction between the other functions mentioned above, rather than as another, further function: Both narratives and rituals function as important "ways of worldmaking" in Nelson Goodman's terms (cf. Nünning and Nünning, "Ways of Worldmaking"), or as "cultural constructions of world or reality" (Dücker 37).[21]

All in all it can be observed that narratives and rituals feature extensive functional equivalences. From the point of view of cultural-historical and functional-historical narrative research, the fact that both narratives and rit-

---

21 As Goodman stresses, the making of new worlds always depends on the existence of old ones – and on their destruction. The most important principles of worldmaking are therefore composition and decomposition, deletion and supplementation, deformation, weighting, and ordering (7-12).

uals present historically variable symbolic forms, which are responsible for constituting cultures as "narrative- and memory-communities" (cf. Müller-Funk) and belief- and "value-communities" (Dücker 31) is probably the most important parallel. From the perspective of a functional approach to history, narrations and rituals prove to be social constructions or media of social self-monitoring and self-understanding, which, for their part, actually create the constitutive characteristics of the respective cultures.[22]

Conversely, one can also put forward the argument that a culture's narratives (cf. Müller-Funk) as well as its rituals "illustrate in miniature the reaches of the entire culture" (Dücker 3). In this lies the "metonymic function of rituals" (ibid., cf. 209) and narratives, which makes both such an interesting research area from the perspective of cultural studies. Just as "theory-based ritual analysis opens a way into an understanding of different cultures" (3), theory-based analyses of narrations, cultural plots and narration patterns provide insights into the attitudes, values and norms of respective cultures.

Rituals as well as narratives can be understood as "indicators of and factors in cultural contexts and systems, their functional-capability, order, and continuity" (Dücker 193). They are both "products of a culture as well as forms and factors of presentation and mediation of their structure" (ibid.). Just as rituals mark the interface between the individual and the collective or the individual history and the collective history (cf. 30, 74) and, in doing so "take on a bridging function between the individual, the collective, and the cultural" (185), the narration patterns and plots common in a respective culture mediate between the individual, society and the overall culture which generates these narratives (cf. Bruner, "Transactional Self" 93f.). Just as rituals are created by a culture, a culture is created by its rituals. This chiasm is also pertinent to the relation between culture and narrative: Every culture creates its own culture-specific narrations and plots, while narratives, for their part, both constitute and modify the respective culture at the same time (cf. Müller-Funk).

---

22 For the notion of literature/narrative and, by extension rituals as media of cultural self-reflection, see Voßkamp.

Epilogue: New Directions in Postclassical Narratologies and Their Potential Usefulness for Ritual Studies

Looking back at the question asked at the beginning, the following conclusion can be made for the time being: "rearrangements in theory-design," Luhmann has observed, "must be judged above all by the consequences they bring about and by whether certain aspects can be presented in a better or worse way than before by means of the new arrangement" (57). Thus, the following question arises: what are the benefits of abandoning the peaceful coexistence and the reciprocal obliviousness which has hitherto been practised in narrative theory and ritual studies and to instead make use of approaches, insights and categories from narrative theory in ritual studies and conversely, to make use of the insights of ritual studies in narrative research? There are a number of good reasons in favour of taking a closer look at the interfaces between narratives and rituals merely outlined here and of continuing the suggested cooperation between ritual sciences and narrative theory.

For the time being one could refer to Gregory Bateson and soberly observe that two descriptions are usually better than one. Just as binocular vision does not just imply a mere quantitative enhancement but an improvement of quality, namely a perception of depth and three-dimensional vision, so the examination of the "rituals"-phenomenon from the point of view of both ritual studies and narrative theory leads to a "thicker" description, in Clifford Geertz's sense.

In the same way as ritual studies are able to sharpen our awareness of those aspects of narratives which have thus far been neglected in narrative theory, new developments and approaches from postclassical narrative theory can also be of use in ritual studies. On the one hand, this heuristic benefit is based on the fact that narrative theory directs focus to those dimensions of rituals and ritual narrations which have received relatively little attention so far – namely the narrative structures of rituals, the function of narrations as elements of rituals, and the perspectivity or multi-perspectivity of rituals.

On the other hand, the interfaces discussed above between narratives and rituals serve as a kind of features-matrix or a pattern of analytical categories which can be beneficial for the comparative analyses of rituals, ritual narrations, and the histories of their performances in different cultures (cf. Dücker 46). In the context of culturally-comparative ritual examinations, the following questions arise from the point of view of narrative theory:

- To what extent do the narrative structures of certain rituals vary in different cultures?
- What differences are there with regard to narrative structures of different rituals or types of rituals?
- What are the typical characteristics of the respective culture with regard to the relationship between rituals and narratives?
- What functions do narratives as elements of rituals fulfil in varying cultural contexts?
- What is the relationship between narrations which are integrated into rituals and the norms and values which are made visible and explicit in ritual?
- How can narratological models be used in order to sufficiently describe the different forms of perspectivity and multi-perspectivity, which are characteristic of particular rituals and ritual narrations in different cultures?
- When analysing rituals as media events, what narrations are propagated through the media by means of ritual in different cultures and what culture-specific functions do these narratives fulfil? (cf. Dücker 59; Grimes).

In light of the multitude of interfaces that can be found between narratives and rituals on various levels, there is much to be said in favour of the hypothesis that ritual studies and narrative research are able to complement each another in a useful way. In the same way that the descriptive concepts and analytical methods developed by ritual studies might prove useful to narrative research, so too might the analytical categories and models of narrative theory be able to provide ritual studies with fresh impulses. In any case, the phenomena which both disciplines deal with are connected in so many ways that it is high time narrations were analysed from the point of view of ritual studies, and rituals from the perspective of narrative theory.

References

Assmann, Aleida. *Erinnerungsräume. Formen und Wandlungen des kulturellen Gedächtnisses.* München: Beck, 1999.
Barthes, Roland. "Introduction to the Structural Analysis of Narratives." *Image Music Text.* Transl. S. Heath. New York: Hill and Wang, 1977 [1966]. 79-124.
Bell, Catherine. *Ritual: Perspectives and Dimensions.* New York, Oxford: Oxford UP, 1997.
Birk, Hanne. *AlterNative Memories. Kulturspezifische Inszenierungen von Erinnerung in zeitgenössischen Romanen indigener Autor/inn/en Australiens, Kanadas und Aotearoas/Neuseelands.* Trier: WVT, 2008.
Böhme, Hartmut. "Vom Cultus zur Kultur(wissenschaft). Zur Historischen Semantik des Kulturbegriffs." *Literaturwissenschaft – Kulturwissenschaft. Positionen, Themen, Perspektiven.* Eds. Renate Glaser and Matthias Luserke. Opladen: Westdt. Verlag, 1996.
Braungart, Wolfgang. *Ritual und Literatur.* Tübingen: Niemeyer, 1996.
Bruner, Jerome. "The Transactional Self." *Making Sense: The Child's Construction of the World.* Eds. Jerome Bruner and Helen Haste. London, New York: Routledge, 1990 [1987]. 81-96.
—. "Self-making and World-making." *Journal of Aesthetic Education* 25.1 (1991): 67-78.
—. "The Narrative Construction of Reality." *Critical Enquiry* 18.1 (1991): 1-21.
—. *Making Stories: Law, Literature, Life.* Cambridge, Mass.: Harvard UP, 2003 [2002].
Dücker, Burckhard. *Rituale: Formen – Funktionen – Geschichte. Eine Einführung in die Ritualwissenschaft.* Stuttgart, Weimar: Metzler, 2007.
Durkheim, Emile. *The Elementary Forms of the Religious Life.* Trans. Joseph Ward Swain. London: George Allen & Unwin Ltd., 1915 [1912].
Eakin, Paul John. *Living Autobiographically: How We Create Identity in Narrative.* Ithaca, NY: Cornell UP, 2008.
Echterhoff, Gerald and Jürgen Straub. "Narrative Psychologie. Facetten eines Forschungsprogramms." *Handlung, Kultur, Interpretation* 12.2 (2003): 317-342; 13.1 (2004): 151-186.
Elsbree, Langdon. *The Rituals of Life: Patterns in Narratives.* Port Washington, NY: Kennikat Press, 1982.

—. Ritual Passages and Narrative Structures. New York: Lang, 1991.
Fludernik, Monika. Towards a 'Natural' Narratology. London: Routledge, 1996.
Gladigow, Burkhard. "Sequenzierung von Riten und die Ordnung der Rituale." Zoroastrian Rituals in Context. Ed. Michael Stausberg. Leiden, Boston: Brill, 2004. 57-76.
Goodman, Nelson. Ways of Worldmaking. Bloomington: Indiana UP, 1978.
Grimes, Ronald L. "Ritual and the Media." Practicing Religion in the Age of Media: Explorations in Media, Religion, and Culture. Eds. Stewart M. Hoover and Lynn Schofield Clark. New York: Columbia UP, 2002. 219-234.
Großklaus, Götz. Medien-Bilder. Inszenierung der Sichtbarkeit. Frankfurt a. M.: Suhrkamp, 2004.
Herman, David, Manfred Jahn and Marie-Laure Ryan, eds. The Routledge Encyclopedia of Narrative Theory. London, New York: Routledge, 2005.
Herman, David. "Stories as a Tool for Thinking." Narrative Theory and the Cognitive Sciences. Ed. David Herman. Stanford: CSLI Publications, 2003. 163-192.
—. Basic Elements of Narrative. Malden, MA [et al.]: Wiley-Blackwell, 2009.
Jungaberle, Henrik and Jan Weinhold, eds. Rituale in Bewegung. Rahmungs- und Reflexionsprozesse in Kulturen der Gegenwart. Berlin: Lit Verlag, 2006.
Kreinath, Jens, Jan Snoek and Michael Stausberg, eds. Theorizing Rituals: Issues, Topics, Approaches, Concepts. Leiden: Brill, 2006.
—, eds. Annotated Bibliography of Ritual Theory, 1966 – 2005. Leiden: Brill, 2007.
Lincoln, Bruce. Emerging from the Chrysalis: Studies in the Rituals of Women's Initiation. Cambridge: Harvard UP, 1981.
Luhmann, Niklas. "Intersubjektivität oder Kommunikation. Unterschiedliche Ausgangspunkte soziologischer Theoriebildung." Archivio di Filosofia 54 (1986): 41-60.
Michaels, Axel. "Zur Dynamik von Ritualkomplexen." Forum Ritualdynamik 3 (2003): 1-12.
Müller-Funk, Wolfgang. Die Kultur und ihre Narrative. Eine Einführung. 2nd ed. Wien, New York: Springer, 2008.

Nadj, Julijana. *Die Fiktionale Metabiographie. Gattungsgedächtnis und Gattungskritik in einem neuen Genre der englischsprachigen Erzählliteratur*. Trier: WVT, 2006.

Neumann, Birgit and Ansgar Nünning. *An Introduction to the Study of Narrative*. Stuttgart: Klett, 2008.

Nünning, Ansgar, Vera Nünning and Birgit Neumann, eds. *The Aesthetics and Politics of Cultural Worldmaking*. Trier: WVT, 2010.

—, eds. *Cultural Ways of Worldmaking. Media and Narratives*. Berlin, New York: De Gruyter, 2010.

Nünning, Vera and Ansgar Nünning, eds. *Multiperspektivisches Erzählen. Zur Theorie und Geschichte der Perspektivenstruktur im Englischen Roman des 18. bis 20. Jahrhunderts*. Trier: WVT, 2000.

—. "Ways of Worldmaking as a Model for the Study of Culture: Theoretical Frameworks, Epistemological Underpinnings, New Horizons." *Cultural Ways of Worldmaking. Media and Narratives* .Eds. Vera Nünning, Ansgar Nünning and Birgit Neumann. Berlin, New York: De Gruyter, 2010. 1-25.

Nünning, Vera. "A 'Usable Past': Fictions of Memory and British National Identity." *Journal for the Study of British Cultures* 10.1 (2003): 27-48.

Oppitz, Michael. "Montageplan von Ritualen." *Rituale Heute. Theorien – Kontroversen – Entwürfe*. Eds. Corina Caduff and Johanna Pfaff-Czarnecka. Berlin: Reimer, 1999. 73-95.

Ryan, Marie-Laure and Marina Grishakova, eds. *Intermediality and Storytelling*. Berlin: De Gruyter, 2010.

Ryan, Marie-Laure. *Possible Worlds, Artificial Intelligence and Narrative Theory*. Bloomington: Indiana UP, 1991.

—. *Narrative Across Media: The Languages of Storytelling*. Lincoln, NB: U of Nebraska P, 2004.

Sax, William. "Agency." *Theorizing Rituals: Issues, Topics, Approaches, Concepts*. Eds. Jens Kreinath, Jan Snoek and Michael Stausberg. Leiden, Boston: Brill, 2006. 473-481.

Schacter, Daniel L., Donna R. Addis and Randy L. Buckner. "Remembering the Past to Imagine the Future: The Prospective Brain." *Nature Reviews: Neuroscience* 8 (2007): 657-661.

Segal, Robert A., ed. *The Myth and Ritual Theory: An Anthology*. Malden, MA, Oxford: Blackwell, 1998.

Stausberg, Michael. "Reflexive Ritualisation." *Zeitschrift für Religions- und Geistesgeschichte* 56 (2004): 54-61.

—."Reflexivity." *Theorizing Rituals. Issues, Topics, Approaches, Concepts.* Eds. Jens Kreinath, Jan Snoek and Michael Stausberg. Leiden: Brill, 2006. 627-646.

Sugiyama, Michelle Scalise. "On the Origins of Narrative. Storyteller Bias as a Fitness-Enhancing Strategy." *Human Nature* 7.4 (1996): 403-425.

—. "Narrative Theory and Function: Why Evolution Matters." *Philosophy and Literature* 25 (2001): 233-250.

Voßkamp, Wilhelm."Literaturwissenschaft und Kulturwissenschaft." *Interpretation 2000. Positionen und Kontroversen. Festschrift zum 65. Geburtstag von Horst Steinmetz.* Eds. Henk de Berg and Matthias Prangel. Heidelberg: Winter, 1999. 183-199.

Wulf, Christoph. "Die Erzeugung des Sozialen in Ritualen." *Die Neue Kraft der Rituale.* Ed. Axel Michaels. Heidelberg: Winter, 2007. 179-200.

Zapf, Hubert. *Literatur als kulturelle Ökologie. Zur kulturellen Funktion imaginativer Texte an Beispielen des amerikanischen Romans.* Tübingen: Niemeyer, 2002.

Obama's American Narrative: A Narratological Approach to Complex Rituals

ROY SOMMER

1. INTRODUCTION

It is not difficult to see why closer collaboration between narrative theory and ritual studies is possible and desirable. Scholars in both fields study cultural practices, storytelling and ritual behaviour. What is more, the theoretical and methodological origins of the systematic study of rituals and narrative lie in structuralism. Close collaboration between narrative theory and ritual studies is thus facilitated by the use of similar or even identical terms and concepts, a shared terminology that functions as a cross-disciplinary lingua franca. Examples of terms that are equally at home in indices of books in either field include the dynamics of self and other, memory and identity, (imagined) communities and (invented) traditions, performativity and performance, values and taboos, authority and authenticity, interactivity and communication, intentionality and meaning, emic and etic perspectives, liminality and subversion, myth and structure, message and speech act, sign and symbol.

Surprisingly, despite these similarities narrative and ritual have rarely been studied in combination. This is not to say that there is no relevant research at all. Compared to the attention other cultural practices that contribute to the formation and shaping of personal or collective identities have received, however, the forms and functions of ritual have been rather neglected in literary theory and, more specifically, in narratology. The lack of an entry on ritual in the *Routledge Encyclopedia of Narrative Theory* (Herman et al.), the most comprehensive resource of its kind, is a case in point. Although narratives and rituals often seem to occur in related or similar contexts, possibly share certain features, and may serve similar purposes, a theory that links narrative and ritual – already called for by Thomas Pavel, one of the founders of structuralist narratology – has yet to be developed (cf. Pavel). Conversely, ritual studies have sometimes used narratological terminology, yet without a systematic interest in the narrative nature or the narrativity of their objects of study.

Like the other contributions to this volume, this chapter proceeds from the assumption that the cultural, social and aesthetic phenomena that constitute the object of narratology and ritual studies, as well as the kinds of questions they ask, the methodological challenges they face, and even the preliminary answers they provide, have much in common. In fact, experts from both fields share a number of theoretical premises and methodological principles that make the architecture of their inquiries strikingly similar. These confluences informing both fields of study – and thereby creating the potential for interdisciplinary collaboration – are most obvious in two areas:[1] on the one hand, the conceptual modelling of relationships between underlying structural patterns (myths, narrative grammars) and concrete forms (rituals, stories), on the other hand the analysis of cultural functions of narratives and rituals as means of cultural self-reflection and collective identity formation.

The focus on the notion of deep structures and the shared interest in cultural functions, further explained in section two, will provide a conceptual framework for the case study in section three. This explores the uses of storytelling in United States presidential elections, with a focus on Barack Obama's campaign in 2008. The presidential elections are described as complex rituals that are not only designed to find a new political leader, but also engender collective reassurance in the wider context of cultural self-fashioning and nation-building. An analysis of narrative elements in Barack Obama's speeches illustrates how storytelling is embedded in contexts that may be usefully studied from a ritual theory perspective. This allows us to

---

1   There are also many overlaps with respect to solutions for definition and classification, and a shared insight into the importance of framing.

hypothesize that – with respect to American presidential elections – narrative is a key component of ritual design.

2. THE STRUCTURALIST HERITAGE: CONFLUENCES IN NARRATIVE RESEARCH AND RITUAL STUDIES

Borrowed from everyday language, the term ritual has acquired a wide variety of meanings that are shaped by the disciplines involved in ritual studies, from sociology to anthropology. The consensus now is that no single definition can subsume all types of rituals, old or new, in all types of societies, traditional or modern. Taking his cue from classification theory, Snoek (4ff.) therefore replaces classical monothetic definitions with the related notions of fuzzy sets or polythetic classes. The former is partly based on continuous characteristics, the latter assemble sets of features that do not have to be present in all phenomena belonging to one class. Snoek – like Michaels (3f.) in an earlier paper – argues that "(almost all) the characteristics of the class of phenomena usually called 'rituals' in fact *are* either polythetic or fuzzy or even both" (Snoek 7). This allows for a less rigid approach to classification and definition that is content with listing recurrent features, i.e. features that are not essential elements, but typical of most rituals.[2]

These family resemblances include, according to Michaels (4f.), embodiment (rituals require human agents performing more or less intentional actions), formal behaviour that can be imitated and repeated, framing (this includes, for instance, signs that signal the beginning and end of a ritual, but also cognitive framing, i.e. the fact that participants are aware of performing a ritual), transformation (participants acquire a new status or new competencies) and – frequently – a transcendental effect. Michaels further

---

2   See Snoek (7): "Once this is accepted, the task is no longer to search for the few essential characteristics of 'rituals,' which unambiguously distinguish between them and everything else, but rather to sum up as large as possible a collection of characteristics which are typical for most rituals, or at least for those being considered in a particular project."

proposes a distinction between ritualized behaviour in everyday life on the one hand, and complex rituals on the other. The latter are rather static and thus convey a sense of security, authority and legitimacy (cf. 6). They are generally performed in public and emphasize the collective over the individual (cf. 8). From the emerging perspective of ritual dynamics, however, it is worth pointing out that rituals tend to be less static than has traditionally been assumed, although it seems reasonable to suspect that the degree of complexity is closely related to the flexibility of a ritual's design and structure.

Turning to narratological terminology, the situation is slightly different but no less complex, particularly from an outside perspective. "Narrative" and "narration" are certainly more technical terms than "ritual" – outside academic circles people prefer to speak of "stories" and "storytelling." Depending on one's theoretical approach, however, one may choose among several complementary definitions. Some of these are more oriented towards fictional narrative, while others seek to define narrative as broadly as possible. There have been numerous descriptions of the uses and functions of narrative in specific discursive contexts, as well as definitions of narrativity, the quality that unites all and only narratives.[3]

Among recent proposals, David Herman's distinction between four basic elements of narrative – "situatedness, event sequencing, worldmaking/world disruption, and what it's like" (14) – provides an excellent starting point for a discussion of the relevance of storytelling in rituals. Firstly, he introduces an aspect largely absent from narratological discourse, i.e. the emic perspective of the storytellers and audience involved in narrative communication, a perspective that is also vital for ritual studies (cf. 4). Secondly, Herman acknowledges intentionality more explicitly than most narratological definitions of narrative, encouraging interpreters to "draw inferences about the communicative goals that have structured the specific occasion of the telling, motivating the use of certain cues in favour of others and shaping the arrangement of the cues selected" (17). Acknowledging the relevance of intentionality is important, as the motivation behind the creation of narrative artefacts and ritualist behaviour has gained more prominence in critical discourse. Having said this, studies of both narrative

---

3   For surveys of narratological definitions of narrative see Richardson and Ryan, as well as the introduction to this volume.

design and ritual design are less interested in reconstructing the intentions behind cultural practices than in the constraints to which these practices are subjected. Thirdly, Herman's approach is specifically designed to facilitate transdisciplinary collaboration. He connects literary studies with research on personal experience narratives and other types of non-fictional storytelling, whereas other theories of narrative are designed specifically for the analysis of literary fiction.

Proceeding from these preliminary definitions of ritual and narrative, which are primarily intended to prepare some common terminological ground for the envisioned cross-disciplinary project, we will now turn to the conceptual parallels between approaches to narrative and ritual that retain a structuralist dimension. Both lines of approach are interested in processes of transformation: how does a narrative grammar produce a story, or a myth a ritual? Such approaches to rituals and stories are firmly grounded in the structuralist tradition. They rest on the premise that all narrative artefacts or all kinds of ritual behaviour can be reduced to a limited number of core elements, and that the combination of these elements follows a limited number of rules. The ultimate goal of such approaches is a grammar that describes all visible phenomena as surface structures that are manifestations of underlying principles or deep structures.

The most prominent model of deep narrative structures was proposed by Claude Lévi-Strauss, whose structuralist approach to myth had a major impact far beyond his own field of anthropology.[4] In postclassical narratology, the universalist quest for foundational myths or narremes and grammatical rules that account for all possible realizations of the underlying principle has now been superseded by more pragmatic approaches to ritualist behaviour and storytelling. It is probably fair to say that for most narratologists the point of reference in linguistics is no longer transformational grammar and syntax but pragmatics and cognitive linguistics. This is, however, due to a shift in research interests rather than in shortcomings of the structuralist paradigm. The distinction between surface structures and deep structures remains illuminating if one is studying narrative in highly formalized contexts such as those afforded by complex rituals.

---

4 For a brief survey of Lévi-Strauss's notion of deep narrative structures and its reception in structuralist narratology see Rimmon-Kenan (11ff.).

Lévi-Strauss's critical paradigm also exhibits its explanatory power in studies of ritual design. In their introduction to a recent collection of articles, Karolewski, Miczek and Zotter argue that even though contemporary ritual designers appear to enjoy considerable creative freedom when inventing alternative wedding ceremonies or burial rites, the results are frequently reminiscent of more traditional practices.[5] The authors further suggest that habitual determination (*Prägung*) of participants may be responsible for this, as well as the need to create practices that can clearly be identified as rituals – otherwise the new rituals would not fulfil their intended functions (whatever these may be). These habitual and functional constraints on creativity allow one to consider ritual design as a process of selection, combination and transformation of established and new features that can be clearly identified (both by participants and observers) as variations belonging to an established class or type of ceremonies or rites.

Generic fiction is in this respect similar to complex rituals that draw on a limited number of obligatory elements that may only be modified within well-specified limits: it is based on established formal and thematic patterns that consist of dramaturgical elements such as actantial roles or recurrent conflicts, as well as of dramaturgical rules that govern possible combinations. This is not to say that such narratives merely repeat a formula. Even the most formulaic genres are dynamic in that they allow for slight variations. Such changes, introduced by individual narratives belonging to the genre, will always be evolutionary rather than revolutionary, but they are nonetheless required to appeal to the intended audience.

The focus on processes of selection and combination of elements from a large, but ultimately limited pool of possibilities provides a conceptual link between studies of ritual design and formalist or structuralist approaches to

---

5 See Karolewski et al. (8): "Auf den ersten Blick erscheint es, als seien der Kreativität der Ritualbegleiter keine Grenzen gesetzt, wenn sie solch ‚neue' Rituale entwerfen. Verschiedenste rituelle, religiöse und auch aus populären Kontexten stammende Elemente stehen zur Auswahl, um neu zusammengesetzt zu werden. In der Praxis weisen diese Rituale jedoch häufig starke Ähnlichkeiten mit bereits aus ‚traditionellen' Kontexten bekannten Strukturen auf. Das dürfte zum einen auf die habituelle Prägung der an der Gestaltung Mitwirkenden selbst zurückzuführen sein, zum anderen aber darauf, dass bei den Beteiligten die Erkennbarkeit des ‚fertigen Produktes' als Ritual gewährleistet sein soll."

narrative. The latter assume that there is a limited number of narrative universals that account for narrativity. The more generic a narrative, the easier it is to establish functional links between its elements and to specify the rules that govern their selection and combination. Famous examples include Vladimir Propp's analysis of Russian folktales or Umberto Eco's study of James Bond novels. In both cases, archetypal scenarios establish generic conventions to which each individual narrative adheres. Such an approach is best suited to highly formalized types of narratives such as fairy tales and spy thrillers, while its usefulness in analyses of literary fiction, which seeks to subvert generic conventions and formulaic patterns, is rather limited.

Structuralist approaches in classical narrative theory were mainly interested in the underlying elements and rules that produce new narratives. In analogy to the structuralist study of natural languages, story grammars were devised with the ultimate goal of identifying and classifying universally applicable structures and patterns. The relationship between narratological categories and the empirical, extratextual world, however, was largely neglected. In a thought-provoking article on the deficiencies and unrealized potential of structuralist narratology, Thomas Pavel argues that a more dynamic theory of plot is needed that will help to explain "not only the architecture of plot but also the principles of its movement" (68). While narrative theorists like Peter Brooks have found inspiration for such a theory mainly in the psychoanalytical or psychological models proposed by Sigmund Freud and Jaques Lacan, Pavel envisages a link between Russian formalism, French sociology and American anthropology: "In what could be called the Propp-Eliade-Turner hypothesis, the well-knit, richly articulated folktale must be correlated with the presence of ritual" (67). He puts special emphasis on Victor Turner's anthropological work as a stimulus for a more dynamic narratological theory of plot: "[A] fully relevant theory of plot must as well make use of the rich anthropological notions of social drama and ritual, and learn to relate formal literary structures to the cultural texture that makes them possible" (ibid.).

For the present discussion, the notion of a cultural texture that facilitates the emergence of literary or narrative structures is of particular importance, as rituals themselves can be regarded as products, elements and visible expressions of that cultural texture, a virtual code that defines a community, a culture, a nation. Rather than seeking a key to a better understanding of fictional plots, I would like to emphasize the analogy between narratives and rituals suggested by Pavel's metaphor – both are highly conventionalized sign systems that carry the DNA of the culture from which they emerge. Using the slightly less metaphorical linguistic analogy of narrative grammar introduced above, one might also say that both narratives and rituals are surface structures in which deep structures become manifest. Methodologically, then, narratology and ritualogy – i.e. the structuralist study of narratives and rituals – proceed from similar assumptions.

The structuralist approach seems particularly helpful in the context of the current debate on ritual dynamics. The concept of static, more or less invariable rituals has recently been challenged by the new paradigms of ritual dynamics and ritual design proposed by Gregor Ahn ("Ritualdesign," "Ritual Design").[6] While the former has its focus on the interdependence of change and continuity (Ahn, "Ritual Design" 601), the latter designates an intentional act, describing "processes of adapting, transforming and re-organizing or composing already existing elements out of different religious or secular traditions into the frame of an already known type of ritual" (603). Ritual design is concerned with creating alternative versions of existing rituals (such as the re-invention of wedding ceremonies or burials for a secular society). It also helps to adapt existing rituals to new contexts, for instance when migrant communities need to re-establish their cultural traditions in a diasporic situation (cf. 601). In this sense, ritual design can be distinguished from the invention of new rituals that have no traditional predecessor or cultural counterpart.

The initial appeal of structuralist narratology lies in its promise of rigorous theorizing and an almost scientific degree of objectivity. This "austere grammatical project, aimed at the discovery of regularities in literary behaviour" (Pavel 64), however, failed to link knowledge about textual regularities to the extratextual world and thus to provide the "powerful tool for textual interpretation" (ibid.) that many structuralists, including Pavel himself, had initially hoped for. While Pavel – writing at a time when structuralism was still the dominant paradigm in narrative research – sought to overcome this shortcoming by turning to anthropology, more recent developments in narratology have addressed the core issue by adding new items to the narratological agenda. Postclassical narratology still incorporates the classical structuralist approach, but extends it with a host of con-

---

6   See also the impressive collection of articles edited by Harth and Schenk.

textual narratologies that are either based on corpora or interested in the cognitive processes of producing and reading narratives. This development can be seen in analogy with the development of pragmatics in linguistics – a programmatic turn towards the uses and functions of narrative.

What, then, are the purposes of narrative? Why do people tell stories? There are as many functions as there are types or kinds of narrative, from conversational storytelling to literary fiction. Generally speaking, narrative is now widely regarded as a way of world-making, a means of understanding and sharing lived experience, as well as of conveying, storing, sharing and remembering information, an important contribution to individual self-fashioning and collective identity formation, community maintenance and nation building. In their introduction to an interdisciplinary collection of essays on the idea of narrative in the human sciences, as the subtitle has it, Hinchman and Hinchman (xvii) suggest how individual stories may assume a social function: "The stories that individuals create often strike variations upon a repertoire of socially available narratives that, in turn, legitimize the community and guarantee its continued existence."

The term "repertoire" echoes the structuralist notion of deep structures – the storyteller appears as a mythmaker who has access to the cultural texture or DNA, to use a more fashionable metaphor, and revives the core myths and master narratives for the sake of his or her community. Storytelling as an activity that requires communication between teller and audience thus facilitates social cohesion. It is no coincidence, though somewhat surprising, that the purposes ascribed to narratives are reminiscent of the social and cultural functions generally ascribed to rituals. What is more, the relationship between the storyteller and his or her story, as described by Hinchman and Hinchman, privileges the cultural repertoire over the creativity of the individual by restricting the function of storytelling to a form of cultural recycling. While such a reductive view of narrative cannot account for complex works of art such as modernist fiction or postmodern narrative experiments, it highlights functional equivalences between collective narratives and rituals.[7]

---

7   The term collective narratives (*Kollektiverzählungen*) designates flexible narrative constellations of non-canonical, non-fictional stories that are based on recognizable, recurrent patterns and contribute to communal identity formation (see Sommer, "Kollektiverzählungen" 230ff.).

The emphasis on cultural functions offers a viable alternative to the study of personal motivations or intentions on the part of the creators or designers of narratives and rituals. One reason why the author has long been excluded from narratological inquiry lies in the disciplinary provenance of narratology as a branch of literary studies. When in 1946 Wimsatt and Beardsley renounced the intentional fallacy of earlier literary criticism and founded a new formalist school (New Criticism), they paved the way for a new dogma that culminated in a famous phrase by Roland Barthes: the death of the author. The rise of narratology in the 1960s is at least partly due to the fact that it offered a genuine alternative to the traditional method of hermeneutic interpretation. Instead of trying to understand texts, narratologists were content with exploring narrativity for narrativity's sake. Once the quest for meaning is abandoned in favour of explorations of the nature of narrative, however, authors and their actual or possible intentions are no longer relevant. Authorial intention loses its traditional role as a source of textual meaning.

More recently, postclassical narratologies have begun to reconsider intentionality: "No theory can eliminate the cognitive impulse to assume that *someone* wrote a narrative for *some intentional purpose*, which, at the very least, constrains fast, unconscious reading processes" (Gibbs 249; italics in original). Both corpus-based and process-oriented contextual narratologies have opted for a more pragmatic approach to concepts of authorship, context or intention than their structuralist predecessors.[8] The re-evaluation of the authorial function as a critical concept acknowledges that narratology's technical vocabulary contains phrases such as narrative device, technique or strategy, as well as terms like focalization, authorial voice and intended audience, which all imply creative activity, and that it is hardly possible to speak of narrative design without considering the possibility of a designer.

This is not to say, however, that intentionality is set to become the focus of narratological research. The intentionalist turn in narrative theory, if one can speak of such a development, does not coincide with a lack of interest in narrative patterns, structures and principles. In fact, the generic and pragmatic constraints that influence the creative process imply that the idea of a narrative grammar as such was not wrong, but that the structuralist no-

---

8 For the distinction of corpus-based and process-oriented contextual narratologies see Sommer, "Merger."

tion of grammar itself may have to be reconsidered. While the distinction between deep structures and surface phenomena still retains high analytical value, a shift from a grammatical description of transformation rules to a modular network – or another more suitable metaphor – might help free structuralist approaches to narrative and ritual design from their inherent limitations.

3. COMPLEX RITUALS AND STRATEGIC STORYTELLING: OBAMA'S AMERICAN NARRATIVE

United States presidential elections are complex rituals, or rather a complex of rituals that combines rites of passage, initiation rites and ritual ceremonies. Traditional ceremonies such as the inaugural oath and invocation, or more recently added elements such as TV duels and polls, form the core of the complex of rituals that accompanies the campaigns, from the nomination of the candidates to the parade that concludes the inauguration on Election Day. It is this ritualist character of presidential elections, with their carefully staged dramaturgy of controversies, conflicts and compromises, that helps to create that sense of unity in diversity, of historical continuity and collective destiny, that is commonly regarded as characteristic of American cultural identity.

By combining traditional and carefully designed new elements, these rituals not only frame the process of electing or re-electing a political leader. They also serve to reassure the electorate – the American people, the American nation, as political rhetoric has it – of their unity, a unity founded on shared beliefs, values and ways of life. There is also a transcendental aspect to American presidential elections that is markedly different from elections in more secular democracies such as France or Germany. In Germany, for instance, the public profession of faith and membership of a Christian church, without which no American president would be voted into office, would alienate large parts of the (atheist, Muslim or decidedly secular) electorate, and would thus be regarded – even by the most conservative politicians – as unsuitable for political discourse. In the United States, however, the candidates' speeches would be incomplete without invocations of God's blessings and references to a sacred or higher truth; in fact, it is hardly possible to imagine an outspoken atheist winning the elections. Campaigns typically include carefully staged and televized visits to church and, in the inauguration ceremony, the presidential oath sworn over the Holy Bible. Religion clearly matters more than elsewhere in the Western world – Obama was accused of being a Muslim (his middle name is Hussein), and he had to respond to charges of racism against a minister of his church.

While all independent nations make extensive use of public rituals to legitimate, demonstrate and reinforce political power, the role of storytelling – just like the role of faith – in political rhetoric varies among cultures. German politicians appear to be less inclined to tell stories than their counterparts in the United States. Storytelling – from personal experience narratives told by campaign helpers to support their candidates to narrative elements or episodes in the candidates' speeches – is an integral part of American election campaigns. In this ritualized rhetorical duel the better story often plays a decisive role, as recent elections have shown. George Bush prominently employed imperialist rhetoric of good and evil in order to justify his war effort, but also made good use of an old narrative genre that helped his conservative voters to forgive him his former drug-taking habits and alcoholism: the conversion narrative, deeply rooted in Christian tradition, provides a pattern for self-righting and self-improvement or rather, as critics might object, righteous self-making and self-marketing. Barack Obama (with the help of excellent ghost-writers and spin doctors) has time and again proved that he, too, understands the power of stories as means of overcoming – or downplaying – racial divisions and creating momentum for a campaign that appears to be a losing battle. As will be shown below, his speeches frequently contain carefully crafted narrative passages that are an integral part of the dramaturgical staging of his public persona.

Why stories? Designed to exemplify abstract arguments and to give weight to programmatic statements, few rhetorical devices are more effective than stories when it comes to sharing experiences (true or invented) and eliciting emotional response. Stories, according to Herman's definition, show us what it is like to experience a certain situation, and by making references to others' stories and experiences, successful storytellers like Barack Obama portray themselves as someone who is compassionate, empathetic and – above all – able to listen to and understand the concerns of the common people. While a rational argument based on figures and data appeals to the mind, stories appeal to the heart, and more often than not it is the latter effect that decides elections. Embedded in complex rituals in an even more complex world, simple stories – the sinner turned saint, the loving husband who tucks in his wife at night – promise hope and comfort. Above all, they allow voters to be persuaded that their future president understands them, and that he (or she) is good at heart.

Obama's first election campaign is an interesting case for both ritual design theory and narrative theory. In "America is not the World," a song from the album *You Are the Quarry* (2004), British singer Morrissey had imagined America as a racist, patriarchal and homophobic pseudo-democracy "where the president is never black, female or gay." As Obama himself openly admitted in his Acceptance Speech at the Democratic Convention, he was faced with serious obstacles (he is careful not to mention racial prejudices explicitly): "I get it. I realize that I am not the likeliest candidate for this office. I don't fit the typical pedigree, and I haven't spent my career in the halls of Washington."[9] One of the many challenges, then, that Obama had to face during his election campaign was to prove that he was neither insensitive to racial issues nor – in order not to alienate his black and white supporters – a partial representative of the black community. Instead of taking sides, he chose to portray himself as the embodiment of the American promise (the title of his Acceptance Speech), a promise given to *all* Americans.

Obama's candidacy thus required a careful but thorough rethinking of what it meant to be an American in 2008, and this formidable task – preparing the electorate "for the work of remaking America," as the Inaugural Address had it – was achieved by means of a combination of ritual design and narrative design. Through a wide variety of marketing strategies and symbolic gestures, from an innovative use of social media to the symbolic choice of Abraham Lincoln's Bible for the swearing-in ceremony, the election campaign carefully shaped the public image of the future president. It was in Obama's speeches, however, that the new master narrative began to take shape – the unlikely candidate and his speech-writers demonstrated that they were not only excellent rhetoricians, but gifted storytellers as well.

From a generic perspective, one can distinguish five kinds of narrative in the speeches – life stories, biographical stories, personal experience narratives, anecdotes and what I would like to call micro-stories. Life stories consist of stories of formative events told by the individual himself or her-

---

9   http://obamaspeeches.com.

self; they focus on the teller's experience, and have what Linde (278) calls "extended reportability": for instance stories about career milestones, marriage, childbirth, divorce, major illness, or religious or ideological conversions. Biographical stories differ from life stories in that they are not about one's own life but about that of another person, whereas personal experience narratives are about one's own life, but only recount specific episodes that are not designed to form a coherent account of the self. Thus, one might say that a life story is a configuration of personal experience narratives. Formal features of anecdotes are short, entertaining narratives that usually focus on the interaction between two interlocutors in a single scene and often culminate in a punch line (cf. Bauman 22).

I am using the term micro-story not as a synonym for flash fiction but as a broader generic category that subsumes very short narratives that do not fully tell, but merely imply a story or a network of stories that make up a complex narrative.[10] In order for micro-stories to work, the implied story needs to be instantly recognizable. For instance, when Obama talks about "the faces of those young veterans who come back from Iraq and Afghanistan" ("The American Promise"), he triggers mediated images and personal experience stories of war atrocities; when he imagines "that young student who sleeps just three hours before working the night shift" (ibid.) he creates a micro-story that might trigger personal memories of one's own student days and the stories these memories are made of.[11]

On March 18, 2008, Barack Obama addressed an audience at the National Constitution Center in Philadelphia, Pennsylvania. His speech, titled "A More Perfect Union,"[12] was a response to the controversy surrounding his former pastor, Reverend Jeremiah Wright, who had been accused of harbouring racial prejudices. The publication of excerpts from Wright's

---

10 Flash fiction is a literary subgenre that designates very short short stories.
11 All examples are taken from the "American Promise" speech (see http://obamaspeeches.com).
12 The title is an intertextual reference to the Preamble of the United States Constitution: "We the People of the United States, in Order to form a more perfect Union, establish Justice, insure domestic Tranquility, provide for the common defence, promote the general Welfare, and secure the Blessings of Liberty to ourselves and our Posterity, do ordain and establish this Constitution for the United States of America."

sermons by ABC News follows the ritual of mediatized election campaigns in which every aspect of a candidate's public and private life comes under scrutiny. Obama's speech condemns Wright's allegations, but also confirms the responsibility of the white community to address racial discrimination.[13] In a personal experience narrative quoted from his book *Dreams From My Father*, Obama recounts the story of his first service at Trinity:

People began to shout, to rise from their seats and clap and cry out, a forceful wind carrying the reverend's voice up into the rafters [...]. And in that single note – hope! – I heard something else; at the foot of that cross, inside the thousands of churches across the city, I imagined the stories of ordinary black people merging with the stories of David and Goliath, Moses and Pharaoh, the Christians in the lion's den, Ezekiel's field of dry bones. Those stories – of survival, and freedom, and hope – became our story, my story; the blood that had spilled was our blood, the tears our tears; until this black church, on this bright day, seemed once more a vessel carrying the story of a people into future generations and into a larger world. Our trials and triumphs became at once unique and universal, black and more than black; in chronicling our journey, the stories and songs gave us a means to reclaim memories that we didn't need to feel shame about [...] memories that all people might study and cherish – and with which we could start to rebuild (294).

This passage testifies to the almost mythical power of stories and storytelling – narratives connect past and future as well as community and individual, they help us transcend race and coalesce into a new master narrative, a variation of the underlying narrative structure, the myth of the American Dream. In Obama's agenda, the key to a "coalition of white and black; Latino and Asian, rich and poor, young and old" lies in the power of progress and change: "The profound mistake of Reverend Wright's sermons is not that he spoke about racism in our society. It's that he spoke as if our society was static; as if no progress has been made."

---

13 "In the white community, the path to a more perfect union means acknowledging that what ails the African-American community does not just exist in the minds of black people; that the legacy of discrimination – and current incidents of discrimination, while less overt than in the past – are real and must be addressed."

Of course, Obama never uses terms like master narrative or comments on the rhetorical façade of his speech or on his use of narrative design; his strategy in all speeches is to give space to an emic perspective, the point of view of ordinary Americans imagining a better future for themselves as individuals but also for their fellow Americans, their economy, their nation. In phrases such as "we may have different stories, but we hold common hopes" the word "story" with its more positive connotations routinely replaces polarizing phrases such as "political conviction" or "party affiliation" in an attempt to turn a clash of opinions into an exciting and morally uplifting story-sharing exercise ("patriotism has no party").

Obama's speech concludes with a biographical story of Ashley Baia, a campaign worker (Appendix 1). The following extract also demonstrates another peculiarity of ritualized narrative: the narrative subgenres mentioned above often occur in hybrid forms, for instance when personal experience narratives are linked to a life story, or when a biographical story turns into an anecdote, as in the story of Ashley. During a meeting of campaign workers a few months earlier, Baia had disclosed that as a nine-year-old she had eaten sandwiches for a year to support her mother who was suffering from cancer and experienced financial difficulties. This life story, that motivates her political engagement, is retold (and thus turned into a biographical narrative) by Obama who construes Ashley's experience as an example of how a white person can overcome difficult circumstances without blaming others for her situation, or even turning racist. In a surprising twist, Obama then tells how her story motivated a black man to join the campaign: "I am here because of Ashley."

This anecdote emphasizes the point that racial divisions can be overcome if the shared goal – mutual recognition, a stronger union and, ultimately, perfection – is kept in mind. It is more than that, however. The combination of narrative and dramaturgical strategies – the girl's perspective, the generic transition from biographical story to anecdote, the change of tenses to increase immediacy and credibility, and, above all, the emotional punch line – "I am here because of Ashley" – lend the story a high degree of tellability and emotional appeal. Ashley's personal experience narrative has not only been widely remediated ("I am here because of Ashley" has become a slogan that has found its way onto mugs and T-shirts), but also been followed up by an American success story: Ashley served as a Field Director in the 2012 campaign. It will perhaps never be possible to ascertain who helped turn the poor girl, the student volunteer and role model, into a prototypical Obama story. Whoever deserves the credit, this is narrative design at its best.

As I have shown in an earlier analysis of the "Election Night Victory Speech," Obama also uses biographical storytelling – a condensed account of the life of Ann Nixon Cooper, a black woman who was born a generation after the end of slavery and now, at the age of 106, bears witness to America's progress (Appendix 2) – to capture the experience of change that is the emotional force behind the famous slogan associated with his campaign ("yes, we can"); he even predicts that stories surrounding his candidacy will provide a new master narrative for subsequent generations (cf. Sommer, "Kollektiverzählungen" 233ff.). Both the longer life stories, such as that of Ann Nixon Cooper, and the brief narratives that I have termed micro-stories are an excellent means of creating a narrative effect that has been described by Suzanne Keen (xiv) as "broadcast strategic empathy": "Broadcast strategic empathy calls upon every reader to feel with members of a group, by emphasizing common vulnerabilities and hopes through universalizing representations." Although Keen's focus is on fiction, and thus on the authorial intentions behind the narrative design of novels, the effect of universalizing representations is also heavily exploited in non-fictional narrative, especially in economic discourse where storytelling primarily serves marketing and branding.

This is, of course, the main purpose of many of Obama's life stories, biographical stories, personal experience narratives, and micro-stories that form, in fact, a new post-racial American master narrative. Time and again, Obama reminds himself (or rather his audiences) of the American Dream and the vision of unity across races, generations, faiths, and beliefs, the "more perfect union" promised in the title of the Philadelphia speech that originates in the Preamble of the American Constitution. In "The American Promise," micro-stories of anonymous individuals – an old woman, a bankrupt businessman, homeless veterans, impoverished families[14] – that rhetor-

---

14 "This country is more decent than one where a woman in Ohio, on the brink of retirement, finds herself one illness away from disaster after a lifetime of hard work. This country is more generous than one where a man in Indiana has to pack up the equipment he's worked on for twenty years and watch it shipped off to China, and then chokes up as he explains how he felt like a failure when he

ically represent American society as a whole are linked to his own life story, and to that of America: "I will never forget that in no other country on Earth is my story even possible. It's a story that hasn't made me the most conventional candidate. But it is a story that has seared into my genetic makeup the idea that this nation is more than the sum of its parts – that out of many, we are truly one."

4. CONCLUSION: NARRATIVES AND RITUALS

These selected examples are typical of Obama's combination of rhetoric and narrative. His speeches and stories are an essential part of that complex ritual – or series of complex rituals – in which the American president is elected into office. Quadrennially, the United States presidential elections include the nomination process with primaries and caucuses, in which the parties' delegates are elected for the national conventions, the modification of delegate selection rules, the selection of the parties' presidential nominees, the allocation of Electoral College electors, the election process, and finally the inauguration ceremony. Using the definition proposed by Michaels, it is easy to describe the ritualist nature of these processes and activities. They involve formal behaviour at all stages, embodiment (the candidates represent different sets of values and ideas), as well as transformation (the transferral of power). They even bear traces of transcendentalism, for the mandatory appeal to higher values, the ritualist invocations of God's blessing in the candidates' speeches, and the structure of the swearing-in ceremony all substantiate the claim that this is not an exclusively secular affair.

In fact, United States presidential elections are highly semanticized cultural practices that offer rich material for anyone interested in studying ritual and narrative (and also rhetoric) in combination. It would certainly be interesting to see how a close analysis of ritual design in Obama's campaign would relate to the findings of a narratological reading of the speeches. More issues have only been mentioned in passing. The political process is

---

went home to tell his family the news. We are more compassionate than a government that lets veterans sleep on our streets and families slide into poverty; that sits on its hands while a major American city drowns before our eyes."

accompanied by a campaign that involves opinion polls, media coverage, TV duels, and fieldwork by numerous volunteers. All these activities must be considered as parts of the ritual, as they contribute to the cognitive framing of the political process. According to the terminology developed in narrative theory (cf. Sommer "Initial Framings"), these aspects fall under the umbrella term "contextual framing." Rhetoric and storytelling, essential tools in this framing process, are regarded as "textual framing." A joint research project between narratologists and ritual studies experts might explore the interplay between textual and contextual framing and thus shed light on the question how complex rituals are designed, performed and remediated in contemporary media cultures.

APPENDIX 1

Remarks of Senator Barack Obama: "A More Perfect Union"
(Philadelphia, PA, March 18, 2008)

[...]
There is one story in particularly that I'd like to leave you with today – a story I told when I had the great honor of speaking on Dr. King's birthday at his home church, Ebenezer Baptist, in Atlanta.

There is a young, twenty-three year old white woman named Ashley Baia who organized for our campaign in Florence, South Carolina. She had been working to organize a mostly African-American community since the beginning of this campaign, and one day she was at a roundtable discussion where everyone went around telling their story and why they were there.

And Ashley said that when she was nine years old, her mother got cancer. And because she had to miss days of work, she was let go and lost her health care. They had to file for bankruptcy, and that's when Ashley decided that she had to do something to help her mom.

She knew that food was one of their most expensive costs, and so Ashley convinced her mother that what she really liked and really wanted to eat more than anything else was mustard and relish sandwiches. Because that was the cheapest way to eat.

She did this for a year until her mom got better, and she told everyone at the roundtable that the reason she joined our campaign was so that she could help the millions of other children in the country who want and need to help their parents too.

Now Ashley might have made a different choice. Perhaps somebody told her along the way that the source of her mother's problems were blacks who were on welfare and too lazy to work, or Hispanics who were coming into the country illegally. But she didn't. She sought out allies in her fight against injustice.

Anyway, Ashley finishes her story and then goes around the room and asks everyone else why they're supporting the campaign. They all have different stories and reasons. Many bring up a specific issue. And finally they come to this elderly black man who's been sitting there quietly the entire time. And Ashley asks him why he's there. And he does not bring up a specific issue. He does not say health care or the economy. He does not say education or the war. He does not say that he was there because of Barack Obama. He simply says to everyone in the room, "I am here because of Ashley." By itself, that single moment of recognition between that young white girl and that old black man is not enough. It is not enough to give health care to the sick, or jobs to the jobless, or education to our children.

But it is where we start. It is where our union grows stronger. And as so many generations have come to realize over the course of the two-hundred and twenty one years since a band of patriots signed that document in Philadelphia, that is where the perfection begins.

[...]

APPENDIX 2

Election Night Victory Speech
(Grant Park, Illinois, November 4, 2008)

[...]

This election had many firsts and many stories that will be told for generations. But one that's on my mind tonight is about a woman who cast her ballot in Atlanta. She's a lot like the millions of others who stood in line to make their voice heard in this election except for one thing – Ann Nixon Cooper is 106 years old.

She was born just a generation past slavery; a time when there were no cars on the road or planes in the sky; when someone like her couldn't vote for two reasons – because she was a woman and because of the color of her skin.

And tonight, I think about all that she's seen throughout her century in America – the heartache and the hope; the struggle and the progress; the times we were told that we can't, and the people who pressed on with that American creed: Yes we can.

At a time when women's voices were silenced and their hopes dismissed, she lived to see them stand up and speak out and reach for the ballot. Yes we can.

When there was despair in the dust bowl and depression across the land, she saw a nation conquer fear itself with a New Deal, new jobs and a new sense of common purpose. Yes we can.

When the bombs fell on our harbor and tyranny threatened the world, she was there to witness a generation rise to greatness and a democracy was saved. Yes we can.

She was there for the buses in Montgomery, the hoses in Birmingham, a bridge in Selma, and a preacher from Atlanta who told a people that "We Shall Overcome." Yes we can.

A man touched down on the moon, a wall came down in Berlin, a world was connected by our own science and imagination. And this year, in this election, she touched her finger to a screen, and cast her vote, because after 106 years in America, through the best of times and the darkest of hours, she knows how America can change. Yes we can.

America, we have come so far. We have seen so much. But there is so much more to do. So tonight, let us ask ourselves – if our children should live to see the next century; if my daughters should be so lucky to live as long as Ann Nixon Cooper, what change will they see? What progress will we have made?

[...]

REFERENCES

Ahn, Gregor. "Ritual Design – an Introduction." *Ritual Dynamics and the Science of Ritual*. Ed. Gregor Ahn. Wiesbaden: Harrassowitz, 2010. 601-606.

—. "'Ritualdesign' – ein neuer Topos der Ritualtheorie?" *Ritualdesign. Zur kultur- und ritualwissenschaftlichen Analyse 'neuer' Rituale*. Eds. Janina Karolewski, Nadja Miczek, and Christof Zotter. Bielefeld: Transcript, 2012. 29-44.

Bauman, Richard. "Anecdote." Herman et al. 22.

Gibbs Jr. and W. Raymond. "Intentionality." Herman et al. 247-249.

Harth, Dietrich and Gerrit Jasper Schenk. Eds. *Ritualdynamik. Kulturübergreifende Studien zur Theorie und Geschichte rituellen Handelns*. Heidelberg: Synchron, 2004.

Herman, David. *Basic Elements of Narrative*. Malden and Oxford: Wiley-Blackwell, 2009.

Herman, David, Manfred Jahn, and Marie-Laure Ryan. Eds. *Routledge Encyclopedia of Narrative Theory*. Abingdon and New York: Routledge, 2005.

Hinchman, Sandra K. and Lewis P. Hinchman. "Introduction. Toward a Definition of Narrative." *Memory, Identity Community. The Idea of Narrative in Human Sciences*. Eds. Lewis P. Hinchman and Sandra K. Hinchman. Albany, NY: State U of New York P, 2001. xiii-xxxii.

Karolewski, Janina, Nadja Miczek, and Christof Zotter. Eds. *Ritualdesign. Zur kultur- und ritualwissenschaftlichen Analyse ‚neuer' Rituale*. Bielefeld: Transcript, 2012.

—. "Ritualdesign – eine konzeptionelle Einführung." Karolewski et al. 7-28.

Keen, Suzanne. *Empathy and the Novel*. Oxford: Oxford UP, 2007.

Linde, Charlotte. "Life Story." Herman et al. 277-278.

Michaels, Axel. "Zur Dynamik von Ritualkomplexen." *Forum Ritualdynamik – Diskussionsbeiträge des SFB 619 der Ruprecht-Karls-Universität Heidelberg* 3 (2003): 1-14.

Obama, Barack. *Dreams from My Father: A Story of Race and Inheritance*. Edinburgh et al.: Canongate, 2007 [1995].

—. "A more Perfect Union." Philadelphia, PA. March 18, 2008.

http://obamaspeeches.com/E05-Barack-Obama-A-More-Perfect-Union-the-Race-Speech-Philadelphia-PA-March-18-2008.htm (07.03.2013).

—. "Election Night Victory Speech." Grant Park, Illinois. November 4, 2008. http://obamaspeeches.com/E11-Barack-Obama-Election-Night-Victory-Speech-Grant-Park-Illinois-November-4-2008.htm (03.07.2013).

—. "First Inaugural Address." January 20, 2009. http://obamaspeeches.com/P-Obama-Inaugural-Speech-Inauguration.htm (07.03.2013).

—. "The American Promise. Acceptance Speech at the Democratic Convention." Mile High Stadium, Denver, Colorado. August 28, 2008. http://obamaspeeches.com/E10-Barack-Obama-The-American-Promise-Acceptance-Speech-at-the-Democratic-Convention-Mile-High-Stadium-Denver-Colorado-August-28-2008.htm (07.03.2013).

Pavel, Thomas. "Narratives of Ritual and Desire." *Victor Turner and the Construction of Cultural Criticism: Between Literature and Anthropology*. Ed. Kathleen Ashley. Bloomington: Indiana UP, 1990. 64-70.

Prince, Gerald. *A Dictionary of Narratology*. Lincoln, NB: U of Nebraska P, 2003.

Richardson, Brian. "Recent Concepts of Narrative and Narratives of Narrative Theory." *Style* 34.2 (2000): 168-175.

Rimmon-Kenan, Shlomith. *Narrative Fiction: Contemporary Poetics*. London: Routledge, 2002.

Ryan, Marie-Laure. "Narrative." Herman et al. 344-348.

Snoek, Jan, "Transfer of Ritual." *Journal of Ritual Studies* 2.1 (2006): 1-10.

Sommer, Roy. "Initial Framings in Film." *Framing Borders in Literature and Other Media*. Eds. Werner Wolf and Walter Bernhart. Amsterdam/New York: Rodopi, 2006. 383-406.

—. "Kollektiverzählungen. Definitionen, Fallbeispiele und Erklärungsansätze." *Wirklichkeitserzählungen. Felder, Formen und Funktionen nicht-literarischen Erzählens*. Eds. Christian Klein und Matías Martínez. Stuttgart: Metzler, 2008.

—. "The Merger of Classical and Postclassical Narratologies and the Consolidated Future of Narrative Theory." *Diegesis. Interdisciplinary E-Journal for Narrative Research* 1.1 (2012). 143-157. http://www.diegesis.uni-wuppertal.de/index.php/diegesis (31.03.2013).

II. Historical Case Studies of Different Media and Cultural Contexts: Ritual and Narrative in Depth

Depicting Sacrifice in Roman Asia Minor: Narratives of Ritual in Classical Archaeology

GÜNTHER SCHÖRNER

1. THE STUDY OF NARRATIVE IN CLASSICAL ARCHAEOLOGY[1]

The study of narrative in classical archaeology, and this means of course pictorial narrative in a rather specific sense, dates back to the second half of the 19th century. In one of the first contributions, Carl Robert analysed pictorial narrative in his book *Bild und Lied* of 1881, in which he differentiates between three different types of narration, each of them belonging to one specific period in Greek art history:[2]

---

1   I am very grateful to Prof. Dr. Vera Nünning and Prof. Dr. Gregor Ahn (Collaborative Research Centre "Ritual Dynamics," Heidelberg) for accepting my paper. For discussion and extremely helpful advice and comments I thank G. Ahn (Heidelberg), V. Nünning (Heidelberg), Marie-Laure Ryan (Mainz – Bellvue/CO) and Roy Sommer (Wuppertal). Thanks are also due to Martin Zettersten for improving my English text.
2   See Robert, especially 3-51; for the history of research on this topic, see Stansbury-O'Donnell 1-17.

- complete narration
- situational narration
- cyclical narration.

This classification was further developed by Fritz Wickhoff,[3] but the next major step in studying the modes of pictorial narration was made by Kurt Weitzmann in his 1947 analysis of book illustration in late antiquity, *Illustrations in Roll and Codex*. He concentrated on questions of the representation of time and space. Thus he replaced the term "complete" with "simultaneous," emphasizing that one picture shows multiple moments of one story. Instead of Robert's *Situationsbilder* he used the term "monoscenic," in order to stress the unity of time and place in one single picture.[4] These studies remain highly influential in classical archaeology, with Robert's (and Wickhoff's) terminology enjoying popularity in Germany and Austria, while Weitzmann's is used in English speaking countries.

Over the past fifty years, new efforts to understand pictorial narration in antiquity have called this tripartite model into question.[5] The main result of these studies is that a more detailed schema replaced the older one. This improved categorization discerns eight instead of three types of pictorial narration:[6]

- monoscenic
- synoptic/simultaneous
- progressive
- unified
- cyclical
- continuous
- episodic
- serial.

---

3   See Wickhoff, "Wiener Genesis"; cited mainly as Wickhoff "Römische Kunst."
4   For corrections of Robert's and Wickhoff's terminology, see Weitzmann 33-36.
5   See Bielefeld; von Blanckenhagen 78-83; Hanfmann; Himmelmann-Wildschütz; Carter; Kaeser; Meyboom; Snodgrass; Brilliant; Raeck; Stewart; Boardman; Shapiro, "Old and New", "Narrative Strategies"; Small. The limitation on Greek iconography in these studies is astonishing; see footnote 14 below.
6   See Stansbury-O'Donnell 5-8; Stähli 253-258.

The first three categories are valid for pluriscenic pictures, especially painted or relief friezes. The other five terms were used for single picture series like *metopes* or framed paintings.

While this terminology equips archaeologists with a sophisticated framework for classifying narrative pictures primarily with respect to their representation of time and space, it has several drawbacks. One of the main problems is that this terminology is mostly used by archaeologists only.[7] Thus, the analysis of narrative in classical archaeology has become isolated and unapt for the recent scientific discussion.

This problem has been recognized as such in the last twenty years. Therefore, current studies have started to adopt literary theories of narration, mainly structural analysis as conducted by Roland Barthes[8] or – less often – semiotic approaches like those of Umberto Eco.[9]

The most important contributions are the introduction to the volume *Narrative and Event in Ancient Art* edited by Peter J. Holliday[10] and Mark D. Stansbury-O'Donnell's *Pictorial Narrative in Ancient Greek Art*. For German archaeology, the proceedings of a conference in 2000 "Zum Verhältnis von Raum und Zeit in der griechischen Kunst" can be mentioned,[11] especially the contribution by Adrian Stähli on "Erzählte Zeit, Erzählzeit und Wahrnehmungszeit. Zum Verhältnis von Temporalität und Narration speziell in der hellenistischen Plastik."

Despite these efforts the study of pictorial narrative in classical archaeology is characterized by various short-comings: Structural analysis was applied very late with a delay of thirty years in comparison to modern philology.[12] Newer post-structuralist/post-classical approaches have not been

---

7   For an exception see Dehejia.
8   See Barthes, "Introduction à l'analyse structurale" (English version: "Introduction to Structural Analysis"); see also Stähli 244-254.
9   See Eco, *Role of Reader*; "Zeit der Kunst," and *Lector in Fabula*.
10 See Holliday, *Narrative*, especially Introduction.
11 See Bol; see also the contributions of, for example, Maderna and Strawczynski in Bol's edited volume.
12 The situation in classical philology is similar; see Schmitz 37-75.

adopted at all.[13] In addition, there is a classical archaeology-specific problem: Roman art with its rich picture universes is highly underrepresented in these newer studies on narrative, which mainly concentrate on Greek vases and Greek architectural sculpture.[14]

This chapter is an attempt to adopt methodological approaches to narratology and narrativity developed in the recent decades in an intermedial context by analysing depictions and descriptions of sacrifice in different media. It concentrates on the narrative content of the most explicit and detailed visual representation of this ritual in Roman Asia minor, the theatre frieze in Hierapolis representing a sumptuous sacrifice in honour of Artemis Ephesia.

2. A CASE STUDY: THE HIERAPOLIS FRIEZE

2.1 Description

Hierapolis, modern day Pamukkale, was one of the most important cities in Roman Asia minor and the centre of the inner-Anatolian region of Phrygia. In the city's rich and dense network of public buildings, the theatre was one of the most important structures. It was built during the reign of the emperor Hadrian in the first half of the 2nd century and renovated under Septimius Severus at the beginning of the 3rd century.[15] At this time, the *scaenae frons*, the front of the stage, was rebuilt as an impressive three story-façade with elaborate sculptural decoration forming the greatest sculptural complex of Roman Asia minor.[16]

---

13 One seeming exception is Giuliani, but he never cites any narratological literature apart from Lessing's Laokoon. For criticism on Giuliani's approach see Stähli 250f., note 35.

14 Only the columns of Traian and Marcus Aurelius were read as narratives (with all the emerging problems); see Baumer; Hölscher and Winkler; Huet; Galinier; Hölscher, "Säule des Marcus Aurelius"; Koeppel; Krierer; Elsner.

15 See de Bernardo-Ferreri; Çubuk; d'Andria 124-126 (includes a bibliography with older literature); Sobrà and Masino.

16 Fundamental is d'Andria and Ritti passim; see also Stupperich 222-227.

Apart from mythological friezes, a procession and sacrifice to the goddess Artemis Ephesia is depicted (see figure below). This section of the frieze is situated on the northernmost part of the *scaenae frons* decorating both sides of one doorway and the left front of one of the gates.[17] It starts with three young women standing with their left hands elevated in a gesture of salutation and adoration and looking to the right side, the direction in which the frieze continues. Their clothing and especially their hairstyle characterize them as girls or young women (d'Andria and Ritti 143-146, pl. 37). The following slab is decorated with a relief depicting two women and the statue of Artemis Ephesia (146-149, pl. 38). The goddess shows the typical features of the Ephesian Artemis: motionless; both arms bent with two lions sitting on her forearms; an elaborate headdress; a special form of skirt, the *ependytes*; and the *polymasteia*, an ornament on her chest resembling many breasts, but probably representing the collected testicles of sacrificed bulls.[18] The statue stands on a decorated base with two deer beside her legs. It is an object of veneration. To the left, a woman, whose head is covered, strews incense into a fire burning on an altar crowned with a kind of canopy. To the right, a second woman sprinkles water on Artemis' head using a branch.

After this section of veneration the action changes; the relief of the following slab depicts a man dressed in a *chiton* and *himation* guiding a bull or ox to the right (150, pl. 39,1). This assistant holds a club in his right hand and a rope in his left, to which the animal is tied. The subject of driving an animal to sacrifice is repeated on the next slab, but here the servant is standing motionless beside a tree (150f., pl. 39). These four panels described are attached to the north wall of the theatre.

---

17 For localization see d'Andria and Ritti 1-3.
18 For the typical iconography of Artemis Ephesia, see Fleischer, "Artemis von Ephesos" and "Artemis Ephesia."

Fig.1: The Hierapolis Frieze: Sacrifices and procession in honour of Artemis Ephesia

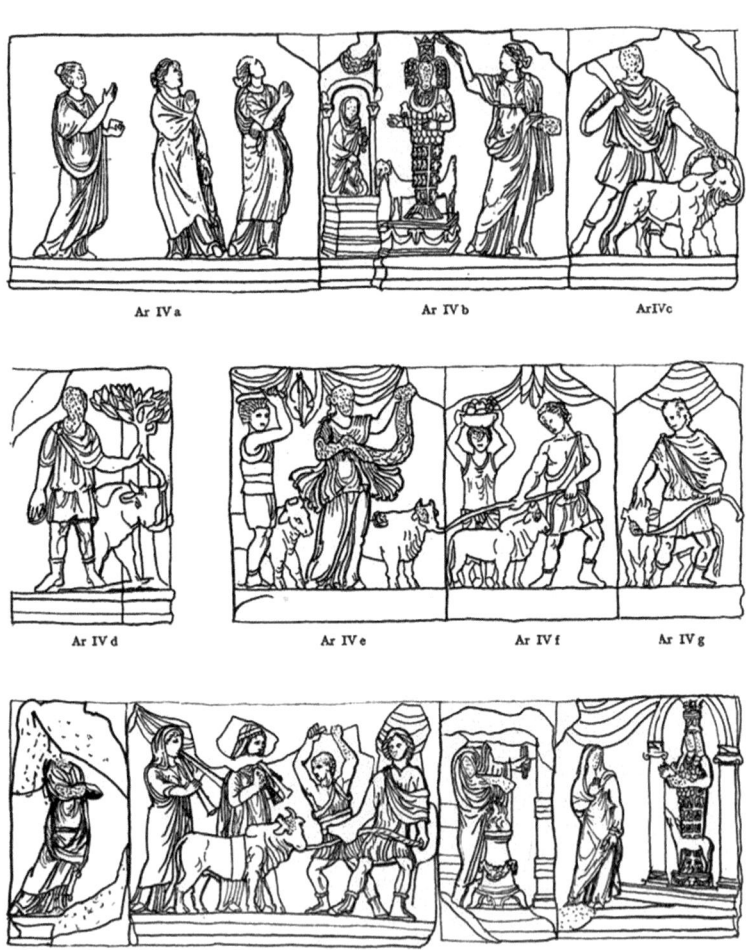

D'Andria and Ritti 97

The slabs on the opposite wall of the doorway continue with the sacrificial cortege: A boy wearing an *exomis* with a broad girdle brandishes a club over his head driving another bull (151f., pl. 40,1). Next to him, a woman in long floating garments presents a garland. The bull in front of her is guided by an attendant depicted on the next slab (153, pl. 40,2). He pulls two animal offerings following the rightward movement of the parade. A young servant in a sleeveless *chiton* standing behind one of the bulls holds a basket of fruit in his raised hands (154f., pl. 41 and 42,1). A fifth man with a bull is depicted on the next slab. This figure concludes the sacrificial procession of cult attendants and bulls.

The following sequences are located on the front of the gate and were highly visible from the audience. It starts with a woman in long garments. Unfortunately the relief is damaged, thus the attributes and the general action is hard to detect. The next slab abounds in acting persons and actions (155-157, pl. 42,2): Two girls with covered heads are playing double-flutes. An attendant in a *chiton* and *himation* holds a bull by a rope. The standing animal is adorned with a belt around its waist in a way most sacrificial animals are decorated. The sacrifice is actually going to be executed: a second attendant in *exomis* and broad girdle lifts his arms, ready to strike a blow with an axe or club – unfortunately not identifiable – to kill the bull.

The following sequence is very similar to that at the beginning. A person at a flaming altar offers incense holding a scroll in his left hand (157f., pl. 43,1). There are, however, some significant differences. Firstly, the altar is cylindrical, which stands in contrast to the rectangular construction on the slab seen before. Secondly, and more importantly, a man wearing a *chiton* and *himation* is now acting as a priest. The sequence closes with a woman worshipping the statue of Ephesian Artemis against an architectural backdrop (158-160, pl. 43,2). This statue resembles the statue in the first part of the frieze wearing a complicated headdress, the usual chest ornament and the *ependytes*; even the lions on the forearms and the deer beside the statue are identical. The architectural framing of the acting persons and of the statue, however, is completely different.

2.2 Structuralist Analysis

After the description of the relief, the first step in analysing the narrative of the representation will be to define the microstructure and macrostructure of the frieze, following the classical structuralist approach.

According to Roland Barthes, the microstructure of narration consists of two basic units, functions and indices.[19] Functions can be further differentiated into nuclei and catalyses. Nuclei are the most important components describing an open-ended action on which the narrative is mounted (Barthes, "Introduction" 247). Barthes stresses that nuclei consist of two elements, an agent and an object or a person acted upon. By means of this definition, many nuclei can be identified on the sacrificial frieze:

- three girls praying
- woman offering incense
- sprinkling the statue of Artemis Ephesia with water
- pulling and driving of bulls
- killing an animal
- man offering incense
- adoring Artemis Ephesia.

Roland Barthes calls the second kind of function catalyses ("Introduction" 248). He defines catalyses as elements that explain the nuclei. It could be disputed whether there are any catalyses on the frieze. Since driving the bulls is the main function, the girl with a garland could be identified as catalysis. The same holds true for the boy carrying a fruit basket and the two women playing the flute.

Besides the functions, indices form the other main component of narrative (Barthes, "Introduction" 249). Among these integrative units a distinction is drawn between indices proper and informants; the indices refer to anything outside of the direct narrative, and the indicators locate the narrative in time and place. Taken as a whole these units are much less frequent than functions. Thus the architectural settings, the tree and the curtain that covers the uppermost part of the second half of the frieze fixing the worship of Artemis Ephesia in place are informants. The curtain as informant is particularly important because by this identical rendering of the background, the procession, the animal sacrifice and the second sacrifice of incense and adoration in front of the statue of Artemis Ephesia are spatially connected. Indices are much harder to detect, but because units can belong to two dif-

---

19 See Barthes, "Introduction" 244-250. See also Stansbury-O'Donnell 18-31; Stähli 245-252.

ferent classes at the same time, the nuclei "driving a bull" or "sacrificing a bull" can be regarded as indices to an expensive and opulent sacrifice, to piety, luxury and abundance.[20]

The composition of the frieze is very simple; thus the viewer can rapidly discover the functions. The actions are easy to identify, so there is little doubt about the general character of the content, the depiction of the worship of Artemis Ephesia by means of adoration, offering incense and sprinkling water, a procession with animal sacrifice as goal and a final act of veneration with adoration and offering incense again. The narrative could be classified as functional because of the preponderance of functions in general and nuclei in particular. Due to this multitude of nuclei, the main task of the viewer is to decide how they relate to each other.

From the perspective of a structural analysis, the nuclei form three sequences linked by a logical relation:[21] The first sequence consists of the worship of Artemis Ephesia, comprising the girls expressing adoration for her and the women offering incense and performing a lustration. The second sequence contains the cortege including the sacrifice, and the third sequence depicts the second worship scene with the second offering of incense and the second adoration in front of a statue. This structure was independent of the installation of the slabs on different parts of the *scaenae frons*, thus abstaining from establishing a correspondence between topic and locale.[22]

At this point of the argument it is possible to specify the type of pictorial narration according to the terminology used in classical archaeology:[23] As the frieze is conceptually composed of one picture, it could be defined as monoscenic, synoptic or progressive, especially because no actant is repeated and shown twice or more. Trying to classify the frieze further leads to a most virulent and tricky question: the question of temporal and spatial continuity. Is there a progression in time or do all actions occur simultane-

---

20 For the interpretation of sacrifice: see Hölscher, "Geschichtsauffassung" 281-287.
21 For a definition of sequence see Barthes, "Introduction" 253; d'Andria and Ritti 160-165 discern only two sequences.
22 See sketch in d'Andria and Ritti 2f.
23 See footnote 5.

ously? Is there a change of locations or are all actions performed in one place?

The first sequence should be characterized as happening in one place and at the same time following the Aristotelian rules of the unity of time and place (d'Andria and Ritti 160). The second sequence cannot be interpreted as such. Although the aforementioned curtain points to the unity of space, the procedure of sacrifice is composed of two consecutive steps: first the driving of the bulls to the altar, or the place where the sacrificial animals were killed, and then the killing itself. Therefore, the unity of time is not maintained in this sequence. It is retained within sequence III. The veneration scene, however, can be connected to the sacrifice scene by means of the curtain. This detail links both sequences spatially. By doing this the procession and the sacrifice on the one hand, and the adoration of Artemis Ephesia on the other, must be located in the same area. Space of action and space of narration should not be confused, but sequences II and III generally depict progression in space from the start of the cortege to the place of sacrifice next to a temple of Artemis.

The spatial relationship between sequence I and sequence III is of great importance for the correct interpretation of the frieze. Do both acts of worship to Artemis happen at the same place? Here the slightly varied depiction of the statues of Artemis Ephesia and the different architectural setting indicate that the two veneration sequences are performed in two different places (d'Andria and Ritti 164). It is hard to assume which places are meant exactly but one could be – hypothetically – identified as the Artemis temple at the fringes of Ephesos, and the other as a second place of worship within the city.[24]

To summarize, the frieze depicts a series of actions divided into three sequences. From one series to the other the unity of time and space is not maintained; even within a single sequence time and space can vary. According to the categorization of types of pictorial narration dealt with earlier, the frieze is an example of progressive narration. This is defined by E. Harrison and especially Stansbury-O'Donnell (144) as a narrative work in which multiple episodes are integrated into a single pictorial field in which no figures are repeated, but in which time and space develop. The progression is realized both in time and space, so that the direction in which the

---

24 For the ambiguous localization see d'Andria and Ritti 164f.

procession moves defines the advancement not only in space, but also in time. Therefore, the structure of time in the pictorial narrative is completely synchronous. The time of narration matches that of the events and also that of the viewer's experience of the frieze when moving from left to right as indicated by the figures on the frieze themselves.

Having pinpointed the narrative microstructure of the frieze as mainly based on functions, we were able to categorize its macrostructure identifying the depiction as a progressive narration. In doing so we followed the main archaeological discourse of pictorial narrative whereby the correlation of the time of the story, the time of the depiction and even the time of the viewer are taken into consideration.

2.3 Postclassical Approaches

More recent studies of narrative are less concerned with describing structural features of the story; instead, they focus on a wide range of different aspects, such as the features of narrative and narrativity, the functions of narratives in various contexts and cultures as well as the analysis of narratives in different media. As mentioned above, these postclassical approaches[25] were never adopted in classical archaeology despite the fact that intermediality plays an especially important role. The following is therefore a completely novel attempt at coming to terms with archaeological objects of study.[26]

---

25 First mentioned in Herman, "Scripts, Sequences and Stories" 1046-1059. For Methods and issues see Fludernik; Herman, Introduction; A. Nünning, "Narratology or Narratologies?"; Herman and Vervaeck 103-176. For a recent collection of essays see Fludernik and Alber. For the development of postclassical approaches, see Phelan; Shang 132-134.

26 For transmedial approaches see Herman, "Towards a Transmedial Narratology"; Ryan, Introduction and "Theoretical Foundations"; Wolf, "Problem der Narrativität"; Wolf, "Cross the Border"; Ryan, "Defining Transmedial Narrative"; Wolf, "Narratology and Media(lity)" (with bibliography). For a summary of recent research, see Mahne (not for pictures); Wolf, "Narrative and Narrativity"; Steiner, "Pictorial Narrativity"; Nanay; Hoogvliet (with bibliography).

According to some scholars narrativity has become the central term in modern narratology[27]. Werner Wolf gives one definition of narrativity: "Fähigkeit, das Narrative im Verein mit einer bestimmten Geschichte zu evozieren oder zu vermitteln" ("Problem der Narrativität" 38). Narrative and narrativity have often been used as a variable, somewhat fuzzy quality. The main problem lies in the exact definition of narrativity and its characteristics. Trying to answer this question at least helps to get a better insight into the narrative strategies applied. Recent work in this field has led to different approaches to grasp the narratological content and the degree of narrativity in a story represented in different media. In this part of my chapter the focus lies on the question whether the Hierapolis frieze can be characterized as a narrative in a different sense to how classical archaeologists use the term. Thus we have to analyse if the representation of the rituals as they were depicted on the Hierapolis frieze can claim narrativity as a particular quality. For doing this we apply three of the most eminent transmedial frameworks in narratology developed by Marie-Laure Ryan, Werner Wolf, and David Herman:

a) Marie-Laure Ryan: dimensions of narrativity
b) Werner Wolf: narrem-based explanation of narrative and narrativity.
c) David Herman: narrative ways of worldmaking.

Ryan presents a fuzzy definition of narrative.[28] In a scalar model she sees eight conditions as constitutive of narrative in a transmedial context:

1.) Narrative must be about a world populated by individuated existents.
2.) This world must be situated in time and undergo significant transformations.
3.) The transformations must be caused by non-habitual physical events.
4.) Some of the participants in the events must be intelligent agents who have a mental life and react emotionally to the states of the world.
5.) Some of the events must be purposeful actions by these agents.
6.) The sequence of events must form a unified causal chain and lead to closure.

---

27 Term coined by Greimas.
28 See Ryan, "Theoretical Foundations" 4, *Avatars of Story* 7-9, "Towards a Definition" 29f., "Defining Transmedial Narrative" 66f.

7.) The occurrence of at least some of the events must be asserted as fact for the storyworld.
8.) The story must communicate something meaningful to the audience.

To proceed strictly in sequence: The Hierapolis frieze shows a detailed picture of a world with many human actors and objects. One problem, however, lies in the question whether the actors are purely generic or individuated agents. In this regard it is significant that no figures seem to have portrait features. Only one figure, the sacrificing *togatus* in sequence III, is damaged and left without a head, thus a secure decision is not possible. Because none of the women performing rituals in the first half of the frieze are depicted as having individual traits, it seems highly plausible that the man offering incense is a generic anonymous agent, too. Therefore, the frieze is not meant to commemorate one specific historical event, but represents a figural translation of an ideal type of sacrifice.

Conditions 2 and 3 are fulfilled, as the actions depicted show a temporal progression and are not habitual. The formal and pragmatic dimensions of narrative expressed by the conditions 6, 7 and 8 are realized in the Hierapolis monument in a rather unambiguous manner: it is evident that the frieze communicates an important meaning, simply because many other representations of sacrifice existed in Roman Asia minor. Despite its limited degree of narrativity, the frieze presents no "bad picture": it illustrates piety and the effort made to perform it. Since everything that is depicted in pictorial representation is factual – it is impossible to depict something that did not happen within the storyworld – all rituals performed are facts.

It is clearly more difficult to answer the question whether the conditions 4 and 5 are met. It depends mainly on whether a specific goal could be developed in the narrative. One possible theme could be the spread of the cult of Artemis within a single city or even from one city to another if the veneration sequence III is read as a representation of the foundation of a new sanctuary inaugurated by performing different rituals. Regarding condition 4, however, neither the mental life nor the emotional reactions of the agents are depicted.

It is one of the important conclusions of more recent contributions to narrative and narrativity that narrative is not absolute, but relative:[29] a rep-

---

29 See footnote 25.

resentation – picture or text – can be more or less narrative. According to the classification proposed by Ryan, the Hierapolis frieze should not be regarded as a full narrative, because not all conditions are met. Since the man in sequence III could not be identified as an individuated person, the Hierapolis frieze is less narrative for missing one of the most important requirements of narrativity. However, the frieze possesses narrativity in the sense that the sequences and actions can easily be constructed into a narrative succession, if the viewer provides common agents and logical connections. What matters is the viewer's ability to extrapolate them from the images.

Wolf considers narrative as a cognitive frame and favours a pluri-componential approach to narrative and narrativity.[30] Like Ryan, Wolf proposes a scalar concept of narrativity, especially in a transmedial context ("Cross the Border" 86). He defines fairy tales as a prototype narrative (87) because they possess the full range of narratological characteristics called narratemes.[31] Thus the degree of narrativity existing in a specific verbal or – in this context more interesting – pictorial representation depends on the number of narratemes realized. The catalogue of narratemes is basically divided into three groups – qualitative narratemes, content narratemes and syntactic narratemes (87-91).

Qualitative narratemes indicate meaningfulness, representationality and experientality, i.e. they are very similar to conditions 6-8 posed by Ryan. The Hierapolis frieze clearly fulfils the narrateme of representationality, and depicts a "possible world" in a rather simple manner. The extent of experientiality, however, is debatable because none of the agents offers clues to the viewers to re-experience the world depicted and become engaged with it. Content narratemes designate the existence of clearly given, specific anthropomorphic characters who are able to choose consciously, perform multiphase actions, or are involved in a number of happenings concluding in some external results. These narratemes mainly designate the plot and can be associated with the spatial, temporal and mental dimensions as Ryan describes them. Here we meet difficulties in individualizing the agents and identifying the meaning of the rituals performed.

---

30 See Wolf, "Problem der Narrativität," "Cross the Border."
31 Term coined by Prince 46.

New aspects for the analysis of the Hierapolis frieze are offered by the syntactic narratemes, predominantly concerning the level of the story. Wolf defines them as thematic unity, causality, clear chronology and – above all – teleology. These particular narratemes are not realized in the Hierapolis frieze. The Aristotelian unity of beginning, middle and end is only maintained if one reads the frieze as the depiction of how the cult of Artemis Ephesia spread in Asia Minor. It means that the viewer has not only got to read the frieze, but also to extrapolate and make inferences. This is true for the chronology of the actions in equal measure: the sequence of the different ritual stages could be detected only by minute analysis of pictorial details, and even then it is hard (or impossible) to determine how much time lies between the sacrifice by the woman in sequence I and the sacrifice by the man in sequence III. The most important flaw regarding the narrativity of the frieze, however, is the lack of teleology as one of the main narratemes: the goal of the rituals depicted can only be specified on the basis of conjectures such as that the frieze represents cultic dissemination.

Thus it should be evident that the Hierapolis frieze is, according to the methodology of Wolf, no prototypical narrative because not all narratemes are met. Since this approach to narrative sees narrativity as a gradable concept, however, the question arises to what extent the application "narrative" to the Hierapolis frieze is justified. Although the depiction of sacrifice displays certain narratemes, it lacks others. Mainly because of being deficient in respect to syntactic narratemes, the Hierapolis frieze requires a high amount of conjecture to construct a story or "narrativization" as Wolf calls it ("Cross the Border" 95). This points to the result that the Hierapolis frieze possesses only a limited degree of narrativity.

Another method to define narrative in an explicit transmedial sense has been developed by Herman,[32] followed by V. Nünning and others.[33] They both rely on the ground-breaking work *Ways of Worldmaking* by N. Goodman. In this context narrative is characterized in a double sense: Firstly as a cognitive scheme dealing with change, action and time, and, secondly, as a

---

32 See Herman, "Narrative Ways," *Basic Elements*, "Stories, Media." I am very grateful to Vera Nünning for calling this approach to my attention and for bringing several important essays to my knowledge.
33 See A. Nünning, "Making Events"; Sommer. Writing the passage on worldmaking I heavily benefited from comments and references made by Vera Nünning.

gradual concept. Therefore it is essential for this approach (like those of Ryan and Wolf) to specify elements which are essential for a prototypical narrative.

According to Herman and others,[34] these elements are:

- situatedness
- worldmaking / world disruption
- sequentiality / linearity
- experientiality (what it's like).

The first characteristic points to the specific context, in which the "story" is told. In the case of the Hierapolis frieze it is the polis world of Roman Asia minor with its culture of theatres, religious traditions, and sumptuous festivals. The theatre as the place of display has to be taken into account, because it is highly probable that this very place was the locale for sacrificial processions such as the one depicted. The context helps to fill the remaining gaps: spectators could amend the representation very easily by making use of their first-hand testimony.

Sequentiality is observed in so far, as the scenes are grouped next to each other. Because the order in which we have to read the sequence is not entirely determined, the Hierapolis frieze meets this condition to the extent that a time sequence could be developed on the basis of interpretation. The depiction could be recognized as sacrifice, however, even if it is "read" in the opposite direction to how it was described before. The gist of the frieze – representation of piety and the efforts made to venerate Artemis – could be understood without considering the correct time sequence. Thus, sequentiality is not given or essential, but has to be deduced according to the knowledge and experience of each spectator.

One of the most important questions for the worldmaking-approach is, of course, whether the Hierapolis frieze constitutes a narrative world. Herman's explanation that "these events are such that they introduce some sort of disruption or disequilibrium into a story world involving humans or human-like agents" facilitates the answer ("Narrative Ways" 73). Instability

---

34 See Herman's preface (IX-XIII), his list of elements (XVI), as well as pages 9-21 in *Basic Elements*.

or disturbances are not depicted, and it may be doubted whether any picture without further explanation by textual comments could achieve this.

The last characteristic – experientiality – points to the subjective experience as a mental state in the sense of Butler and Fludernik, who stress qualia and consequently also the nature of consciousness.[35] The resulting emphasis on conveying a particular experience entails that, like other pictorial representations of rituals in antiquity, the Hierapolis frieze does not fulfil this condition.

The "worldmaking approach" produces the result that the Hierapolis frieze is not a narrative or only a narrative in a very limited sense. In this it is similar to the outcome achieved by the two other methods to detect and quantify narrativity in a transmedial context. Thus it should be evident that the Hierapolis frieze is not a narrative or possesses only a limited number of narrative qualities.

Each of these postclassical methodologies offer very important insights into the way the ritual is depicted: the dimensions-approach by Ryan offers a clear framework for detecting the amount of narrativity the depicted story holds. The narratemes developed mainly by Wolf are especially suitable for analysing the depiction both on the level of *histoire* and on the level of *discourse* adding understanding of further essential dimensions like teleology. The most sophisticated worldmaking-approach is – in my opinion – not fully applicable to purely visual depictions because two of the four elements postulated for a prototypical narrative can be excluded in advance as they cannot easily be realized by pictures without text. The most important contribution for a better understanding lies in stressing the context – a point neglected by the approaches centred on dimensions and narratemes.

3. COMPARISON: THE STORY OF ANTHIA AND HABROCOMES

Having discussed the Hierapolis frieze at length, it is now time that the pictorial series be contrasted to a literal representation of a ritual contemporary to the relief. In his novel, *The Ephesian Tale of Anthia and Habrocomes*, Xenophon of Ephesos, a local writer who lived during the 2nd century, pro-

---

35 See Fludernik 15-19 and passim.

vides a sketch of a festival to venerate Artemis Ephesia by performing a procession.[36] This episode is part of the first book, when the two protagonists meet for the first time:

> A local festival of Artemis was underway, and from the city to her shrine, a distance of seven stades, all the local girls had to march, sumptuously adorned, as did all ephebes who were the same age as Habrocomes; he was about sixteen and already enrolled among the ephebes, and he headed the procession. For the spectacle there was a large crowd both local and visiting, for it was customary at this assemblage to find husbands for the girls and wives for the ephebes. The procession marched along in file, first the sacred objects, torches, baskets, and incense, followed by horses, dogs, and hunting equipment, some of it martial, most of it peaceful [....] each of the girls was adorned as for a lover. Heading the line of girls was Anthia, daughter of Megamedes and Euippe, locals. Anthia's beauty was marvellous and far surpassed the other girls. She was fourteen, her body was blooming with shapeliness, and the adornment of her dress enhanced her grace. Her hair was blonde, mostly loose, only little of it braided, and moving as the breezes took it. Her eyes were vivacious, bright like a beauty's but forbidding like a chaste girl's; her clothing was a belted purple tunic, knee-length and falling loose over the arms, and over it a fawnskin with a quiver attached, arrows [....], javelins in hand, dogs following behind. Often when seen at the shrine, the Ephesians worshipped her as Artemis, so also at the sight of her on occasion the crowd cheered; the opinions of the spectators were various, some in their astonishment declaring that she was the goddess herself, others that she was someone else fashioned by the goddess, but all of them prayed, bowed down, and congratulated her parents, and the universal cry among all spectators was "Anthia the beautiful!". As the crowd of the girls passed by, no one said anything but "Anthia" but as soon as Habrocomes followed with the ephebes, as lovely as the spectacle of the girls had been, at the sight of Habrocomes they all forgot about them and turned their gaze to him, stunned at the sight and shouting "Handsome Habrocomes! Peerless likeness of a handsome god!" And now some added, "What a match Habrocomes and Anthia would make!" These were opening moves in Eros' stratagem. They were both quickly aware of each other's reputation; Anthia longed to see Habrocomes and Habrocomes, hitherto insensible to love, wanted to see An-

---

36 See O'Sullivan; Elsner 233f. (with bibliography).

> thia. And so when the procession was over, the whole crowd repaired to the shrine for the sacrifice, the order of the procession was dissolved, and men and women, ephebes and girls, gathered in the same spot. There they saw each other. Anthia was captivated by Habrocomes, and Habrocomes was bested by Eros. He kept gazing at the girl and though he tried, he could not take his eyes off her: the god pressed his attack and held him fast. Anthia too was in a bad way, as with eyes wide open she took in Habrocomes' handsomeness as it flowed into her, already putting maidenly decorum out of her mind: for what she said was for Habrocomes to hear, and she uncovered what parts of her body she could for Habrocomes to see. He gave himself over to the sight and fell captive to the god. After the sacrifice they parted painfully, complaining about being parted so soon, [and] because they wanted to see each other they kept turning around and stopping, and found many an excuse for delay.[37]

This love story is of course a fully narrative text possessing a great amount of narrativity. But even the description of the festival is conceptualized as a narrative, because it is the specific procession Anthia took part in, and thus a coherent plot is developed with a beginning, a change of places, a series of actions and a somewhat surprising end. First, women and men form different files, but having reached the sanctuary they all come together. Thus even in a relatively short text the narrative character is easier to detect and describe than in a detailed and elaborated relief frieze like that from the theatre at Hierapolis.

All the features of different postclassical approaches are clearly met. This holds true for the conditions regarding spatial, temporal, and mental dimension, which are essential for Ryan's definition of narrativity. Also, all narratemes are realized in the story, even those lacking in the Hierapolis frieze: the agents are two clearly defined individuals, so individualization is given. Experientiality is realized by the sensations the two protagonists raise in the onlookers, and by the changes of feeling they undergo during the procession. The unity of time and space is unambiguous with a clear beginning and end. The most important shortcoming of the pictorial frieze, teleology, is present in a double way: the procession serves, in a strictly ritualistic sense, the worship of the goddess moving from the temple to a

---

37 Xen. Eph. I 2.2-I 3.3. Text and Translation: Henderson 213-221.

shrine nearby and is – in a more mundane meaning – intended as an opportunity for young men and women to meet, like Anthia and Habrocomes do. The story of Anthia and Habrocomes could be interpreted as successful "worldmaking"; even elements of instability or disturbance are easily detected (the power of Eros and the search of the beloved one). It is harder to look for qualia but the description of the mental state of both Habrocomes and Anthia gives clear hints towards comprehending their particular experiences. It is noteworthy, however, that these qualities are realized in the love story and not in the narration of the procession.

Still, it is puzzling that literal descriptions of sacrifices always come as narratives. There are no instructive descriptions as in a recipe: "first you have to offer incense and wine, then a bull has to be killed etc." All texts are part of the narration of one single event. Even one of the most accurate reports of a Roman sacrifice written by Dionysios of Halicarnassus refers to the sacrifice in the context of the *ludi Romani* conducted in the 6th century B.C. in Rome by the dictator Aulus Postumius.[38] This has to be seen in strong contrast to pictorial representations in general.

4. CONCLUSION

Most depictions of sacrifice in *Asia Minor* concentrate mainly on one single action or function: killing the bull or having the bull tied up. Thus only a very short sequence of the ritual is represented in a very unrealistic manner and with a reduced number of human actors. In the sense of Roland Barthes, the sacrifice is condensed to one single function or one single index. Further stages of the sacrifice can be indicated, but not narrated. Therefore, pictorial representations have to be set in contrast to literal texts narrating sacrifice. Rareness or lack of narrativity in pictorial representations of sacrifices is a feature specific to Asia Minor. Here, narrative is mainly limited to myth; events of daily life or of the *Lebenswelt* were not narrated. It is very difficult to find explanations for this cultural habitus. One could be that the past was seen as providing orientation for future actions, while present-day actions were seen as not worth narrating. This attitude contrasts with sacrificial representations in Rome, where depictions

---

38 For the text see Schörner 83-86 (with bibliography).

of this ritual were embedded in biographical narratives not only of the emperors but also of magistrates, priests and other people. The postclassical approaches with explicitly transmedial validity, which were applied to the study of the Hierapolis frieze, all lead to the result that this picture series is not a narrative in its proper sense. It possesses narrative qualities only to a limited degree. The term "narrative" should be used very carefully in an iconographic-archaeological sense, but the dictum of W. Steiner stated twenty years ago is still valid: "the typical art-historical usage of the term 'narrative painting' is very loose" (*Pictures of Romance* 8).[39] The Hierapolis frieze (and many other Roman picture series) needs a great amount of extrapolation or "narrativization" based on prior context-based knowledge. The adoption of postclassical methodologies in classical archaeology could not only make a substantial contribution to a closer look at allegedly well-known monuments but could help keep in touch with important discourses in other disciplines which focus on the study of culture.

REFERENCES

Barthes, Roland. "Introduction à l'analyse structurale des récits." *Communications* 8 (1966): 1-27.
—. "An Introduction to the Structural Analysis of Narrative." *New Literary History* 6 (1975): 237-272.
Baumer, Lorenz E., Tonio Hölscher, and Lorenz Winkler. "Narrative Systematik und politisches Konzept in den Reliefs der Traianssäule. Drei Fallstudien." *Jahrbuch des Deutschen Archäologischen Instituts* 106 (1991): 261-295.
Bielefeld, Erwin. "Zum Problem der kontinuierenden Darstellungsweise." *Archäologischer Anzeiger* (1956): 29-34.
Von Blanckenhagen, Peter H. "Narration in Hellenistic and Roman Art." *American Journal of Archaeology* 61 (1957): 78-83.
Boardman, John. "The Greek Art of Narrative." *Eumusia. Ceramic and Iconographic Studies in Honour of Alexander Cambitoglou*. Ed. Jean-Paul Descoeudres. Sydney: Meditarch, U of Sydney, 1990. 57-62.

---

39 Quoted in Wolf, "Problem der Narrativität" 25.

Bol, Peter C., ed. *Zum Verhältnis von Raum und Zeit in der griechischen Kunst. Passavant-Symposion 8. Bis 10. Dezember 2000*. Möhnesee: Bibliopolis, 2003.

Brilliant, Richard. *Visual Narratives. Storytelling in Etruscan and Roman Art*. Ithaca: Cornell UP, 1984.

Carter, John. "The Beginning of Narrative Art in the Greek Geometric Period." *The Annual of the British School at Athens* 67 (1972): 25-58.

Çubuk, Nizami. *Hierapolis. Tiyatro Kabartmaları*. Istanbul: Arkeoloji ve Sanat Yayınları, 2008.

D'Andria, Francesco, ed. *Atlante di Hierapolis di Frigia. Hierapolis II*. Istanbul: Ege Yayinlari, 2008.

D'Andria, Francesco, and Tullia Ritti. *Hierapolis Scavi e Ricerche II: Le Sculture del Teatro. I Rilievi con i Cicli di Apollo e Artemide*. Rom: Bretschneider, 1985.

De Bernardo Ferreri, Daria, ed. *Il teatro di Hierapolis di Frigia. Restauro, Architettura ed Epigrafia*. Genova: de Ferrari 2007.

Dehejia, Harsha V. "On Modes of Visual Narration in Early Buddhist Art." *Art Bulletin* 72 (1990): 374-392.

Eco, Umberto. *The Role of the Reader. Explorations in the Semiotics of Texts*. Bloomington: Indiana UP, 1979.

—. "Die Zeit der Kunst." *Zeit. Die vierte Dimension in der Kunst. Ausstellung Kunsthalle Mannheim – MuMoK Wien 1985*. Ed. Michel Baudson. Weinheim: Acta Humaniora, 1985. 75-83.

—. *Lector in Fabula. Die Mitarbeit der Interpretation in erzählenden Texten*. München: Hanser, 1987.

Elsner, Jaś. *Roman Eyes. Visuality & Subjectivity in Art & Text*. Princeton: Princeton UP, 2007.

Fleischer, Robert. "Artemis von Ephesos und verwandte Kultstatuen aus Anatolien und Syrien." *Études Préliminaires aux Religions Orientales dans l'Empire Romain 35*. Leiden: Brill, 1973.

—. "Artemis Ephesia." *Lexicon Iconographicum Mythologiae Classicae II*. München/Zürich: Artemis, 1984. 755-763.

Fludernik, Monika. *Towards a 'Natural' Narratology*. London: Routledge, 1996.

Fludernik, Monika, and Jan Alber, eds. *Postclassical Narratology: Approaches and Analyses*. Columbus: Ohio State UP, 2010.

Galinier, M. "La colonne de Marc Aurèle: Réflexions sur une gestuelle narrative." *La colonne aurélienne. Geste et image sur la colonne de Marc Aurèle à Rome*. Eds. John Scheid and Val Huet. Turnhout: Brepols, 2000. 141-161.

Giuliani, Luca. *Bild und Mythos. Geschichte der Bilderzählung in der griechischen Kunst*. München: Beck, 2003.

Goodman, Nelson. *Ways of Worldmaking*. Indianapolis: Hackett, 1978.

Greimas, Algirdas J. "Éléments d'une grammaire narrative." *L'Homme* 9.3 (1969): 71-92.

Hanfmann George M.A. "Narration in Greek Art." *American Journal of Archaeology* 61 (1957): 71-78.

Harrison, Evelyn B. "Direction and Time in Monumental Narrative in the 5th Century B.C." *American Journal of Archaeology* 87 (1983): 237-238.

Henderson, Jeffrey, ed. and trans. *Daphnis and Chloe*. by Longus. *Anthia and Habrocomes*. by Xenophon of Ephesus. Cambridge: Harvard UP, 2009.

Herman, David. "Scripts, Sequences, and Stories: Elements of a Postclassical Narratology." *Transactions and Proceedings of the Modern Language Association of America* 112 (1997): 1046-1059.

—. Introduction. *Narratologies: Perspectives on Narrative Analysis*. Ed. David Herman. Columbus: Ohio State UP, 1999. 1-30.

—. "Towards a Transmedial Narratology." *Narrative across Media: The Languages of Storytelling*. Ed. Marie-Laure Ryan. Lincoln, NB: U of Nebraska P, 2004. 47-75.

—. "Narrative Ways of Worldmaking." *Narratology in the Age of Cross-Disciplinary Narrative Research*. Eds. Sandra Heinen and Roy Sommer. Berlin: de Gruyter, 2009. 71-87.

—. *Basic Elements of Narrative*. Malden: Wiley-Blackwell. 2009.

—. "Stories, Media, and the Mind: Narrative Worldmaking through Word and Image." *Foreign Literature Studies* 4 (2010): 42-50.

Herman, Luc, and Bart Vervaeck. *Handbook of Narrative Analysis*. Lincoln, NB: U of Nebraska P, 2005.

Himmelmann-Wildschütz, Nikolaus. *Erzählung und Figur in der archaischen Kunst*. Wiesbaden: Steiner, 1967.

Holliday, Peter J., ed. *Narrative and Event in Ancient Art*. Cambridge: Cambridge UP, 1993.

—. Introduction. *Narrative and Event in Ancient Art.* Ed. Peter Holliday. Cambridge: Cambridge UP, 1993. 3-13.

Hölscher, Tonio. "Die Geschichtsauffassung in der römischen Repräsentationskunst." *Jahrbuch des Deutschen Archäologischen Instituts* 95 (1980): 265-321.

—. "Die Säule des Marcus Aurelius: Narrative Struktur und ideologische Botschaft." *La Colonne Aurélienne. Autour de la Colonne Aurélienne. Geste et Image sur la Colonne de Marc Aurèle à Rome.* Eds. John Scheid and Val Huet. Turnhout: Brepols, 2000. 89-105.

Hoogvliet, Margriet. "How to Tell a Fairy Tale with Images: Narrative Theories and French Paintings from the Early Nineteenth Century." *Relief* 4 (2010): 198-212.

Huet, Valerie. "Stories One Might Tell of Roman Art. Reading Trajan's Column and the Tiberius Cup." *Art and Text in Roman Culture.* Ed. Jaś Elsner. Cambridge: Cambridge UP, 1996. 8-31.

Kaeser, Berthold H. "Zur Darstellungsweise der griechischen Flächenkunst von der Geometrischen Zeit bis zum Ausgang der Archaik. Eine Untersuchung an der Darstellung des Schildes." *Diss.* Bonn U, 1976/81.

Koeppel, Gerhard. "The Column of Trajan. Narrative Technique and the Image of the Emperor." *Sage and Emperor. Plutarch, Greek Intellectuals, and Roman Power in the Time of Trajan, 98 - 117 A.D.* Ed. Philip A. Stadter. Leuven: Leuven UP, 2002. 245-257.

Krierer, Karl R. "Konzept, Struktur und narrative Methode der Bildprogrammatik römischer Triumphsäulen. Trajanssäule und Mark Aurel-Säule." *Krieg und Sieg. Narrative Wanddarstellungen von Altägypten bis ins Mittelalter. Internationales Kolloquium im Schloss Haindorf, Langenlois 29. - 30. Juli 1997.* Ed. Manfred Bietak. Wien: Verl. d. Österr. Akad. d. Wiss., 2002. 161-173.

Maderna, Caterina. "Augenblick und Dauer in griechischen Mythenbildern." *Zum Verhältnis von Raum und Zeit in der griechischen Kunst. Passavant-Symposion 8. bis 10. Dezember 2000.* Ed. Peter C. Bol. Möhnesee: Bibliopolis, 2003. 275-298.

Mahne, Nicole. *Transmediale Erzähltheorie: Eine Einführung.* Göttingen: Vandenhoeck & Ruprecht, 2007.

Meyboom, Paul G.P. "Some Observation on Narration in Greek Art." *Mededelingen van het Nederlands Instituut te Rome. Antiquity* 5 (1978): 55-82.

Nanay, Bence. "Narrative Pictures." *The Journal of Aesthetics and Art Criticism* 67 (2009): 119-129.

Nünning, Ansgar. "Narratology or Narratologies? Taking Stock of Recent Developments, Critique and Modest Proposals for Future Usage of the Term." *What is Narratology? Questions and Answers Regarding the Status of a Theory*. Ed. Tom Kindt. Berlin: de Gruyter, 2003. 239-275.

—. "Making Events – Making Stories – Making Worlds: Ways of Worldmaking from a Narratological Point of View." *Cultural Ways of Worldmaking. Media and Narratives*. Eds. Vera Nünning, Ansgar Nünning and Birgit Neumann. Berlin: de Gruyter, 2010. 191-214.

Nünning, Vera. "The Making of Fictional Worlds: Processes, Features, and Functions." *Cultural Ways of Worldmaking. Media and Narratives*. Eds. Vera Nünning, Ansgar Nünning and Birgit Neumann. Berlin: de Gruyter, 2010. 215-243.

O'Sullivan, James N. *Xenophon of Ephesus. His Compositional Technique and the Birth of the Novel*. Berlin: de Gruyter, 1995.

Phelan, James. "Narrative Theory 1966-2006: A Narrative." *The Nature of Narrative*. Eds. James Phelan, Robert Scholes and Robert Kellogg. Oxford: Oxford UP, 2006. 283-336.

Prince, Gerald. "Revisiting Narrativity." *Grenzüberschreitungen. Narratologie im Kontext/Transcending Boundaries: Narratology in Context*. Eds. Walter Grünzweig and Andreas Solbach. Tübingen: Narr, 1999. 43-51.

Raeck, Wulf. "Zur Erzählweise archaischer und klassischer Mythenbilder." *Jahrbuch des Deutschen Archäologischen Instituts* 99 (1984): 1-25.

Robert, Carl. *Bild und Lied. Archäologische Beiträge zur Geschichte der griechischen Heldensage*. Berlin: Weidmann, 1881.

Ryan, Marie-Laure. Introduction. *Narrative across Media: The Languages of Storytelling*. Ed. Marie-Laure Ryan. Lincoln, NB: U of Nebraska P, 2004.

—. "On the Theoretical Foundations of Transmedial Narratology." *Narratology beyond Literary Criticism*. Ed. Jan C. Meister. Berlin: de Gruyter, 2005. 1-23.

—. *Avatars of Story*. Minneapolis, MN: U of Minnesota P, 2006.

—. "Towards a Definition of Narrative." *The Cambridge Companion to Narrative*. Ed. David Herman. Cambridge: Cambridge UP, 2007. 22-35.

—. "Defining Transmedia Narrative: Problems and Questions." *Enthymena* 4 (2011): 65-71.
Scheid, John, and Val Huet, eds. *La Colonne Aurélienne. Autour de la Colonne Aurélienne. Geste et Image sur la Colonne de Marc Aurèle à Rome*. Turnhout: Brepols, 2000.
Schmitz, Thomas A. *Moderne Literaturtheorie und antike Texte. Eine Einführung*. Darmstadt: Wiss. Buchges., 2002.
Schörner, Günther. "Sacrifice East and West: Experiencing Ritual Difference in the Roman Empire." *Reflexivity, Media, and Visuality*. Ed. Udo G. Simon. Wiesbaden: Harrassowitz, 2011. 81-99.
Shang, Biwu. "Plurality and Complementarity of Postclassical Narratologies." *Journal of Cambridge Studies* 6 (2011): 131-147.
Shapiro, Harvey A. "Old and New Heroes. Narrative, Composition, and Subject in Attic Black-Figure." *Classical Antiquity* 9 (1990): 114-148.
—. "Narrative Strategies in Euphronios." *Euphronios. Atti del Seminario Internazionale di Studi. Arezzo, 27-28 Maggio 1990*. Ed. Mario Cygielman. Firenze: Ed. Il Ponte, 1992. 37-43.
Small, Jocelyn P. "Time *in* Space: Narrative in Classical Art." *Art Bulletin* 81 (1999): 562-575.
Snodgrass, Anthony M. *Narration and Allusion in Archaic Greek Art*. London: Leopard's Head Press, 1982.
Sobrà, Giorgia, and Filippo Masino. "La Frontescena Severiana del Teatro di Hierapolis di Frigia. Architettura, Decorazione e Maestranze." *La Scaenae Frons en la Arquitectura Teatral Romana. Actas del Symposium Internacional Celebrado en Cartagena los Días 12 al 14 de Marzo de 2009 en el Museo del Teatro Romano*. Ed. Sebastian F. Ramallo Asensio. Murcia: Univ.; Fundación Teatro Romano de Cartagena, 2010. 373-412.
Sommer, Roy. "Making Narrative Worlds. A Cross-Disciplinary Approach to Literary Story-Telling." *Narratology in the Age of Cross-Disciplinary Narrative Research*. Eds. Sandra Heinen and Roy Sommer. Berlin: de Gruyter, 2009. 88-108.
Stähli, Adrian. "Erzählte Zeit, Erzählzeit und Wahrnehmungszeit. Zum Verhältnis von Temporalität und Narration speziell in der hellenistischen Plastik." *Zum Verhältnis von Raum und Zeit in der griechischen Kunst. Passavant-Symposion 8. bis 10. Dezember 2000*. Ed. Peter C. Bol. Möhnesee: Bibliopolis, 2003. 239-264.

Stansbury-O'Donnell, Mark D. *Pictorial Narrative in Ancient Greek Art.* Cambridge: Cambridge UP, 1999.

Steiner, Wendy. *Pictures of Romance: Form against Context in Painting and Literature.* Chicago, IL: U of Chicago P, 1988.

—. "Pictorial Narrativity." *Narrative across Media: The Languages of Storytelling.* Ed. Marie-Laure Ryan. Lincoln, NB: U of Nebraska P, 2004. 145-177.

Stewart, Andrew. "Narrative, Genre, and Realism in the Work of the Amasis Painter." *Papers on the Amasis Painter and His World: Colloquium Sponsored by the Getty Center for the History of Art and the Humanities and Symposium Sponsored by the J. Paul Getty Museum.* Malibu: J. Paul Getty Museum, 1987. 29-42.

Strawczynski, Nina. "La représentation de l'événement sur la céramique attique: quelques stratégies graphiques." *Zum Verhältnis von Raum und Zeit in der griechischen Kunst. Passavant-Symposion 8. bis 10. Dezember 2000.* Ed. Peter C. Bol. Möhnesee: Bibliopolis, 2003. 29-45.

Stupperich, Reinhard. "'Dionysos in Comics.' Mythologische Theaterbühnenfriese der Kaiserzeit im griechischen Osten." *Skeniká. Beiträge zum antiken Theater und seiner Rezeption. Festschrift zum 65. Geburtstag von Horst-Dieter Blume.* Eds. Susanne Gödde and Theodor Heinze. Darmstadt: Wiss. Buchges., 2000. 207-231.

Weitzmann, Kurt. *Illustrations in Roll and Codex. A Study of the Origin and Method of Text Illustration.* Princeton: Princeton UP, 1947.

Wickhoff, Franz. Einleitung. *Die Wiener Genesis.* Eds. Wilhelm von Hartel and Franz Wickhoff. Prag: Tempsky, 1895.

—. "Die Römische Kunst: Die Wiener Genesis." *Die Schriften von Franz Wickhoff.* Ed. Max Dvořák. Berlin: Meyer & Jessen, 1912.

Wolf, Werner. "Das Problem der Narrativität in Literatur, Bildender Kunst und Musik: ein Beitrag zu einer intermedialen Erzähltheorie." *Erzähltheorie transgenerisch, intermedial, interdisziplinär.* Eds. Vera Nünning and Ansgar Nünning. Trier: WVT, 2002. 23-104.

—. "Narrative and Narrativity: A Narratological Reconceptualization and Its Applicability to the Visual Arts." *Word & Image* 19 (2003): 180-197.

—. "'Cross the Border – Close that Gap': Towards an Intermedial Narratology." *European Journal of English Studies* 8 (2004): 81-103.

—. "Narratology and Media(lity): The Transmedial Expansion of a Literary Discipline and Its Possible Consequences." *Current Trends in Narratology*. Ed. Greta Olson. Berlin: de Gruyter, 2011. 145-180.

"He had just finished presenting the burnt offering ...": Narrative and Ritual in the Context of Saul's Failure (1 Sam 13-14)

JOACHIM VETTE

1. INTRODUCTION

The narratives in the first book of Samuel provide rich opportunity for narrative analysis. Readers encounter many detailed characterizations, a wealth of direct speech and complex plots full of conflicts. All this is also true for the narratives in 1 Samuel 13-14. They describe how Israel's first king Saul stumbles from one crisis into the next while continually losing authority. At the same time, his son Jonathan establishes himself as the next sympathetic protagonist and potential successor. This transfer of power is symptomatic for the books of Samuel as a whole. A sequence of different dynasties runs through the stories, beginning with Eli and his ill-bred sons who are followed by Samuel and his sons (1 Sam 1-7). The house of Samuel is succeeded by Saul and then his son Jonathan (1 Sam 8-15). David is next in line, and much of the text is devoted to who among David's sons will follow him on the throne (1 Sam 16 – 2 Kings 2). Almost every dynastic turn is characterized by conflicting interests, opportunism and the inability to let go of or hold on to power. The same is true for the transfer of authority from Samuel to Saul and finally to Jonathan.

Within this context, 1 Sam 13-14 is characterized by a plethora of varying rituals. The two chapters refer to the blowing of the shofar, a burnt offering (ʿōlāh), a peace offering (šᵉlāmîm), a sign of divine favor, the use of the Ark of the Covenant, an oath, a collective sacrifice, and the casting of lots to determine divine judgment. No other narrative in the Old Testament contains this many rituals. The texts in 1 Sam 13-14 are thus ideally suited for a discussion of the relation between Old Testament narrative and ritual. Following a few introductory remarks on Old Testament narrative poetics as well as ritual in the Old Testament, I will present a detailed narrative reading of 1 Sam 13-14 with special emphasis on the rituals mentioned there. I propose that the descriptions of ritual are the narrative strategies that communicate both the loss and the gain of power.

1.1 Narrative Poetics

It is not a matter of course to connect poetics with narrative texts. Based on the classic distinction between lyrical, dramatic, and epic texts, we cannot help but notice that lyrical and dramatic texts have traditionally been at the forefront of poetic interest (Lämmert 9). As a subgroup of epic texts, narratives were only at the fringes of poetic research until the beginning of the 20th century. The lack of stringent formal categories, especially when compared to lyrical texts, was one reason for the lack of narrative poetic studies. The classic statement by E.M. Forster sums it up: "The novel is most distinctly one of the moister areas of literature" (Forster 25). If we include not only the novel but all shapes of narrative texts, analysis of this "genre" is further complicated by a lack of clear terminology and analytical method (Wehrli 83).

According to Eberhard Lämmert, a definition of "narrative" should describe the wide range of texts that might conceivably belong to this category "ungeachtet des etwaigen Vorwiegens eines Typus in einer Zeit, bei einem Volk oder einem Dichter" (Lämmert 16). The most important feature of any narrative is the construction of a discourse, in which a narrator presents to a reader characters engaged in a plot occurring in a specific context of space and time (cf. 21). A narrative thus "narrates something," as in the phrase "to tell a story." The statement that the narrative narrates something sketches the two main categories of narrative analysis: the story and the telling, or narrative content and narrative shape. This distinction has been described with a host of varying terminology: "fabula-sujet" (Todorov), "story-discourse" (Chatman), "histoire/diégèse-récit" (Genette), "Stoff-Erzählung" (Kayser), "source-discourse" (Sternberg). Narrative poetics is the description of the various relationships between narrative content and narrative shape. On this relationship Lämmert writes:

Die Spannung zwischen dem vorgespiegelten realen Geschehen und seiner erzählerischen Bewältigung beruht zunächst auf der Spannung zwischen realer und sprachgetragener, d.h. intentionaler Wirklichkeit schlechthin. Sprache kann Gegenstände und Vorgänge nicht nachahmen, sondern nur andeuten und soweit bewusst machen, als es für den jeweiligen Zweck der Aussage notwendig ist. Durch Andeutung jedoch macht der Sprecher das Ganze aus seiner Perspektive sichtbar. *Mit seiner Auswahl aus dem unbegrenzten Ganzen, das ihm real oder fiktiv zur Verfügung steht, erstellt er ein begrenztes Ganzes*, getreu dem Gesetz, dass alles Bilden und insbesondere das Bilden von Menschenhand ein Weglassen sei. Sind diese Prinzipien der Andeutung und der Auswahl für jede Art sprachlicher Weltdarbietung verbindlich, so müssen sie auch an allen Phänomenen der Erzählkunst gleichermaßen aufweisbar sein (23; emphasis J.V.).

A narrative discourse is not the imitation of a non-discursive reality; it is rather the construction of a unique narrative reality. The source material for each narrative is selected from a vast universe of possible events, actions, characters and settings (Lämmert's *"unbegrenztes Ganzes"*). Yet the unique task of narrative poetics does not lie in identifying the sources and historical context for the material in the story (such as a certain ritual); instead, narrative analysis describes what material is selected and how the material is used, shaped, and communicated to the reader *within* the discourse.[1] Analytical description, however, is not the end of the matter; it leads to interpretive synthesis. In this creative and often playful endeavor,

---

1 "Was die Quellenforschung mit dem Odium der Stoffhuberei belastet hat, war das Sich-Zufrieden-Geben mit den bloßen Feststellungen stofflicher Bezüge. Tatsächlich ist damit nichts für die künstlerische Erfassung und noch sehr wenig für die literarhistorische getan. Die eigentliche Arbeit müsste jetzt beginnen. Warum ergriff der Dichter diesen Stoff, was reizte ihn? Wie und wozu verarbeitete er ihn? [...] Die sorgfältige Analyse der Art, wie die Quelle im Ganzen oder in Einzelheiten benutzt wird, die eingehende Beobachtung und Ausdeutung aller Änderungen versprechen reiche Erkenntnisse für das Werk einerseits und darüber hinaus für das Wesen des Poetischen, andererseits für die Erkenntnis des Dichters, der Strömung, der Epoche" (Kayser 60).

the reader constructs the meaning and intention of the narrative text. As Sternberg states: "our primary business as readers is to make purposive sense of it, so as to explain the *what's* and the *how's* in terms of the *why's* of communication." (*Poetics* 1)[2]

1.2 Narratology and the Old Testament

Once we define narratives as stated above, we realize that more than one third of all texts in the Old Testament can be classified as narrative. It is thus no surprise that narrative studies also turned to the Old Testament, especially from the 1970s on. Given Sternberg's proposal, narrative analysis of Old Testament narratives should try to describe *how* the story is told in order to explain *why* the story is told. Instead of succumbing to "Stoffhuberei" ("the stench of source fixation," see above) and spending all interpretive energy on constructing the possible historical context for the material used in the telling, narrative analysis aims to understand the mechanisms that shape the discourse itself. It will tend to focus on the final form of the Masoretic Text as a unified text.[3] Whether or not reading the text as a homogenous unit is plausible will depend on whether the many oddities in the text can be worked into an overall construct of textual intention. The interpreter should never forget that Old Testament narratives are indeed texts that were edited and combined over time. Certain aspects of the text will always remain visible as traces of textual growth. Yet even though the controversy between synchronic and diachronic observations continues in unabated controversy, there can be no doubt that Old Testament studies also need to be concerned with the shape of the narrative discourse.

I cannot provide an overview over the wealth of Old Testament narrative readings in this context. A precise description of methodology also exceeds the limits of this chapter. I have attempted both a survey and a de-

---

2   The fact that the same source material can be shaped into a variety of different narratives raises the question: why did the "narrator" present the story in this manner if he could have also done it differently?

3   As with canonical approaches, as proposed for example by Sanders, we must acknowledge that there is more than one canonical text (see also Zenger; Tov). The various textual families (the Septuagint or the Samaritan Pentateuch) are separate discourses to be interpreted each on their own terms.

scription of methodology elsewhere (Vette, "Survey"; *Samuel und Saul*). In the following, I will present a close reading of 1 Sam 13-14 with special emphasis on the ritualized actions mentioned there.

1.3 Rituals in the Old Testament

Old Testament texts describe ancient Israelite religion as a highly cultic affair, especially for the pre-exilic period. We frequently encounter rituals in a host of different textual genres.[4] This variety opens up a window into very different descriptions of rituals, into how they are praised and criticized. The priestly writings and the book of Ezekiel are especially concerned with the topic. Sacrifices are the most frequent type of ritual. According to Alfred Marx (573), the texts distinguish between two main forms of sacrifice: a) the whole offering or burnt offering; b) the meal offering. Whereas the burnt offering sacrifices the entire animal (the texts mention cattle, sheep, goats and doves) to YHWH, the meat of the meal offering is distributed among the guests, and only fat and blood are kept for YHWH.

In addition to summoning YHWH's presence, rituals in the Old Testament are a main factor in establishing order. This includes the order of time (structuring chaos through daily, weekly, annual and other rhythms), the order of space (separation of holy and profane or pure and impure areas), and the order of social hierarchy and power structures (avoidance of the chaos of anarchy; see Gertz 551).

Despite the relative wealth of textual descriptions, the attempt to reconstruct Old Testament rituals as historical events remains almost impossible. There is hardly any archaeological evidence, we know of little iconographic material or sacred architecture, and the precise dating of the texts remains a matter of great controversy. Are the texts contemporary to the ritual prac-

---

4 The Old Testament is an important witness to ritual practices in the ancient Near East as a whole. Scholars have often pointed to the continuities between Old Testament and other ancient Near East ritual practices. Compare Koch: "[Es] wird erkennbar, dass zwischen akkadischen und hebräischen Ritualverfahrensanweisungen überraschende Strukturparallelen bestehen. [...] Von daher ergibt sich, daß es einmal an alte Gattung (mündlicher) Ritualverfahrensanweisungen gegeben hat, die wohl auf irgendeine Weise von Babylonien nach Israel hinübergelangt sind."

tices described therein, might they even prescribe these practices, or are they "mere" literary reflections on much older traditions that may not even be familiar anymore? Yet even if we were able to reach a consensus on the dating of individual texts, the texts themselves do not contain enough detailed information that might allow us to reconstruct the particular ritual process. Bibb correctly states:

Even if one could firmly situate the Pentateuchal ritual texts within a particular historical setting, it still would be impossible to observe these rituals in practice. Aside from the historical uncertainties, the texts themselves do not provide enough information to allow the interpreter fully to imagine a real performance. [...] [T]he ritual world constructed by the text is partial, fractured, and ambiguous (41).

This fact becomes especially obvious when considering what texts may have accompanied the ritual act. Scholars have long noted that Old Testament ritual description lacks any mention of related speech acts:

Beim Vollzug der vorgesehenen Begehung scheint kein einziges Wort zu fallen. Kein Sprachgeschehen unterbricht – nach dem Wortlaut der Text – die stillen und ernsten Opferungen und Weihehandlungen, keinerlei Rezitation wird laut; nicht von flehen oder Gebet an die Gottheit; nichts von Kommunikation zwischen den aktiv am Kult Beteiligten, kein Spruch des Segens (Koch 75).

We should treat the assumption with caution that all rituals in the Old Testament were "silent events," and that the temple in Jerusalem was a "sanctuary of silence" (Knohl), in which the priest did not speak at all. Is it truly plausible to think that no one ever spoke in the temple only because the texts contain no reference to such speech? The richness of biblical and extra-biblical liturgical poetry points to the high estimation in which liturgical texts were held. If, however, the spoken word is constitutive for the reconstruction of ritual meaning (Sundermeier 260), then any attempt to understand the meaning of a ritual as a historic event is faced with insurmountable difficulties (Gertz 551). Approaching Old Testament rituals as historic events leads scholars to a dead end.

1.4 Beyond the Reconstruction of History: Ritual Theory and Narrative Strategy

We can nevertheless incorporate insights from ritual studies in general in order to see more clearly the role and function of rituals *in narrative*.

According to Gorman, rituals serve to avoid chaos and stabilize order in a given society, should order be threatened or damaged (41). Rituals play a constructive role by giving shape to boundaries and hierarchies that shape the community celebrating the ritual. The ritual is a model of a desired outcome, a *telos* towards which the community should move. Instead of simply enforcing the status quo, rituals are instruments of change, as they embody the vision a society is aiming for (Altmann 61-64).

In order to better grasp the strategies of change and the accompanying claims to power promoted by rituals, it is helpful to follow a change of perspective suggested by Catherine Bell. She suggests emphasizing ritualized behavior or action as a whole instead of the individual ritual itself:

[R]itualization is a matter of various culturally specific strategies for setting some activities off from others, for creating and privileging a qualitative distinction between the 'sacred' and the 'profane,' and for ascribing such distinctions to realities thought to transcend the powers of human actors (74).

Instead of attempting to understand a concrete ritual as a closed symbolic system, Bell turns her attention to the question of why certain actions or events are "ritualized," i.e. emphasized and valorized by a variety of different means.[5] Strategies of ritualization elevate the importance of individual actions, increase their value, and strengthen their binding character (140). These actions can then serve to strengthen or to weaken existing structures of power. In this sense, ritualized actions are strategic instruments of political power.[6] Any individual performing a ritual publicly defines and enforces a certain concept of identity and objective.

---

5 Even the use of unusual terminology or loanwords can be seen as strategies of ritualization (Bibb 59).

6 Bibb 52: "When one considers the power-laden relationships that shape and direct ritual interactions, discovering ritualization strategies becomes essential. Ritualization is 'strategic.'"

Many have noted this connection between ritual, publicity and power (Sundermeier 263). Even knowing about the place and time of a ritual is a means of exerting power and defining clear hierarchies (Strausberg 548). Being informed of the precise procedure of a ritual and controlling who participates how in the ritual process further enforces such social stratification and group identity. Sundermeier speaks of the limiting aspect of ritual: "Er [the ritual process] schließt die Teilnehmer als Gruppe zusammen und schließt andere zugleich aus. Er macht Zugehörigkeit und Ausgeschlossenheit sichtbar und vollzieht beides in einem Akt. Segen und Sanktionen liegen nahe beieinander" (263). All ritualized actions have a political dimension. They might be used to define group boundaries, compensate loss of authority, strengthen personal status, enforce agreement and loyalty, or challenge a political opponent and prepare a transfer of power. All these aspects will be part of the narrative world presented in 1 Samuel 13-14.

2. RITUALS AND NARRATIVE DISCOURSE IN 1 SAMUEL 13-14

I will proceed in the assumption that the rituals described in 1 Samuel 13-14 are not simply historical artifacts that embellish the stage design of the narrative, or archival "reports" on ancient historical practices. Instead, these rituals will be read as intentionally shaped elements of the narrative matrix that are used strategically to construct and deconstruct the power relationships between the different protagonists of the story.

2.1 1 Sam 13-14: Introduction

1 Samuel 13-14 narrates Saul's tragic failure. The narratives explain this failure on the basis of several bad decisions made by the king. Readers are thus led through a dramatic reversal of fortune: Saul starts as a youthful hero, filled with the spirit of God, who gathers the people "as one man" (1 Sam 11:7) and liberates the inhabitants of Jabesh-Gilead. He ends as an outcast, rejected first by the prophet Samuel and then by the people as a whole. Saul's rise and his fall are narrated in only three chapters. We can point to a combination of many narrative strategies that work together and lead the reader along the path of accepting this radical reversal (Sternberg

1992). An important foundation is already laid in Samuel's long monologue in chapter 12. The prophet cleverly undermines the relationship between God and his king as well as the king and his people. At the same time, Samuel presents his own sons as potential replacements despite their shortcomings ("...and my sons: Behold, they are with you"; 1 Sam 12:2. Cf. 1 Sam 8:3 and Vette, "Farewell"). Samuel's speech ends with an explicit warning against the imminent destruction of the people and their king Saul ("If you continue in your evil, you and your king will be destroyed"; 1 Sam 12:25). He does not seem to consider a positive development possible. This is the background of the plot in 1 Sam 13-14.

2.2 1 Sam 13-14: Framing the Text

[13,1] Saul was ___ years old[7] when he became king. For two years he was king over Israel.

[...]

[14,47] When Saul had taken the kingship over Israel, he fought against all his enemies on every side-- against Moab, against the Ammonites, against Edom, against the kings of Zobah, and against the Philistines; wherever he turned he routed them. [48] He did valiantly, and struck down the Amalekites, and rescued Israel out of the hands of those who plundered them. [49] Now the sons of Saul were Jonathan, Ishvi, and Malchishua; and the names of his two daughters were these: the name of the firstborn was Merab, and the name of the younger, Michal.
[50] The name of Saul's wife was Ahinoam daughter of Ahimaaz. And the name of the commander of his army was Abner son of Ner, Saul's uncle; [51] Kish was the father of Saul, and Ner the father of Abner was the son of Abiel.
[52] There was hard fighting against the Philistines all the days of Saul; and when Saul saw any strong or valiant warrior, he took him into his service.

The text in 1 Sam 13:1 and 14:47-52 shows clear parallels to the so-called royal summaries [Königsnotizen][8] in 1 and 2 Kings. In highly formalized

---

7 A date is missing in the Hebrew text. A survey of various theories that attempt to explain this absence is found in Stoebe 242-243.

language, the summary communicates basic information about the respective king. The fact that the royal summary for Saul is divided in two parts creates a clear frame around the narratives in 1 Sam 13:2-14:46.

2.3 1 Sam 13:2-15: Plot Structure

Set within the larger framework created by 1 Sam 13:1 and 1 Sam 14:47-52, 1 Samuel 13:2-15 presents us with the first act of the story. Its boundaries are shaped by the repetition of the name of the town of Gibea-Benjamin and the mention of the size of the army in 13:2 and 13:15. Explicit temporal modifiers in 13:8 and 13:10 mark three scenes within this first act (v. 3-7; v. 8-9; v. 10-14). I will refer to these scenes as "escalation," "sacrifice," and "rejection." The rituals of the $š^e lāmîm$ offering and the $'ōlāh$ offering stand at the center of the narrative.

13:2 Exposition
   13:3-7 Escalation
      13:8-9 Sacrifice
   13:10-14 Rejection
13:15 Epilogue

2.3.1 1 Sam 13:2-7: Exposition and Escalation

[2] Saul chose 3000 from all of Israel; 2000 were with Saul in Michmas and on the hills of Beth-El. 1000 were with Jonathan in Gibea Benjamin. He sent the remaining troops each to his own tent.
[3] Jonathan struck the Philistine outpost in Gibea. And the Philistines <u>heard</u> of this. Saul had ordered the sounding of the shofar in all the land and had proclaimed:
   "<u>Hear</u>, Hebrews!"
[4] And all of Israel <u>heard</u> this:
   "Saul has struck the Philistine outpost and all of Israel has become odious among the Philistines."
The troops gathered themselves to Saul in Gilgal.

---

8 Stoebe proposes that the royal summary is a secondary addition to the text, framing a collection of previously independent episodes (246).

⁵ The Philistines had gathered themselves to wage battle with Israel: 3000 chariots and 6000 riders and troops as a many as sand on the shores of the sea. They came up and camped at Michmas opposite from Beit Awen.
⁶ Once everyone in Israel saw that they were in great danger because the troops were under great pressure,
the troops hid in caves, under thorn bushes, in cliffs, caverns and cisterns.
⁷ And the Hebrews ["those that withdraw"] withdrew to the other side of the Jordan to Gad and Gilead.
Saul was still in Gilgal and all of his troops trembled after him.

Following the first part of the royal summary in 13:1, we encounter the expositional statement that Saul had chosen 3000, of which 2000 remained with him and 1000 with Jonathan in Gibea Benjamin. It is interesting that the text chooses the term *ha'am* (troops)⁹ for those "who return each to his own tent." This may indicate that Saul did not gather his entire army, but only a part of it.

Such an intentional reduction of military strength may deliberately contrast the statement in 1 Sam 11:7b-8 ("The fear of the LORD fell upon the people and they all went out *as one man*. And Saul gathered them at Bezek; there were 300,000 from Israel and 30,000 from Judah."). This contrast may be a first hint at Saul's loss of power already at the outset of the narrative. On the other hand, the reduction may activate an intertextual connection between Saul and the judge Gideon, which had already been an important part of Saul's characterization in 1 Sam 11 (see Vette, "Charaktergestaltung"). The motif of an army that is continually reduced is a central aspect to the story of the judge Gideon (Jdg 6-8). In this context, the reduction is a sign of Gideon's increased dependence on YHWH in all of his military actions. If we assume the same context for 1 Sam 13:2, Saul likewise appears as a god-fearing judge (Fokkelmann 27), who – like Gideon – relies not on his own strength, but on YHWH's guidance. The exposition in 1

---

9   The Hebrew text in 1 Sam 13-14 frequently alternates between different terms to describe the Israelites. The terms hāʿām, yiśrāʾel, and ʿibrī are most common. It is difficult to clearly distinguish the meaning of these terms, but it seems plausible to connect ha'am to the troops, yiśrāʾel to the population as a whole, and read ʿibrī as a sarcastic word play (see below).

Sam 13:2 thus remains ambiguous. It remains to be seen what direction the plot will take.

Jonathan appears in 1 Sam 13:2 for the very first time. Informed readers of the books of Samuel obviously know that this Jonathan is the son of Saul, but the attribute "ben Shaul" is not mentioned in this context. The text introduces an undetermined character with no further attributes other than his name ("Given by YHWH"). The text does not define his relation to Saul when he attacks a Philistine outpost. We are only told how the various characters react to this initiative. A three-fold repetition of the verb *šm'* ["hear"] follows a common pattern in Old Testament narrative: statement, repetition, variation (Bar-Efrat 104-106). The statement "the Philistines heard" (1 Sam 13:3b) is followed by the imperative: "Hear, Hebrews."[10] Yet while we are not told what the Philistines heard, the message to the Hebrews is explicated in detail: "Saul has struck the Philistine outpost and all of Israel has become odious among the Philistines" (1 Sam 13:4b). This explication points to an interesting transfer of responsibility. Even though Jonathan had attacked the outpost, Saul takes credit for the action, a fact that is not really surprising given that Jonathan is obviously subordinate to Saul. Important questions, however, are left open. What does Saul intend with his statement that the action stinks from the perspective of the Philistines? What exactly did the Philistines hear? How will they react to Jonathan's action? Whereas the text does not contain any hint as to how we should answer the latter questions, an interesting intertextual connection may provide an answer to the first. The parallel in 2 Sam 16:21 allows us to read Saul's statement "you have become odious" as a deliberate provocation, designed to jostle his troops into action.[11] Saul thus interprets Jonathan's initiative positively and proves himself to be a god-reliant judge, just as Gideon was before him.

---

10 Fokkelmann assumes that Saul is deliberately reminding the people of their past as Egyptian slaves in order to raise their fervor against the Philistines (30). See also Gen 39:14.17; 41:12; 43:32; Ex 1:15 et al.

11 "Ahithophel said to Absalom, 'Go in to your father's concubines, the ones he has left to look after the house; and all Israel will hear that you have made yourself odious to your father, and the hands of all who are with you will be strengthened.'" See also Ex 5:21; 1 Sam 27:12; 2 Sam 10:6 par 1 Chr 19:6.

As the tension in the narrative builds, we encounter the first ritualizing element in the story. To proclaim his message to his troops, Saul sounds the shofar. This instrument appears primarily in ritual contexts. It is blown on occasion of the great theophany at Mt. Sinai (Ex 19-20) and is used by the high priest during Yom Kippur, the highest holy day (Lev 25). It is heard when kings ascend to the throne (1 Kings 1:34) and when the Ark of the Covenant enters the city of David (2 Sam 6). The Old Testament also uses the shofar to elevate the importance of certain military endeavors. Here we clearly see what Catherine Bell refers to as "ritual as creator of formality." By means of ritual enhancement (in this case through the use of a ritual instrument), the military leader signals the heightened importance of the upcoming venture (Bell 140; Bibb 59). Direct parallels are Joshua's siege of Jericho (Jos 6) and Gideon's uprising against the Midianites (Jdg 7). In each case, the use of the shofar signals the leader's divine inspiration and YHWH's support of the action. When the shofar appears also in 1 Sam 13, the text leads readers to believe that Saul stands in one line with Joshua and Gideon and that his plans will meet with equal success.

It is thus surprising when Saul's troops act in complete contrast to those of Joshua and Gideon. In the face of the overwhelming strength of the Philistine army, the Hebrews [in Hebrew: îbrî = "those that withdraw"] live up to the sarcastic wordplay associated with their name. The narrative delights in describing the various hiding places that serve as their refuge. The sounding of the shofar does not summon the troops; instead, the episode ends with Saul's men "trembling after him."

2.3.2 1 Sam 13:8-9: Sacrifice

[8] [Saul] waited seven days until the time appointed by Samuel.
    Samuel, however, had not appeared in Gigal.
And the people dispersed from him [9] and Saul said:
    "Bring me the ʿolāh sacrifice and the šelāmîm sacrifice."
He performed the ʿolāh sacrifice.

Even though summoning the troops had been ritualized by the sounding of the shofar, it had not been successful. The troops lack the cohesion and confidence necessary to withstand the Philistine threat. In this situation, Saul resorts to another sequence of rituals, the ʿolāh sacrifice and the

$š^e lāmîm$ sacrifice. The $'ōlāh$ sacrifice is a whole offering, in which the animal is burnt in its entirety. Neither the owner of the animal nor the priest lay claim to any part of the animal (Kellermann 108). According to the description in Leviticus 1, a lay person brings the designated animal, which must be without blemish, to the altar and presses his hands on the animal's head.[12] Then the animal is slaughtered[13] and dissected, the impure parts (entrails and shanks) are washed and everything is cremated on the altar. As the Old Testament texts describe a variety of different contexts in which this ritual is performed, it is not possible to pinpoint the precise function of the sacrifice.

Outside of the priestly document, the $š^e lāmîm$ sacrifice always occurs together with the $'ōlāh$ sacrifice. It appears in a host of different contexts: when building and using an altar (Ex 20:24), in rituals of lament (Jdg 20:26), upon the inauguration of a king (1 Sam 11:15), in military crisis situations (1 Sam 13:8-9), in connection with the transfer of the Ark of the Covenant to the city of David (2 Sam 6:17f), when purchasing the threshing floor of Arauna (2 Sam 24:25), and on occasion of consecrating the temple (1 Ki 8:63; see Seidel 104). Given this wide range of situations, the $š^e lāmîm$ sacrifice remains an unknown ritual event (Seidel 108). The only factor common to all instances is the close connection to a sacrificial meal. According to Martin Modéus, the $š^e lāmîm$ sacrifice is merely a "marking symbol" without any meaning on its own. Its function lies solely in giving special focus to a certain event.[14] It is thus a prime example of what Catherine Bell refers to as a ritualizing mechanism.

---

12 On the interpretation of this action as a means of identification between the animal owner and the animal see Janowski 219f.

13 The texts differ on who slaughters the animal: the priest, the Levite or the lay person who brought it. See Exo 29:16; Lev 1:5; Lev 8:19; Lev 9:12; Eze 44:11.

14 "By itself, the marking symbol has no meaning, and therefore it has as its only object to create differentiation, to give ritual weight and thereby, assist in the focusing task. Candles, flowers, more or less sacred meals and funny hats are examples of marking symbols that create the sense that something is going on, without in any way pointing out what is going on" (Modéus 77). Compare 380: "Put in another way, the selamim was a resource when a situation called for ritualization. The selamim presents itself as pure action with no meaning."

Even if we survey all the passages mentioning these sacrifices, we will not be able to define the "meaning" of these rituals apart from their use in 1 Sam 13. The historical question leads us to a dead end; a conclusion strengthened by the fact that 1 Sam 13:8-9 mention no details at all about the ritual process itself. Yet if we move beyond the historical question and attempt to understand the sacrifice as part of an intentionally constructed narrative world, we encounter a different situation: already several chapters earlier, in 1 Sam 9:1 – 10:16, both sacrifices are part of the plot. Even though Samuel had been instructed by YHWH to anoint Saul and tell him of God's plans to lead Israel against the Philistine threat, Samuel continually avoids communicating this message.[15] Samuel's avoidance comes to a climax in 1 Sam 10:8:

⁸ *And go down before me to Gilgal! And behold, I will come down to you to perform the 'ōlāh sacrifice and the šᵉlāmîm sacrifice. You shall wait seven days until I come and tell you what you should do.*

This last instruction puts Saul in a situation of complete passivity. Once in Gilgal, he is to patiently await further instructions; he is entirely dependent on Samuel's initiative. Samuel's sole control of the situation is most clearly seen in the ritual process, in which he is the only actor. Saul is left with the role of the obedient listener. His entire future depends on what Samuel will or will not communicate. Saul may be the divinely elected savior of Israel, but outside of Samuel's control he cannot know what to do.

The introductory statement in 1 Sam 13:8 (*"He waited seven days until the time appointed by Samuel"*) and the mentioning of Gilgal create a strong intertextual connection to the earlier scene in 1 Sam 10:8.[16] The concrete Philistine threat now stands in stark contrast to Saul's lack of knowledge of his divinely appointed task. This tension can only be resolved if Samuel finally breaks his silence and marks and confirms Saul's appointment with the ritual sacrifice. As a public statement, the sacrifice can counteract the disintegration of the army and replenish its morale. The rit-

---

15 In 1 Sam 9:19; 9:26 and 9:27 Samuel only announces that he will tell Saul; he never actually does so. This pattern continues in 1 Sam 10:8 (see Vette, *Samuel und Saul*, 154).

16 On the connection between 1 Sam 10:8 und 1 Sam 13 see Long.

ual would signal divine approval and support and legitimize the imminent military venture. There is still hope that Saul will establish himself as a successful leader, even though he is surrounded by "those who withdraw."

Samuel, however, does not appear at the appointed time. In a glaring gap, the text does not explain why the prophet shatters the expectations directed at him by Saul (and the readers of the text). Samuel's continual attempts to undermine Saul's authority and present his sons as an alternative suggest as plausible gap-filling that Samuel is not really all that interested in stabilizing Saul's authority by performing the ritual. In this situation, Saul breaks protocol, countermands Samuel's instructions in 1 Sam 10:8, and performs the sacrifice himself.[17] The narrative thus illustrates the connection between ritual and public power. By assuming the role of the sacrificing agent, Saul makes a public statement about his own claim to power while attempting to strengthen cohesion and loyalty among those surrounding him. At the same time, his action is a clear challenge against Samuel's own claim to power as he is replaced as the sacrificing agent. At this very point the prophet appears.

2.3.3 1 Sam 13:10-14: Rejection

[10] This happened: He had just finished performing the ʻolāh sacrifice:
  Behold: Samuel appeared.
Saul went out towards him to bless him. [11] And Samuel said:
  "What have you done!"
Saul said:
  "When I saw that the troops started to disintegrate and that you did not appear at the appointed time and that the Philistines were gathering in Michmas, [12] I said: 'Now the Philistines are descending to Gilgal and I have not yet sought the face of YHWH.' I pulled myself together and performed the ʻolāh sacrifice."
[13] Samuel said to Saul:
  "You have acted foolishly. You did not heed the commandment of YHWH, which your God commanded you. This is certain: YHWH established your kingdom over Israel for all times. [14] But now your kingdom

---

17 We should note that Saul only performs the ʻolāh offering but not the šelāmîm offering. For an interpretation of this fact see below.

will not last. YHWH has looked for another according to his own heart to appoint him as Nagid over his people. For you did not heed what YHWH commanded."

After not appearing at the appointed time, Samuel appears on stage at the very moment that Saul has completed the first sacrifice. Here, too, the text gives no explanation why the prophet appears there and then. Readers must speculate why Samuel first did not come, only to appear suddenly. Fokkelmann refers to these verses as the *Hintergründigste* that can be found in Old Testament narrative.[18] As the performance of the *š^elāmîm* sacrifice has not yet occurred, Samuel seems to be interrupting the ritual process. Saul's attempt to involve him is met with harsh rejection on the part of the prophet: "What have you done?" (1 Sam 13:11). As justification, Saul basically summarizes the narrative events in 1 Sam 13:4-9 without mentioning the desolate state of troop morale. Readers can connect this fact to Saul's words and thus form a context in which the statement "I pulled myself together" (1 Sam 13:12) is given added force. It seems that Saul never intended to take control of the ritual, but was forced by the circumstances to do so – a defense which, given his current situation, more than wards off the prophetic criticism.

Samuel, however, pays no attention to Saul's arguments. Instead, he lashes out in wholesale dismissal of Saul's entire behavior, motivation and execution in all: "You have acted foolishly!" (1 Sam 13:13). The prophet does not make clear what exactly he is criticizing: the initialization of the ritual, the details of its performance (of which the text says nothing), or the fact that Saul assumed the authority of the sacrificing agent. Samuel twice mentions a divine commandment against which Saul apparently transgressed. Scholars have so far tried in vain to connect this commandment to any known law in other Old Testament traditions.[19] Without knowing what Samuel may be referring to, readers have to create their own contexts to

---

18 Fokkelmann 33: "[T]he text here is even more compressed and hintergründig than practically anywhere else in Samuel."
19 Stoebe states clearly: "Hier wird nicht einmal deutlich, worin das Versagen Sauls eigentlich liegt. [...] [D]as Recht Sauls zum Vollzug des Opfers [wird] sonst nicht bestritten" (252).

understand what is going on. These constructions – this comes as no surprise – vary greatly.[20]

Whether Samuel is speaking on God's behalf when judging Saul, or whether (as so frequently in the past, see Vette, *Samuel und Saul*, 192-194) Samuel and God are not speaking with one voice, remains an open question. The prophet's strange timing, however, as well as the prior events in 1 Sam 9-12 raise the suspicion that Samuel might not be acting selflessly.

A quite different intertextual connection, however, may point the reader in a completely different direction. Martin Modéus has referred to parallels between the narrative of the golden calf (Exodus 32:6) and Saul's sacrifice in 1 Sam 13 (Modéus 304). These are the only two instances in the Old Testament where the *'ōlāh* sacrifice and the *š^elāmîm* sacrifice are used in combination with the verb *ngš* ("to bring forth"). If we follow this lead and read Saul's sacrifice in light of the blasphemy of the golden calf, the narrative might hint at massive criticism against the king's actions.[21] Depending on which aspects of the narrative discourse in 1 Sam 13:2-15 we choose to emphasize, we create a different frame within which to evaluate the king's action. There can be no clear and unambiguous closure of the text at this point. The story continues to oscillate between the two protagonists Saul and Samuel.

---

20 Stolz 85: "Der Text vertritt die Meinung, daß die Prophetie dem Königtum übergeordnet ist."; Fokkelmann 42: We can only understand Saul's mistake in "the dimension of man coram Deo […]. Only by surrendering himself completely to God would he have been able to withstand the test."; Jobling, *1. Samuel* 82: "For this claim by Samuel to carry any conviction at all, the 'commandment' must be understood as follows: 'Thou shalt not, as unauthorized personnel – even as a king – offer the burnt offering. If authorized personnel are unavailable, wait as long as it takes.' If this is what the commandment means, the text fails to say so!"

21 "When Aaron saw this, he built an altar before it; and Aaron made proclamation and said, 'Tomorrow shall be a festival to the LORD.' They rose early the next day, and offered burnt offerings ('olāh) and brought forth (ngš) sacrifices of well-being (šelāmîm); and the people sat down to eat and drink, and rose up to revel. The LORD said to Moses, 'Go down at once! Your people, whom you brought up out of the land of Egypt, have acted perversely'" (Exo 32:5-7, emphasis J.V.).

2.3.4 1 Sam 13:15: Epilogue

[15] Samuel rose and went up from Gilgal to Gibea Benjamin.
And Saul gathered his troops, which he found with him: 600 men.

The geographical reference in the final verse lets us take notice: whereas Gilgal is connected to Saul, Gibea Benjamin points us towards Jonathan (see 1 Sam 13:2), who with his daring attack had displayed exactly the kind of heroism and leadership that Saul is sorely lacking. As Samuel had not mentioned a name when announcing a divinely approved successor ("YHWH has looked for another according to his own heart to appoint him as Nagid over his people," 1 Sam 13:14), the episode ends openly, begging the question who this successor might be and raising the expectation that the continuation of the narrative will answer this question. By moving from Saul's locale to the place where Jonathan resides, Samuel's last action may hint at the possible answer.[22]

2.4 1 Sam 14:1-46: Plot Structure

Judged by Old Testament standards, 1 Sam 14 is a relatively long narrative.[23] It consists of a sequence of various different episodes that are initialized by Jonathan's heroism. His heroic attack against another Philistine outpost with only his weapons carrier at his side is announced in 1 Sam 14:1 and recapitulated in 14:45, thus framing the sequence of episodes as a whole. Each of these episodes centers on a ritualized action (marked in cursive script below):

14:1-5	Exposition
14:6-14	Jonathan's heroic attack
14:15-19	Saul summons the *Ark of the Covenant*

---

22 The details on Saul's and Jonathan's arms purchases that are related in 1 Sam 13:16-23 are beyond the scope of this study. On this topic see Kreuzer 56-73.

23 Given the length of the text, I will only be able to focus on those aspects of the narrative discourse that deal with ritual elements. Interesting readings of the text as a whole are found in Jobling, "Tradition"; McCarthy; Edelman; Ackermann; Craig; Jobling, *1. Samuel* 77-104.

14:20-23   First battle
14:24-30   Saul's *Oath*
14:31-35   Saul's *"Emergency Sacrifice"* ($š^e lāmîm$ offering?)
14:36-45   *Casting Lots*

Given the basic task of ritual to stabilize order, readers might expect each ritual act to successively strengthen Saul's position. The opposite is true. With each episode, Saul's authority crumbles a little more until the troops clearly make a choice for Jonathan and against Saul. 1 Sam 13:15 raised the expectation that Jonathan is Saul's divinely designated successor; 1 Sam 14 confirms this expectation.[24] Several different elements connect the two narratives in 1 Sam 13:2-15 and 1 Sam 14:1-45. The most obvious are: a) both narratives relate the basic conflict between Philistines and Israelites that was announced in 1 Sam 9:16; b) both narratives take their starting point with an act of military valor performed by Jonathan; c) The 600 men mentioned in 1 Sam 14:2 refer back to the final statement in 1 Sam 13:15; d) those troops who had hid so efficiently in 1 Sam 13:6-7 reappear from their hiding places in 1 Sam 14:21-22; e) the $š^e lāmîm$ offering that did not take place in 1 Sam 13:10 finally occurs in 1 Sam 14:31-35 (see the discussion below).

2.4.1 1 Sam 14:1-5: Exposition: Announcement of and Background to Jonathan's Heroic Deed

[1] It happened on that day –
Jonathan, son of Saul, said to the young man who carried his weapons:
     "Come, let us go to the Philistine outpost on the other side."
He had not told his father any of this.
[2] Saul sat on the outskirts of Gibea underneath a pomegranate tree in Migron and the troops that were with him numbered 600 men.
[3] Ahiah ben Ahitub, the brother of Ikabod ben Pinhas ben Eli was the priest of YHWH in Shilo. He wore the Efod.
The troops did not know that Jonathan had left.

---

24 This confirmation is only temporary. The following narratives make very clear that David, not Jonathan is the successor designated by God. But that is another story. Compare Jobling, *1. Samuel* 96.

⁴ In the pass that Jonathan had to traverse on the way to the Philistine outpost there was a cliff wall on the one and on the other side. The one was called Bozez, the other Senna. ⁵ The one cliff rose on the North opposite Michmas, the other rose south opposite Geba.

Both 1 Sam 13 and 1 Sam 14 start with the same event. Both narratives are initialized by Jonathan's foray against a Philistine outpost. In contrast to 1 Sam 13, however, Jonathan is here referred to as "son of Saul." The expectations raised in 1 Sam 13:15 are strengthened at this point: Jonathan is actually the crown prince! It would be no surprise if God had chosen him to be Saul's legitimate successor! The first five verses contain further expositional information.[25] We are well advised to pay close attention, as Old Testament expositions only tend to contain information that will later be taken up in the plot (Bar-Efrat 114-115). The fact that Saul and the troops know nothing of Jonathan's actions and the details of the geographical setting will play an obvious role in later plot development. The reason why the priest is mentioned, however, is not quite as clear.

It seems that the text activates another intertextual connection: the sons of the priest Eli, Hophni and Pinhas, are known as Samuel's rivals from 1 Sam 2-4. They are clearly characterized as corrupt men who abuse their status and misuse rituals to their own advantage, including even the Ark of the Covenant. As a result, the entire family is rejected by God (compare 1 Sam 2:27-36). The last son from this family, Ikabod (Hebrew for "without honor"), represents in his name the fate of the entire family. It can hardly be interpreted as a positive signal that a member of this family now appears at Saul's side instead of Samuel. Fritz Stolz also referred to another possible analeptic element (91): the Efod, a luxurious piece of clothing worn by the priest (see Exo 28) contains two pockets with the necessary equipment for the casting of lots (Exo 28:30). In this manner, the priest's garment mentioned in the beginning of the narrative may already foreshadow Saul's last ritual action at the end of the story.

---

25 On the role of expositions in Old Testament narrative see Vette, *Samuel und Saul* 48-50.

2.4.2 1 Sam 14:6-14: Jonathan's Heroic Deed

⁶ J(h)onathan said to the young man who carried his weapons:
"Come, let us go to the outpost of the uncircumcised. Maybe YHWH will do something for us. There is no obstacle for YHWH to help with much or with little."
⁷ His weapons carrier said to him:
"Do everything that is in your heart. Just go, I will follow you in all that you do."
⁸ J(h)onathan said:
"We will now go over to the men and show ourselves. If they say this: 'Wait until we come to you,' then we will remain in place below them and will not go up to them. But if they say 'Come up!' then we will go up for YHWH has given them into our hands and this will be our sign."

Jonathan makes his actions dependent on the verbal reaction of the Philistines. Only the "correct" Philistine answer will be the sign that he and his weapons carrier can be assured of God's approval and assistance. The judge Gideon had also resorted to requesting a divine sign as a ritualized action to assure divine favor (see Jdg 7). When Jonathan states that there is no obstacle for YHWH "to help with much or with little," he strengthens this intertextual connection to Gideon. Until now, the texts had drawn lines between Gideon and Saul. Now the emphasis shifts to Jonathan. He is shown to be the spirit-filled leader, replacing his father in this role. A spelling variation further drives the point home. In 1 Sam 14:6 and 14:8, the name Jonathan is spelled with an addition *heh* [J(h)onathan]. The *heh* is one of the three letters that make up the divine name (YHWH) and it thus seems likely to interpret this spelling variation as a theomorphic element and as a subtle indication that YHWH's presence is with Jonathan at this moment in time.[26] Without making a transfer of authority from Saul to Jonathan explicit, the narrative in 1 Sam 14:1-8 thus contains several strategies to depreciate the father while elevating the son. The sign that Jonathan requests can be read in this context.

---

26 A similar strategy appears in 1 Sam 18:1-4. Here, too, we encounter J(h)onathan.

2.4.3 1 Sam 14:17-19: Saul Summons the Ark of the Covenant

[17] Saul said to the people who were with him:
"Take a count and see who has left us."
They took a count and behold – Jonathan and his weapons carrier were missing. [18] And Saul said to Ahia:
"Bring me the Ark of God!" (For the Ark of God was this day with the Israelites.)
[19] While Saul was still speaking to the priest, the commotion in the Philistine camp came closer and grew louder. Saul said to the priest:
"Pull your hands back!"
[20] And Saul and his troops around him gathered and went into battle: One sword clashed against the next. Confusion was everywhere. [21] The Hebrews that had previously been with the Philistines and had marched into camp with them – they, too, deserted to the Israel that was with Saul and Jonathan. [22] And every Israelite who had hid himself in the hills of Ephraim had seen that the Philistines were fleeing. They, too, hurried into battle. [23a] And YHWH saved Israel on this day.

Jonathan's successful venture causes great disturbance in the Philistine camp. The text relates the reaction of Saul and the troops who (unlike the readers of the narrative) have no clue what has happened. The intertextual connection to 1 Sam 2-4 that had been activated by mentioning the house of Eli in the exposition is expanded in this context by explicitly mentioning the Ark of the Covenant.[27] Of the various functions of this cultic object,[28] the one mentioned in Num 10:35 is most relevant for the narrative in 1 Sam 14: "Whenever the ark set out, Moses would say, Arise, O LORD, let your enemies be scattered, and your foes flee before you." The Ark embodies

---

27 The shape and the decorations of the Ark are described in detail in Exo 25:10-22 and Exo 37:1-9. Stolz 92, refers to the historical impossibility of the ark appearing in this context: "Historisch ist die Notiz also sicherlich unzutreffend, und der Text trägt diesem Sachverhalt dadurch Rechnung, daß er die Anwesenheit der Lade (um die nur zu berechtigten Zweifel auszuschalten) ausdrücklich betont." This historical impossibility supports my reading that the Ark is mentioned here as a narrative strategy, not as a matter of historical record.
28 A survey of the various functions of the Ark of the Covenant is found in Zobel, 391-404.

YHWH's powerful presence in a critical military crisis; the fear of God emanates from this cultic object, striking despair into the hearts of the enemy. 1 Sam 2-4 turns this expectation on its head. Hophni and Pinhas had led the ark into battle without explicit divine authorization; they had hoped to force God's presence and thus victory over the Philistines. Their hope is thwarted (see 1 Sam 4:3-11): the Philistines win the day, Hophni and Pinhas die on the battlefield and the Ark ends up in the hands of the Philistines. On its own, the Ark displays its awesome power among the Philistine Gods (see 1 Sam 5-6). The narrative makes clear: the Ark is not impotent, but *it resists being used to force God's hand according to human desire. God's actions cannot be controlled by ritualized action.*

Facing the "commotion"[29] in the Philistine camp (1 Sam 14:16), Saul makes the same foolish decision as Hophni and Pinhas. To make matters worse, a member of the house of Eli supports him in this decision. In contrast to Hophni and Pinhas, however, Saul's foolishness immediately becomes apparent as the events make a mockery of his intentions. Readers witness Saul's complete confusion as the king first commands the Ark to be brought to him only to countermand this command almost in the same sentence. The text reads like a parody of ritualized action itself. The irony continues through the following description of the battle. Total military chaos and lack of leadership end with the statement: "And YHWH saved Israel on this day." Saul initializes and interrupts a ritualized action; the ritual is actually cancelled. Without ritual order, the events turn chaotic and still: *God saves Israel!* Just as in 1 Sam 4-6 the text clearly emphasizes God's independence from ritual action. The narrative thus calls the effectiveness and perhaps even the necessity of any ritual action into question.

2.4.4 1 Sam 14:24-30: Saul's Oath

[24] And every Israelite was pressured that day. And Saul took an oath [']lh] in the presence of the troops:
> "Cursed may be all who eat anything until evening. This way, I will take vengeance on my enemies."

And all the people ate nothing.

---

29 The noun hmôn ["commotion"] is only used in 1 Samuel here and in the narrative of Hophni and Pinhas (1 Sam 4:14; 14:16 und 14:18).

²⁵ Honeycombs had appeared in all the land and there was honey on the open field.
²⁶ And the troops came to a honycomb
- behold [hebr.: hnh]: honey dripped from it but none brought their hand to their mouth, for the troops feared the oath. -
²⁷ Jonathan had not heard the oath that his father had taken in the presence of the troops and he stretched out the tip of the spear in his hand, dipped it in the honeycomb, brought it to his mouth and his eyes started to shine. ²⁸ A member of the troops said to him:

"Your father swore to the troops saying: 'Cursed is he who eats something today' – and the troops are weak."

²⁹ Jonathan said:

"My father has disturbed the land. Look: My eyes are shining because I have eaten only a little of the honey. ³⁰ Would that the troops had eaten well from the spoils of their enemies! For now our victory over the Philistines is not great."

If readers expect that Saul will finally distance himself from ritualized action, given his bad experiences thus far, they are disappointed. It almost seems as if Saul is desperately trying to restore the order that is slipping through his fingers through ever new rituals. If we already sensed irony, even sarcasm in the description of Saul's last ritual "performance," this impression grows when he swears his oath. The verb *lh* is directly associated with oaths designed to protect the moral-religious order.³⁰ It is interesting to note that Saul does not refer to the divine name in this oath. It seems as if he expects his oath to become effective on the basis of the power of the spoken word alone. Scharbert thus speaks of "word magic."³¹

The strange connection between not eating and taking vengeance on one's enemies may point to the belief that abstinence can release physical and spiritual energy (Stolz 93; Stoebe 270f.). Saul's actions still have enough normative power to bind the troops to his command. This will be

---

30 'lh "bezeichnet nicht Flüche und Verwünschungen schlechthin, sondern nur bedingte Flüche, die man über andere oder sich selbst ausspricht, um Rechtsgüter oder religiös-sittliche Ordnungen zu schützen" (Scharbert 280).
31 "Wortmagie, die dem gesprochenen und geschriebenen Wort die Macht zuschreibt, das damit Bezeichnete, das Gute oder Böse, wirklich herbeizuführen" (Scharbert 281).

the last time in this narrative that the king's words will have this obligatory force. Already the collective abstinence of the troops is turned to irony in the continuation of the story. Immediately following Saul's oath, the narrative relates how the land is overflowing with honey. The description of the honeycombs is introduced by the Hebrew word *hnh* ("behold"), which frequently indicates a change of camera angle within the narrative. In a "close-up-view," the reader is brought so closely to the honey that he can almost taste it – but the troops have to hold back because they are bound by Saul's oath.

The tension created between the description of the honey and the binding force of Saul's words explodes when Jonathan, who has not heard his father's words, eats without hesitation from the honeycomb. The following dialogue is an intradiegetic (cf. Genette 32-46) commentary on the wisdom of Saul's action: when Jonathan states that his father "has disturbed the land," he is not only resisting a simple command. As he is going against a ritualizing action instituted by his father, he is challenging his father's entire claim to power. By breaking Saul's oath, Jonathan questions Saul's control over the troops. The king's loss of authority is embodied in the failed ritual.

2.4.5 1 Sam 14:31-35: Saul's "Emergency Sacrifice" (š^elāmîm offering?)

³¹ On that day, they struck the Philistines from Michmas to Ajalon and the troops grew very tired. ³² The troops pounced on the spoils. They took sheep, cattle, and calves and slaughtered them on the ground. And the people ate with the blood. ³³ Saul was told:

"The troops are committing a sin against YHWH by eating with the blood!"

He said:

"You are without loyalty. Roll a large stone to me!"

³⁴ And Saul said:

"Go amongst the troops and tell them: 'Each person shall bring his ox and his sheep to me [ngš]. Slaughter it here and eat, but do not sin against YHWH by eating with the blood!'"

And everyone came in the night, each with his ox in hand and they slaughtered it there. ³⁵ And Saul built an altar for YHWH;

This was the beginning of his building an altar for YHWH. / It was a desecration against YHWH to build this altar.

Was Jonathan's action the cause that led the people to move from abstinence to the opposite extreme? The narrative does not explicitly state this, but the direct sequence of events allows this interpretation. Saul is told of what is happening by emphasizing one aspect: eating with the blood is a sacrilege against YHWH. It may be that the narrative here refers back to the $š^e lāmîm$ offering, which is primarily characterized by the fact that only the meat may be eaten, but the blood and the fat are to be left for YHWH alone (see above). In the context of 1 Sam 13:8-9, the sequence 'ōlāh - $š^e lāmîm$ had been interrupted by Samuel's sudden appearance; the $š^e lāmîm$ sacrifice still had to be performed. Here we encounter the sacrifice – but under what circumstances! Urged on by the almost orgiastic frenzy of the bloodthirsty troops, Saul quickly has a stone prepared in order to perform an emergency sacrifice on a makeshift altar. In this manner, the slaughter around him is supposed to receive at least a modicum of ritual propriety.[32] If the immediate context of this ritual is determined by haphazardness, the final narrative commentary in 1 Sam 14:35b makes the summary judgment explicitly clear. The basic meaning of the verb hll is "to start, to begin"; this is how the verse is most often translated. A second meaning of the verb is "to desecrate, to profane." If we follow this meaning in our translation of this admittedly difficult verse, then Saul's actions are utterly condemned.

In this manner, the sequence of rituals itself – from the sounding of the shofar in 1 Sam 13:3 to the emergency sacrifice – paints an impressive, albeit tragic picture of Saul's loss of control and the collapse of social order.

---

32 The use of the verb ngš is striking in this context. It was this verb that created the intertextual connection between 1 Sam 13:8-9 and the sacrilege of the golden calf.

2.4.6 1 Sam 14:36-45: Casting Lots

[36] Saul said:
"Let us go down to the Philistines this night and plunder them until morning. We will leave no one alive!"
They said:
"Do whatever is good in your eyes."
The priest said:
"Let us gather before God!"
[37] And Saul asked God:
"Should I go down to the Philistines? Will you give them into the hand of Israel?"
But on this day he did not answer him. [38] Saul said:
"Come to me, all you leaders of the troops. Recognize the sin among us, here and now. By the life of YHWH, the savior of Israel, even if it should be my son Jonathan: truly, he will die!"
No one from among the troops answered him. [40] He said to all of Israel:
"You shall be on one side and I and my son Jonathan will be on the other side."
The troops said to Saul:
"Do whatever is good in your eyes."
[41] Saul said to YHWH, the God of Israel:
"Grant us clarity."
And the lot fell on Jonathan and Saul, but it did not fall on the troops. [42] Saul said:
"Cast the lot between me and my son Jonathan."
The lot fell on Jonathan [43] Saul said to Jonathan:
"Tell me: What have you done?"
Jonathan told him and said:
"I actually ate a little bit of honey from the tip of my spear. Yes, I must die!"
[44] Saul said:
"God shall do this and more to me: Jonathan, you shall die!"
[45] The troops said to Saul:
"Shall Jonathan die, who has accomplished this great victory in Israel? Far from it! As YHWH lives, not one hair of his head shall fall to the ground; for he has worked with God today."
So the troops ransomed Jonathan, and he did not die.

The sequence of ritualized actions began in 1 Sam 13:8-9 with Saul's desire to seek the face of God. This desire is explicitly mentioned once again at the end of the sequence, providing a frame for the whole. If Saul's attempts to gain clarity in the presence of God are the thread that binds the episodes together, then the failure of the entire course of action becomes very clear: God does not answer Saul. God's silence is the climax of all elements that have subverted the alleged effectiveness of ritualized action: all of the rituals end with nothing.

There is an element of the absurd that enters into the narrative when Saul reacts to the utter failure of all of his ritual attempts by taking recourse to another ritual. By casting lots, he is determined to find out who is to blame for God's silence. Instead of trusting himself to the internal logic of the ritual, however, Saul clearly "stacks the deck" in the upcoming selection process. Although casting lots is mentioned more frequently,[33] two texts parallel Saul's actions in 1 Sam 14:36-45 most closely: Jos 7:10-18 and 1 Sam 10:17-27. It is only in these three narratives that a person is to be determined by the ritual.[34] These are also the only three texts that describe a sequence moving from the whole to ever smaller units until the individual is found. When comparing the three texts, we notice that only Jos 7:14 mentions that YHWH himself commanded the ritual. In Jos 7:10-18 the process is described in great detail: the selection process moves from the tribe to the clan to the family to the individual. The description of each level uses the same terminology: "And he was brought out...and it was indicated." Compared to this methodical selection process, Saul's manipulation of the whole thing becomes very apparent: Saul skips most of the steps described in Jos 7 and reduces the possible outcome to Jonathan, himself and the people as a whole from the very beginning. It is impossible to speak of a "true" casting of lots in this context. The whole process becomes a false front for determining once and for all who is in the position of authority, the father or the son.

This desperate action is Saul's last attempt to hold on to power. And indeed, the ritual ends as he had hoped. Jonathan is publicly identified as the oath breaker. With heavy sarcasm, he confesses his crime: "I actually ate a little bit of honey from the tip of my spear. Yes, I must die!" But when Saul

---

33 See especially Num 33-36; Jos 13-19; Neh 10-11; 1 Chr 6; 1 Chr 24-26.
34 Most of the texts refer to the selection of land. See 1 Chr 24-26 und Neh 10:35.

proclaims his verdict (which is pronounced as the result of a ritual!), he suffers his greatest defeat: the troops reject the authority of the royal verdict and take the side of Jonathan. Where 1 Sam 13:15 only hints at Jonathan's succession, the narrative now makes the transfer of authority from father to son explicit.

3. CONCLUSION

The narratives in 1 Sam 13-14 do not allow us to understand the ritual events described there as meaningful symbolic constructs *in their own respective historical contexts*. As elements of the narrative matrix, however, their importance cannot be overestimated; they are central to understanding the narrative as a whole. In the course of the narrative, readers encounter a continual dismantling of the effective potency of ritualized action. Their ability to guarantee the presence of God, stabilize order, or maintain power is massively called into question. Even more: the ritual actions are the very motor that push the ironic, satiric and tragic aspects of the story. If we look at the unproblematic manner in which Saul accepted and used Jonathan's first military venture (1 Sam 13:3), there was no need for the intense conflict between father and son that took place at the end of the narrative. It was only the sequence of ritualized actions itself that created the situation in which the father had to sentence his son to death and in this verdict lose all of his power.

REFERENCES

Ackermann, James. "Who Can Stand before YHWH, This Holy God? A Reading of 1 Samuel 1-15." *Prooftexts* 11 (1991): 1-24.
Altmann, Peter. *Festive Meals in Ancient Israel*. Berlin: de Gruyter, 2011.
Bar-Efrat, Shimon. *Narrative Art in the Bible*. Sheffield: Almond Press, 1989.
Bell, Catherine. *Ritual Theory, Ritual Practice*. New York: Oxford UP, 1992.
Bibb, Bryan. *Ritual Worlds and Narrative Worlds in the Book of Leviticus*. New York: T&T Clark, 2009.

Chatman, Seymour. *Story and Discourse: Narrative Structure in Fiction and Film*. Ithaca: Cornell UP, 1978.
Craig, Kenneth. "Rhetorical Aspects of Questions Answered with Silence in 1 Samuel 14:37 and 28:6." *Catholic Biblical Quarterly* 56 (1994): 221-39.
Edelman, Diana. "The Deuteronomist's Story of King Saul: Narrative Art or Editorial Product?" *Pentateuchal and Deuteronomistic Studies*. Ed. Jan Brekelmans. Leuven: Leuven UP, 1990. 207-20.
Fokkelmann, Jan. *Narrative Art and Poetry in the Books of Samuel, Vol. II: The Crossing Fates*. Assen: Van Gorcum, 1986.
Forster, E.M. *Aspects of the Novel*. London: Edward Arnold, 1927.
Genette, Gérard. *Die Erzählung*. München: Fink, 1994.
Gertz, Jan Christian. "Ritus/Ritual." *Religion in Geschichte und Gegenwart*. Eds. Hans Dieter Betz et al. Vol. 7. Tübingen: Mohr, 2004. 550-551.
Gorman, Frank. *The Ideology of Ritual: Space, Time and Status in the Priestly Theology*. Sheffield: JSOT Press, 1990.
Janowski, Bernd. *Sühne als Heilsgeschehen: Traditions- und religionsgeschichtliche Studien zur Sühnetheologie der Priesterschrift*. Neukirchen-Vluyn: Neukirchener Verlag, 2000.
Jobling, David. "Saul's Fall and Jonathan's Rise: Tradition and Redaction in 1 Sam 14:1-46." *Journal of Biblical Literature* 95 (1976): 367-76.
—. *1. Samuel*. Collegeville: Liturgical Press, 1998.
Kayser, Wolfgang. *Das sprachliche Kunstwerk*. Bern: Francke, 1951.
Kellermann, Diether. "'olāh" *Theologisches Wörterbuch zum Alten Testament*. Ed. Johannes Botterweck. Vol. 4. Stuttgart: Kohlhammer, 1973. 105-122.
Knohl, Israel. *The Sanctuary of Silence: The Priestly Torah and the Holiness School*. Winona Lake, Ind.: Eisenbrauns, 2007.
Koch, Klaus. "Alttestamentliche und altorientalische Rituale." *Die hebräische Bibel und ihre zweifache Nachgeschichte*. Ed. Erhard Blum. Neukirchen-Vluyn: Neukirchner Verlag, 1990. 75-85.
Kreuzer, Siegfried. "War Saul auch unter den Philistern?" *Zeitschrift für alttestamentliche Wissenschaft* 113 (2001): 56-73.
Lämmert, Eberhard. *Bauformen des Erzählens*. Stuttgart: Metzler, 1993.
Long, V. Philips. *The Reign and Rejection of King Saul: A Case for Literary and Theological Coherence*. Atlanta: Scholars Press, 1989.

Marx, Alfred. "Opfer." *Religion in Geschichte und Gegenwart.* Eds. Hans Dieter Betz et al. Vol. 6. Tübingen: Mohr, 2004. 572-576.

McCarthy, Dennis. "Hero and Anti-Hero in 1 Sam 13:2-14:46." *Institution and Narrative. Collected Essays.* Ed. Dennis McCarthy. Rom: Biblical Institute Press, 1985. 250-59.

Modéus, Martin. *Sacrifice and Symbol: Biblical šĕlamîm in a Ritual Perspective.* Stockholm: Almqvist & Wiksell, 2005.

Sanders, James. *Canon and Community. A Guide to Canonical Criticism.* Philadelphia: Fortress Press, 1984.

Scharbert, Josef. "'lh." *Theologisches Wörterbuch zum Alten Testament.* Ed. Johannes Botterweck. Vol. 1. Stuttgart: Kohlhammer, 1973. 279-285.

Seidel, Theodor. "šᵉlāmîm." *Theologisches Wörterbuch zum Alten Testament.* Ed. Johannes Botterweck. Vol. 8. Stuttgart: Kohlhammer, 1995. 101-111.

Stausberg, Michael. "Ritus/Ritual." *Religion in Geschichte und Gegenwart.* Ed. Hans Dieter Betz et al. Vol. 7. Stuttgart: Kohlhammer, 2004. 547-549.

Sternberg, Meir. *The Poetics of Biblical Narrative. Ideological Literature and the Drama of Reading.* Bloomington, Indiana: Indiana UP, 1985.

—. "The Bible's Art of Persuasion: Ideology, Rhetoric, and Poetics in Saul's Fall." *Beyond Form Criticism. Essays in Old Testament Literary Criticism.* Ed. Peter House. Winona Lake: Eisenbrauns, 1992. 234-71.

Stoebe, Hans-Joachim. *Das erste Buch Samuelis.* Gütersloh: Mohn, 1973.

Stolz, Fritz. *Das erste und zweite Buch Samuel.* Zürich: Theologischer Verlag Zürich, 1981.

Sundermeier, Theo. "Ritus." *Theologische Realenzyklopädie.* Ed. Gerhard Müller. Vol. 29. Berlin: De Gruyter, 1998. 259-265.

Todorov, Tzvetan. *Théorie de la littérature: Textes des formalistes russes.* Paris: Ed. du Seuil, 1965.

Tov, Emanuel. *Der Text der Hebräischen Bibel. Handbuch der Textkritik.* Stuttgart: Kohlhammer, 1997.

Vette, Joachim. *Samuel und Saul. Ein Beitrag zur Narrativen Poetik des Samuelbuches.* Münster: LIT, 2005.

—. "Der letzte Richter? Methodische Überlegungen zur Charaktergestaltung in 1 Sam 11." *Communio Viatorum* 51 (2009): 184-197.

—. "Narrative Poetics and Hebrew Narrative: A Survey." *Literary Construction of Identity in the Ancient World.* Ed. Hanna Liss. Winona Lake: Eisenbrauns, 2010. 19-62.

—. "Samuel's Farewell Speech: Theme and Variation in 1 Samuel 12, Josephus, and Pseudo-Philo." *Literary Construction of Identity in the Ancient World.* Ed. Hanna Liss. Winona Lake: Eisenbrauns, 2010. 325-340.

Wehrli, Max. *Allgemeine Literaturwissenschaft.* Bern: Francke, 1951.

Zenger, Erich. *Einleitung in das Alte Testament.* Stuttgart: Kohlhammer, 1995.

Zobel, Hans-Jürgen, "'ărôn." *Theologisches Wörterbuch zum Alten Testament.* Ed. Johannes Botterweck. Vol. 1. Tübingen: Mohr, 1973. 391-404.

Two Types of Magic in One Tradition?
A Cognitive-Historiographical Case Study on the Interplay of Narratives and Rituals

DIRK JOHANNSEN

1. INTRODUCTION

Magic has a long tradition as a literary topos in the European history of religion. From antiquity onward, scholarly theories and poetic descriptions have suggested magic as a transhistorical and substantive phenomenon, while its alleged historical performances mostly turn out as attributions meant to marginalize or exclude rival parties. Until the modern institutionalization in occult orders, the self-declared magician had, with few exceptions, remained a fictional character, portrayed in varied ways depending on literary or scholarly genre (see Daxelmüller and Otto). In modern day literature, two contradictory types seem to stick out in particular. On the one hand, there is the classical "Faust-type" of character: people skilled in occult knowledge and with high ambitions, learned in the dark arts of performing rituals to evoke demons or craft instruments. The source of their power is a coalition with demonic, non-human entities or, as a heritage of modern occultism, the use of "cosmic" or "spiritual" energies that are channelled by the trained magician – like in Harry Potter's wand-based magic. On the other hand, there are the archetypal "Merlin-type" characters in present-day fantasy literature, who are magical beings themselves. Their magic is not restricted by spells and rituals, but derives or emanates from a source of power intrinsic to them.[1] In scholarly debate, these two basic concepts of superempirical agency have long been identified and seen as mutually exclusive. Nicholas of Cusa, for example, stressed that it is a dangerous misunderstanding to regard magical effects as the result of the magician's peculiar nature. Responsible for the assumed effects produced "is not the fantastic [nature] of the magicians, who allege that by faith and through certain practices a man ascends to a nature of influential spirits who are akin to himself – [...]. [S]uch (magicians) are bound to alliances, and to pacts of unity, with evil spirits" (Hopkins 253).[2] In certain folk religious traditions, however, both concepts of superempirical agency – as an attribute of the practitioner himself and as external entities whose power is mediated by the practitioner – coexist.

This chapter provides a narratologically informed case study on a folk religious tradition in 19th-century southern Norway, in which the concept of *trolldom* seems to imply just this kind of contrasting notions.[3] In Norway, the local oral traditions as well as customs and ritualistic practices have been collected and documented extensively since the 1830s. In the context of the nation-building programme following Danish rule, the skills of the traditional storytellers and the "peasant culture" were discovered as national heritage and led to the establishment of large folkloristic archives.[4]

---

1   The figure of the magician and the concepts of magic in modern literature have only partially been topics in literary studies. Stockhammer distinguishes between several types of magicians within the "supranaturalistic" and fantastic framework of modern literature. Here, a similar dichotomy can be discerned with the charismatic and magical individuals on the one side, and the hypnotists, alchemists and cabbalists on the other side (see Stockhammer).
2   Cf. Nicolaus Cusanus, De Docta Ignorantia, Liber III, c. XI [1440].
3   On the concept of folk religiosity (*folkelig religiøsitet*) as being characterized by a broader spectrum of beliefs and customs than recognized in official (Lutheran) doctrine see Skjelbred (68) and Eriksen.
4   This chapter focuses on sources from the inner Telemark province in southern Norway and claims validity for this region. Where I refer to sources from neighbouring provinces, the motifs were known in Telemark as well. The recordings were done by folklorists and clergy people, but even more by storytellers, peasants and local amateur historiographers. Keeping in mind the political dimen-

Accompanied by a substantial ethnographic corpus, these collections allow a glimpse into 19th-century narrative cultures and their social context, in which *trolldom* is a dominant topic. It has long been noticed that, depending on the sources referred to, *trolldom* is described in a way that seems contradictory (see Lid and Grambo). In the legends, *trolldom* appears as a force intrinsic to certain cunning people. However, this legendary idealization of magical experts contrasts sharply with the actual practice of the same cunning people, as documented in ritual instructions and the ethnographic record. In most folkloristic studies on magic and popular customs, the legends, being fictions, were discounted as meaningful sources. My argument intends to show that despite the apparent dichotomy both rituals and fictional narratives are crucial to the tradition, as only their interplay creates distinct dynamics allowing the tradition to stay in place by renewing its potency and adapting to changing circumstances. In the legends, magic, indeed, comes as a fictional motif, but this motif develops social efficacy. In the following, I will approach the question on the interplay and the respective function of rituals and narratives by applying perspectives from narrative theory and the cognitive science of religion. Two cognitive ritual theories, the ritual competence theory by Thomas Lawson and Robert McCauley and the modes of religiosity theory advanced by Harvey Whitehouse, will be introduced and applied to the historical sources. While the former focuses on ritual syntax, allowing for a classification of ritual forms both in instruction manuals and in narrative descriptions of ritualistic acts, the latter is suited to model the dynamic connections of different types of rituals within a social setting. Although the results are confined to this specific historical setting, the methodological aim is to show how perspectives and models developed in these approaches can be integrated into historiography to provide both a coherent framework and specific instruments for detailed case studies in the history of religions.

---

sion of the enterprise, the collections – primarily the *Norsk Folkeminnesamling* – still provide an excellent corpus for comparative research in narrative cultures. Concerning the criticism of the sources and the question of authenticity see Johannsen (100-111). All translations are mine.

2. RECIPES AND STORIES

The generic term for the semantic field of magic, sorcery, and witchcraft in the southern Norwegian tradition examined is *trolldom*, derived from Old Norse *trolldómr*.[5] Although the term was commonly used to translate "magic" and "witchcraft" since the Middle Ages – leading to mostly overlapping conceptual histories –, the notion of *trolldom* still bears one significant peculiarity in respect to antique and Christian conceptions of magic. The agency is already captured in the term: *trolldom* is what trolls do. Before the national romanticist re-invention of folklore in the late 19th century, the word *troll* denoted not a singular species of legendary entities but was an attribute of uncanny beings and everything opposed to human society (see Hartmann).[6] In the oral tradition of southern Norway, elves or the Hidden People (*huldrefolk*) are *trollfolk*, and so are Sami and Gypsies. Even animals, places or objects can be *troll* (Johannsen 183-187). A famous example are the Black Books, handwritten collections of recipes and formulas including herbal cures and poisons, charms, spells, and rites for calling forth Jesus, saints, Satan or the elves – practices a *trollmann* (sorcerer) or a *trollkvinne* (witch) would be suspected of. More than 150 of these handwritten manuscripts were found in Norway, and although some date back as far as the 15th century, most of them are of relatively recent origin (see Bang; Garstein; Amundsen, *Svarteboken*). They derive from late 18th- and 19th-century peasant culture, even though they bear titles meant to convince the readers of their extraordinary age and value: "Cyprianus Arts. A book written in the Academy of Wittenberg Anno 1345 and later found in the palace of Copenhagen Anno 1665 in a chest of marble, written on parchment."[7] In the oral tradition these manuals were a frequent topic, but had adopted an even darker, "trollish" character which makes the "ex-

---

5 On the concept in Old Norse literature see Raudvere. The loan word "magi" is hardly ever used in the sources examined.

6 *Troll* is a neuter noun that also used to function as an adjective.

7 Norsk Folkeminnesamling: NFS Moltke Moe 106 I. Most of the manuscripts have been digitalized at the IKOS, University of Oslo (http://www.edd.uio.no/ikos/svarteboker/svarteboker.html). The "Black Academy of Wittenberg," where the devil himself teaches, is the motif of a migratory legend (ML 3000) obviously dating back to the Counter Reformation (see Christiansen).

tant Black Books seem naive and prosaic" (Espeland 13-14).[8] In the legends, the books are described as being dangerous not because of their blasphemous content but as mere objects, as they almost seem to bristle with power. They enslave their owners, they cannot be destroyed or got rid of, and opening them calls forth all forms of *trollskap* and leads to insanity – unless one is a *trollmann* already. In that case, however, the content of these books is completely irrelevant, because these legendary figures are in no need of knowledge. Their power is intrinsic to them, as they are *troll* themselves.

In 19th-century Norway, there was a large scene of cunning people. The most famous served as general healers using herbs and homemade drugs – something that was of vast importance in the rural areas where access to conventional medical treatment was rare and mostly too expensive. The borders between these healers and practitioners of more dubious arts were fluid (see Stokker). There were specialists who would take care only of specific ailments or injuries, like curing a sprain by placing the patient's limb on a stump and then pretending to chop wood while reciting a formula to reduce the pain ("knocking the pain off"). Rituals for worldly purposes, like predicting one's future spouse, inducing love, or increasing luck in financial matters were included in the repertoire of some of the healers. In the case of a forest fire, an *ildstemmer* (fire-stopper) was called to perform the odd task of running around the trouble spot reciting charms, so the fire would not be able to cross his path (Hodne, *Trolldom i Norge* 165-195). Most of the rituals described in the historical Black Books are relatively detailed instructions for performing this kind of ritualistic act accurately. Two of the most common themes were staunching blood and catching thieves. Similar to the fire-stoppers, blood-stoppers were mostly specialists, even though the ritual requirements were rather simple. For example, for staunching blood, a "*trollbøn*" (magic prayer) would be declaimed while applying white moss: "Staunch blood and arrest blood for N.N. [the patient], like the stream stood still when Jesus and his 10 disciples went over the water."[9] More elaborate were the rituals for finding thieves by "showing

---

8   Many of the migratory legends of the types ML 3000 – 3025 centre on the Black Book.
9   NFS Moltke Moe 106 I [18th century].

them in the water" (*vise i vannet* or *igjenvise*), that is conjuring an image of the thief on the water's surface:

Make yourself 3 X [crosses] out of rowan tree and go to a small river, where it runs from east to west, on a Friday morning before the sun dawns. Throw the crosses into the water where they cannot float away and read the following words over the crosses: I call you and I beg you, highest Lord Lusefærd [Lucifer] and the Lord Geamataan [?], by your Power and Authority to bring me back what N. [the name of the thief] has stolen from N.N. [the client's name], or that you show me the thief's name and picture here in the water. And that he might become so crazy in his heart and his God and his mind that the earth shakes under his feet in 15,000 devils' name.[10]

The formulaic character is typical of rituals performed in the local community – both by cunning people and laymen. The charms had to be phrased and carried out precisely according to the tradition, calling upon saints, demons or the Hidden People, who in local custom stood side by side with entities from Christian tradition.

Beside the Black Books and the ethnographic record, the oral tradition collected in the 19th century provides additional insight into the conventional notions of *trolldom* and its practitioners. The legendary *trolldom* serves mostly the same purposes as the rituals described, but the ritual acts are hardly ever mentioned. In the legends, a *trollmann* will be called to staunch bleeding, but he will use no formulated charm and certainly not refer to Jesus. A common motif is that he welcomes a messenger with the words: "You can go home again, for the wound is closed already" (Hodne, *Trolldom i Norge* 184). When showing a thief in the water, the legendary *trollmann* will simply point to a bucket for the image to appear, an act causing horror among the spectators. The magical effects are always immediate. In many cases of theft, the *trollmann* even seems to do nothing at all, as in the following legend of one infamous "wise-priest":

Once, it is told, the parish priest called Finkenhagen lost a silver spoon when performing the church service in Tuddal. The people looked for it but could not find it anywhere, so the priest had to continue his journey without the spoon. As he had

---

10 NB Ms.8° 640:a, op. 56 (Cyprianus Frikonst udgivet udi aaredt 1719 [ca. 1780]).

come midway to the hill with the pasture called 'Sveinungshovden' he descended from his horse to rest and said to his companion: "We should wait a moment, he will make him sweat to come after us [sic]." After a short while, a man became visible down in the valley. He came rushing after them with a spoon in one hand and a handkerchief in the other hand, wiping off the dripping sweat. "Here I come with the spoon which you forgot," he said to the priest as he approached. "Yes, that may be so," said the priest and laughed. It turned out that the man had stolen the silver spoon from the priest's room and that he – after the priest left – was unable to find any rest or peace of mind. He *had to* take the spoon and run after the priest.[11]

Instead of describing rituals, the legends focus on portraying the *trollmenn* as powerful and intimidating figures, whose mere presence leads to strong emotional and bodily reactions, allowing them to control other people's behaviour:

[At a dance, the trollmann] Eilev hopped on the bed, and before anyone realized what was going on, the girl hauled to the bed, undressed and laid down beside him, so everyone in the dancing parlour would see it. It took quite a while before she recovered, being embarrassed and getting mocked and laughed at (Flatin 97).

In the legends, magic is not something to be learned. A *trollmann* is somebody who had an encounter with something *troll*; he might have been abducted by elves, been in contact with demons, ethnic minorities, another *trollmann*, or a Black Book (see Mathisen, "North Norwegian Folk Legends" and "Den farlige kunnskapen"). By being with *trolls*, people become *troll* themselves. To understand this concept of magical agency, we have to take a closer look at what precisely the word *troll* refers to within the legends.

3. *TROLL* AS A SEMANTIC VACANCY

Things *troll* are the substrate of mythical legends from 19th-century southern Norway. Telling these legends was considered an art, with proficient

---

11 NFS Klipp VII, p. 64 (Fremskridt Nr. 238, 24/9/1903), Telemark. Emphasis in the original.

storytellers being the keepers of a region's history.[12] In the legends, they present a world inhabited by ghosts and nature spirits, by witches and sorcerers. The stories were meant as entertainment and were subject to controversy and debate. On the one hand, the existence of these beings was doubted by some members of the local community, sometimes understood as allegorical, and their relation to the Christian doctrine was even a theological dispute (Amundsen, "Mellom inderlighet og fornuft" 268-297). On the other hand, stories about Hidden People granting a rich harvest or occupying an alp during the winter months legitimized land claims of those parties within the local community who were known as having a close relationship with these entities (see Solheim). The stories explained genealogies, unusual events and created mysteries to ponder; the range of interpretation, as it is documented in the historical collections, was enormous. In part, this is due to some stylistic features, which can be identified as the conventional patterns of this narrative tradition. Far from being made up spontaneously, the legends told can be shown to follow a strict set of motifs and stylistic rules, which aimed at provoking curiosity and involvement. Regarding the question of what precisely is indicated by the term *troll*, these patterns become visible, as they apply to the representation of superempirical respectively counterintuitive agents in their entirety.[13]

Legends are told from the perspective of the local community. Even if the motifs are those of migratory legends known all over Europe, in the local variants the protagonists are people known by name and family, and the places of the events are precisely specified. The narrative perspective, too, seems bound to the community, and is actively used to construct the "otherness" which defines certain people and beings as *troll*. The legends' conventional perspective is a third-person omniscient point of view with full

---

12 On the storytellers' social position see Bø et. al. (11-60).

13 Instead of "supernatural entities," "culturally postulated superhuman agents," or "intermediate beings" I refer to religious and fantastic entities as counterintuitive, as this term by Pascal Boyer is the only one referring solely to structural features instead of cultural presuppositions or an artificial dichotomy between theological and folkloristic concepts (see Boyer). The underlying theory defines counterintuitivity as "a transgression of a number of ontological features rooted in human cognition" (Severi 816). These features, of course, have to be defined on an empirical base.

access to the characters' emotions and thoughts. The heterodiegetic narrator, however, refrains from any statement concerning the inner life of the superempirical characters in the legends. Although even the spirits of local folklore are highly anthropomorphic and their outer appearance is often described as indistinguishable from ordinary people, their mind remains a black box.[14] Their knowledge and their intentions are never revealed. In episodes describing encounters, this stylistic distance between the narrator and the superempirical beings is maintained by a shift from the conventional zero-focalized point of view to an internal focalization of a human protagonist on the diegetic level, who faces these entities confused and marvelled. In many cases, this sudden shift to a more limited perspective is the only clue to what kind of being the protagonists are dealing with. For example, in one legend two young huntsmen spend the night in a remote cottage in the highlands:

After their meal they cleaned up and rested on the beds they made from fir branches, when suddenly a woman entered, followed by two young girls. The huntsmen became afraid; they thought it strange that somebody would be out here that late. But since they noticed nothing dangerous, they regained some courage. After all, they trusted their rifles. They thought it might be the extraordinarily pretty girls who were said to tend cattle out here. Perhaps they came from the village. Perhaps they lost track of time. Essentially, they did not know what to think (Loupedalen 257f).

Filtered through the protagonists' emotional arousal, questions and doubts, the story suggests a mystery, even if nothing counterintuitive happens. As the visitors are not introduced, in the context of the legends it is already obvious that the two huntsmen have an encounter with something *troll*, in this case the Hidden People.

The technical character of this shift in focalization becomes obvious in the more elaborate legends. The single most dominant motif in the narrative tradition is the story of people who, either for a short time or for the rest of their lives, were taken into the mountain (*bergtatt*). Underground and inside

---

14 In some legends, the female forest spirit *huldra* has a cow's tail, but even this well known trait is not mandatory. This and similar traits are mentioned only where necessary for the plot structure – with the protagonist discovering it in the last moment.

the hills, the Hidden People dwelled, as did their ancestors, the *vættir* and elves of Old Norse literature. According to the motif, the protagonist suddenly stumbles into their home or is allured by their extraordinary beauty and, despite his or her fears and attempts to resist, follows them to their abode. But as soon as the protagonist enters, he or she is lost to society, and therefore to the narrator as well: "Somebody 'taken in' will never again be a proper human being" (Holbek and Piø, 112; see also Feilberg). A typical trait of this legendary motif is the coda, in which the protagonist after some time returns home alienated, mostly unable to utter a meaningful word and yearning to go back to "the mountain," or sometimes empowered as a *trollmann*, with abilities far beyond human reach. Alternatively, he or she stays with the Hidden People and becomes one of them. Remarkably, it never becomes quite clear if this is judged as a good or a bad thing to happen to the people concerned. While the bereaved take a lot of trouble to get them back, for example in fruitless attempts to carry church bells up to the mountain, the storyline provides the abductees with a final word of goodbye, often emphasizing how much better off they are: "to me, it is like Christmas every day" (Johannsen 143-151).

After the initial encounter, the legend's point of view shifts back to the normal zero focalization focusing on the people left behind, while the events in the Hidden People's realm remain untold. The former focalizer is now subject to the same stylistic distance used to characterize all superempirical beings. The moral is ambivalent and so is the character of the *trollfolk*: by artificially restricting the knowledge to the communal consent about these entities, they are constructed as a mystery. A semantic vacancy or blank is installed as the core of these types of legends.[15] The *trolls*' nature and relation to human society are left for the audience to debate, and by doing so, a community's norms, beliefs, and boundaries have to be negotiated. The counterintuitive effects produced by *trollfolk*, with Hidden People vanishing right before one's eyes or the empowered returnees per-

---

15 What is described by Wolfgang Iser as a general operational principle of fictional literature, the gaps or blanks "organizing the readers participation" (203) by "a process set in motion and regulated not by a given code but by a mutually restrictive and magnifying interaction between the explicit and the implicit, between revelation and concealment" (168f.), can for this genre be understood as a narrative technique purposefully applied at the core of the tradition.

forming incredible acts of *trolldom*, come as a result of this ambiguity. With the rule of stylistic distance, their knowledge and abilities are defined as being beyond reach. Every question about "how it is done" leads back to a blank, which is the narrative core of the concept of *troll*, and thus can only be answered by referring to other stories.

4. *TROLLDOM* AND THE FORM OF RITUAL ACTS

Within the folk religious tradition, *trolldom* seems to come in two types. On the one hand, manuals describe elaborate rituals involving formulaic speech, a diversity of items and detailed instructions on how to conduct each step of the ritual. The legends, on the other hand, describe *trolldom* as an intrinsic property of people and beings *troll* with effects achieved immediately. Even if it is assumed that legends focus on the extraordinary outcomes rather than preparatory measures, the absence of rituals is still striking. It seems as if the legendary *trolldom* hardly knows of any formulaic rituals and thus as if two antithetic concepts of magical agency coexisted within the local tradition. This, however, is not the case. The effective agency assumed in the stories about *trolldom* is the same as in the ritual performances, and indeed they constitute a coherent system. The apparent discrepancy is the result of the different ritual forms represented, which both have their respective function in relation to one other.

The gap between the narrative portrayal and the actual performance of acts of *trolldom* can be bridged by applying a cognitive perspective, focusing on the ascription of superempirical agency. The structure of the magical acts can be rendered according to the ritual form hypothesis put forward in the *theory of religious ritual competence* by Thomas Lawson and Robert McCauley. Modelled after Noam Chomsky's *language competence theory*, the theory posits a cognitive processing device called the *Action Representation System*, which checks the well-formedness of notions of actions and generates predictable intuitions about their probable efficacy. The postulated three-slot pattern is one of subject, predicate and object: an agent does something to (or uses something on) a patient [Agent → Instrument (Action) → Patient]. The hypothesis states that religious ritual acts are really like ordinary acts, but include the efficacy of a counterintuitive agent in one of the three possible slots, thus allowing for a non-natural consequence.

Depending on the slot connected to this special agency, thus the prognosis, rituals will be perceived strikingly different.

Special Agent Rituals are those in which the person performing the act has a ritually mediated connection to a counterintuitive agent. Examples are the sacraments of the Catholic Church, which normally have to be given by an ordained member of the clergy. Ordained priests stand in the apostolic succession, which provides a direct and – in theory – unbroken link to the enabling acts performed by God, allowing them to act on His behalf when giving the sacrament. Rituals, in which the special agency is exercized via a person, are acts which, indirectly, are conducted by the counterintuitive agent and are therefore not reversible by human means. Furthermore, for the effect to stay in place, no repetition is needed. The effect of a ritual like matrimony or baptism is lasting.[16] Lawson and McCauley condense the intuitive consequences of this form of rituals in the so-called *Principle of Superhuman Agency*: *Special Agent Rituals* will be relatively rare and infrequently performed, emotionally arousing happenings, coded in episodic memory.

In contrast to *Special Agent Rituals*, *Special Instrument Rituals* as well as *Special Patient Rituals* have a rather different ritual profile, as they both tend to be repeated frequently. In these forms of rituals, the counterintuitive agent is referred to in the action/instrument slot (like when using magical gestures, charms, spells, talismans, relics etc.) or in the patient slot, when it becomes the receiving part of a ritual (say sacrifices to a god). As the actors are humans who are not acting on behalf of a supporting superempirical agency, the attributed effect is usually less intense and lasting, requiring constant updates. The *Principle of Superhuman Agency* predicts that these two forms of rituals will, due to their frequency, come with less emotional arousal on average and be coded in semantic memory. Where several slots provide ritually mediated connections to counterintuitive agents, like baptism involving a priest as the agent and holy water consecrated by a priest as the instrument, the initial appearance is the one more direct, i.e., the entry with the fewest enabling rituals. This additional rule, the *Principle of*

---

16 The theory does not state that exceptions from this inner logic, like emergency baptism, are a theological problem, but that these exceptions will eventually lead to controversy, as they contradict intuitive (and often "theologically incorrect") assumptions derived from the ritual form (Slone 57).

Superhuman Immediacy, implies that the attributed efficacy of rituals tends to fade if no new connections to the counterintuitive agents are established (Lawson and McCauley 26ff.)

The ritual form hypothesis allows rituals to be classified according to the element of the (either performed or described) act perceived as crucial for their efficacy and thus rated as not exchangeable. It is the form rather than the type in which ritualistic acts from the Black Books differ from those represented in the legends. The acts of *trolldom* described in the manuals and the ethnographic record are in virtually all cases either *Special Instrument Rituals* or *Special Patient Rituals*. The ritual form does not require the performer to be a special agent with counterintuitive attributes or skills. Any person of certain learning and with access to the required objects will in principle be able to execute the magical procedures. Required are either items with a connection to counterintuitive agents or a direct addressing of these agents. Neither in the manuals nor in the ethnographic record is there a sharp distinction between entities from the Christian traditions and those from a more folk religious background, as a connection to both of them is able to provide the sufficient "magical essence"; while God's power is utilized by crucifixes and charms, hosts or splinters from church altars, soil from graveyards may either refer to God, as it is consecrated, or to the (un-)dead. In the 19th century, many families owned pieces of silver tableware like spoons or jugs which were considered as elfin silver, former property of the Hidden People and thus still connected to their special agency. These items were said to unfold healing powers and used to administer medicine.

In the legends, *trolldom* is performed by special agents, and thus the formulas and items used are exchangeable and even dispensable. It is the practitioner who is connected to the counterintuitive entities. The folk religious spectrum remains in place, as this connection can be due to an encounter with the Hidden People or due to having visited the black academy of Wittenberg. *Trollmenn*, witches, and the wise priest (*visepræst*), "who can do more than just eat," stand side by side in the legends, and while their social status might differ, the extraordinary effects produced largely overlap. So although the narrative representations and the actual ritual performances seem to imply different notions of magic, the magical agency is still the same; in both cases, it leads back to the narrative substrate, the counterintuitive agents of the legends and the biblical stories, only that the rituals written down in the Black Books refer to them in the performance slots, while the legendary *troll* people incorporate them.

Having identified this connection, it becomes possible to take a closer look at the respective function of legends and rituals within the folk religious frame of thought and the general dynamics of the tradition. Both legendary motifs and conventional rituals are rather static in nature. They are documented as being relatively consistent over decades. And over the decades, they began to be questioned. "These words were powerful once" is a sentence often heard by ethnographers when asking about charms and spells. Consistent with Lawson's and McCauley's prediction, the *Principle of Superhuman Immediacy*, with every new generation, the superempirical agency referred to in the ritualistic acts seems to grow further apart. The legends of counterintuitive agents lose relevance and emotional impact where the connections to everyday life are not frequently renewed. However, the prediction that magical rituals and the oral tradition therefore will become extinct in the coming years, made already in the 18th century and repeated in every following generation, has proven incorrect. While the decline of belief in the "old traditions" is a frequent topic, later scholars observed that beliefs and practices that are ridiculed at one time can come to full bloom again in the following generation. External factors aside, one key to this phenomenon lies in the interplay of narratives and rituals. A case example will serve to illustrate the evolving dynamics, when both forms of magic enter into a synthesis.

5. THE CASE OF SPÅ-EILEV

One of southern Norway's most famous magical experts in the second half of the 19th century was Eilev Olsen Hagen (1814-1891), known by the name of Spå-Eilev (*Scry-Eilev*). Born as the son of a day labourer in Hjuksebø, Sauherad, in the province of Telemark, he rapidly ascended the social ladder by becoming widely known as a professional soothsayer – and a legendary *trollmann*. He became the charismatic protagonist of hundreds of local legends. Eilev Olsen's peculiar career took off in 1838, when he became involved in a law suit.[17] The case started out as a bagatelle, after a local peasant was accused of having stolen barley from his neighbour's barn. Since the accused had a bad reputation, the outcome seemed clear – at least until the accused's daughter broke a barrier of silence not even the accused had dared to touch. She revealed that her father was only blamed for one reason, which was that the key witness for the prosecution, Eilev Olsen, had "shown him in the water." The 24-year-old day labourer had used a magical technique to spot the thief. The trial now unexpectedly became Norway's last witch trial (*trolldomsprosess*), with Eilev Olsen being accused and dozens of witnesses summoned to court, almost all of them being familiar with Eilev's activities. It was put on record that he was a blasphemer who threatened to curse his enemies and who demanded to be worshipped, and he frequently acted as a soothsayer. Eilev Olsen tried to defend himself by stating that he "might have told fortunes" now and then using playing cards, but "if he had done so" then just for entertainment purposes. He had certainly not shown anyone "in the water." The voices of the witnesses could not be ignored, and on April 22, 1839 the court sentenced Eilev Olsen to three years of hard labour and subsequent exile. The verdict was based on the old witchcraft laws from the *Norske Lov*, put in place in 1687 and almost forgotten in the early 19th century. The judge himself, however, forgot about a minor detail: the witchcraft laws were set up under Danish rule, but as Norway had been under Swedish crown since 1814, substantial revisions were in progress. The ruling was appealed and on August 19, 1839, Eilev Olsen was acquitted of all charges, although the High Court (*Høyesterett*) did not fail to comment that his soothsaying acts were reprehensible, even if no longer chargeable. The *trolldom* act was officially repealed in 1842.

Concerning the concepts of magical agency, the most revealing passage in the sixty pages of court documents preserved is the local judge's question whether anyone had ever *seen* Eilev perform an act of *trolldom*. One

---

17 The following three records of this case are preserved in the Riksarkiv in Oslo: Høyesterett L. Nr 1-17, 1. sesjon 1840. Pk. nr. 3., Sak Nr. 52. / Høyesterettsdommer for 1840. Justisdepartmentets forskjellige protokoller nr. 58. Sak. nr. 52 / Høyesteretts voteringsprotokoll 1. sesjon 1840, S. 21/22 sak nr. 52.18. Februar 1840. No page numbers are given; all quotes following are from these manuscripts. On the process see Hodne, "Trolldomssaken mot Spå-Eilev."

person stepped forth and declared he had seen Eilev once "lie motionless on a bench the whole day and when being asked about that, he said he was confused." So when asked for the indicated ritual act, the witnesses only reported an incident where he had done virtually nothing – which obviously seemed suspicious. Otherwise, only two clues regarding the nature of his practices were given. In a side note of the High Court documents it is mentioned that when telling the fortunes he used a printed manual, which might be a reference to one of the popular prints of Black Books from Copenhagen.[18] Furthermore, it was reported that Eilev first worked as a soothsayer after a journey undertaken half a year earlier. In the years to come, the story of this journey became a legend. Eilev himself is said to have told how he met a Sami girl in Northern Norway and stayed with her for some time. It is a common variant of the "taken into the mountain"-motif: in local folklore the Sami were considered *trollfolk*, so he had become a *trollmann* by being with a *troll*.[19]

As the trial had made him famous, in the following fifty years he became a highly frequented and at the same time feared soothsayer and sorcerer. In a time of economic crisis, he moved up from being a day labourer to being a landowner with his own tenants. In dozens of legends, so many "one could easily write a substantial book just about him," he was portrayed telling fortunes, controlling people, and causing harm over vast distances (Flatin 97). The court proceedings – in which the local community had testified against Eilev – were not forgotten, but reinterpreted. Now it was told that he was the victim of a conspiracy, but due to his skills and wit easily got off the hook, leaving the judge stultified. The most common motif was still him finding thieves by "showing them in the water." This ritual practice is depicted as a sort of gimmick, as Spå-Eilev is almost omniscient anyway:

---

18 Popular versions of magical manuals were printed in Copenhagen since the beginning of the 19th century (Espeland 14).

19 The most extensive published collections of legends on Spå-Eilev can be found in Qvisling, Gunnhejm and Flatin. A large collection of unpublished legends can be found in the *Rikard Berge Håndskriftsamling* (Telemark Fylkesmuseum, Skien) and the *Norsk Folkeminnesamling*.

In Slemdal, something was stolen. A girl named Ingeborg from Sauherad was employed at the neighbour's farm. The man who was stolen from went to her and asked her, since she knew Spå-Eilev, if she could persuade him to identify the thief. Indeed, Ingeborg went to Hjuksebø, where Eilev lived. He was standing outside the barn threshing. But as she went down there, she became so afraid she trembled all the way and her heart pounded as if it would burst. As she came to him, Eilev said: "You came because of a theft, and it seems strange that Olav, who is the son in Tingulvstad, does not understand who the thief is. He should realize who steals from him." Then Eilev began to tell her what the thief's home looked like, what the thief looked like and so on, and asked: "Do you think that, by this, you can find out who the thief is?" (He said no name). Ingeborg answered: "I guess I know who it is." "If you are not sure I can show him to you." "No! Anything but that!" – Ingeborg burst out. But Spå-Eilev called his wife to bring him a bowl of water, which she did. "Do you know the man sitting down there in the bowl?" Eilev asked. Ingeborg stared into the water and saw a man she knew, as clear as if she were looking at him face to face. "If you want I can mark him for you; I can put his eye out or something like that." Ingeborg called out: "For God's sake, don't do that!" "Well, sure, I can just leave it be," Eilev said (Gunnhejm 107f.).

As a legendary figure, Spå-Eilev is represented according to the stylistic conventions of the narrative tradition. While the storyline follows the local girl, his character is built up as enigmatic and powerful by a description of the girl's strong bodily reaction to his presence. Although she is the one making a request, he remains in control, answering before the question is uttered. By ignoring her wishes and showing the thief in the water, he demonstrates both his superempirical abilities and his social dominance. Spå-Eilev's intentions and the range of his power remain ambiguous; his thoughts and emotions are generally hidden from the narrator's point of view, while the clients and other members of the local community serve as focalizers. The legends match the prediction of Lawson's and McCauley's *Principle of Superhuman Agency*. Spå-Eilev's acts of *trolldom* are always depicted as singular, outstanding episodes. The legends simulate emotional arousal by focussing on the emotional impact of the sorcerer as a special agent. When he makes a thief appear on the water's surface, the clients tremble and feel horror; if he reads their minds, they are stunned; just encountering him comes with descriptions of fear, fascination, and often stupor. What Eilev does, in contrast, seems random. Where legends were collected in several variants, the course of action is interchangeable and the superempirical effects produced always seem the immediate result of his intrinsic powers, such as when he answers questions not even posed yet.

By the end of the 19th century, some of his late clients described to the lay folklorist Christian Gunnhejm what happened during the consultation. Years after Eilev Olsen's death those clients showed themselves deeply impressed by his personality and skills, even marking the consultation as a watershed moment in their lives. The accounts recorded by Gunnhejm can be classified as *memorates*: autodiegetic narratives of personal experience that mirror the legends both in style and in content (see Honko). The situations described are similar, with Eilev seemingly anticipating the clients' visit and most of their questions. His fortune telling, however, gains a distinct ritualistic component, as the clients report how he read coffee grounds when giving advice on everyday problems. And of course Spå-Eilev's magical leitmotif is mentioned, even though never performed. Asked by a client about his future spouse the client remembers Eilev offering to "show" her: "If you want I can show her to you in a cup of water; but since she is so far away, it would not do her any good" (Gunnhejm 105). As often as the offer is given, it is turned down due to the carefully announced side effects. Against the background of the legends, which conventionalized him as a charismatic authority, the consultation was an experience worth reporting anyway. Within the narrative frame he had developed a social potency. Gunnhejm suggests that Eilev's extraordinary success as a soothsayer was the outcome of his legendary reputation rather than being its cause: "Many did not dare otherwise but to return the stolen goods as soon as they heard Spå-Eilev had gotten involved" (88). In this way, his practice and the stories about his practice together might have constituted a self-affirming system, where the formulaic rituals, even if performed, indeed played an almost negligible role.

6. REJUVENATING THE TRADITION

As the case of Spå-Eilev illustrates, both forms of *trolldom* – as legendary acts of special agents and as special instrument or special patient rituals – are deeply intertwined within the local tradition. Although both the legendary motifs and the conventional rituals are static in nature, in their interplay they develop dynamic qualities and social efficacy. The mechanism of this process, in the centre of which stands the ascription of a special agency to a member of the community, can be explained by a cognitive model elaborated by Jesper Sørensen, based on Harvey Whitehouse's *modes of religiosity* theory (see Sørensen).

The *modes theory* addresses the interaction of different forms of rituals with systems of belief and social structures (see Whitehouse). Similar to Lawson and McCauley's case for the rituals, Whitehouse argues for two cognitive attractor positions within religious systems, deduced from two modes of transmission of religious content, one connected to episodic, one to semantic memory. The *imagistic mode* centres on emotionally arousing, infrequently performed rituals. The level of arousal leads to an episodic encoding of the event. The performers will remember this specific performance in great detail, leading to increased social cohesion and "spontaneous exegetic reflexions" about the ritual experience. As the episodic memories will be retrieved in narrative form, choices of narrative style, genre and patterns will influence these reflexions. If the rituals become routine, the theory predicts a progressive shift to the *doctrinal mode* attractor position, as the performance will be coded in semantic memory and certain interpretations will be established as authoritative. This leads to the strong bonds between participants sharing the experience being reduced, and resources set free for the elaboration of complex systems of belief imparted by organized specialists. The doctrinal mode is no stable outcome either, as the more complex and less experiential cluster of beliefs, hierarchies and rituals will, according to Whitehouse, lead to a "tedium effect." With less personal involvement and references to an individual's life, a reversal of the process is initiated. As the two modes are meant as attractor positions, a religious tradition will oscillate between these poles.[20]

As Jesper Sørensen has pointed out, the *modes theory* may help to identify "both cognitive and social pressures" on the tradition, which lead to the ascription of charismatic authority (181). The special instrument rituals as documented in the Black Books and the ethnographic record are part of a

---

20 It is hard to estimate on which scale of historical processes the dynamics postulated in the *modes theory* actually occur, as it was developed in an anthropological context. For the purpose of this study, however, it may serve as a heuristic model. For applications on different scales see Whitehouse and Martin.

dogmatic system, in which trained magical experts, most of them coming from family traditions, were concerned with clear-cut domains and dealt with a sophisticated apparatus of formulas and recipes referring to folk religious entities. Failing rituals, an increasing amount of instructions, interpretations and forms of specialism will tend to decrease the efficacy accorded to these rituals (168). Weakness of the dogmatic system combined with the cognitive propensity for essentialist thinking will, according to Sørensen, set the stage for charismatic conceptions which allow for the tradition to refocus. As the accused in a highly unusual lawsuit, the soothsayer Eilev Olsen became the subject of stories, which adopted the stylistic patterns from the oral tradition. As a legendary *trollmann* empowered by a transforming encounter, Spå-Eilev does not only stand in a tradition of cunning people, but *embodies* this tradition. In the stories, he performs the traditional special instrument acts as a special agent, renewing their connection to the active principle and reducing them to their bare minimum. Not being bound by doctrines and recipes, his narratively constructed authority stabilized and rejuvenated the system.

7. CONCLUSION

The legends attach emotional arousal and memorable episodes to traditional ritual acts. Their narrative core was identified in the concept of *troll* as having no positive attributes, but being a semantic vacancy established by a set of conventional stylistic patterns mandatory to this specific oral tradition. With contemporaries narratively constructed as *trollpeople*, they provide a general reference to the superempirical agencies of the folk religious frame of thought without already subscribing to a particular theory of magic. As simulated *special agent acts* the stories only add a necessary component for the ritualistic tradition to stay in place. They *recharge* the rituals with meaning and efficacy. The narrative tradition, thus, can be identified as a crucial element of ritual performances – even if the legends hardly ever mention the ritual acts in detail. Far from being mere illustrations, the episodes told legitimize and rejuvenate the folk religious tradition, allowing for it to adapt to changing circumstances, doctrines and the life worlds of new generations.

The aim of this chapter was to show how a historiographical approach benefits from a mixed approach of narrative and ritual theories. Seen individually, the rituals and narratives of the tradition examined are relatively static, and a focus on either one of them will suggest beliefs and performances to be equally static. The historical studies derived from this perspective will therefore always identify external factors as the crucial component for historical developments. A theoretically informed approach can do more than just provide interpretations of stories and customs at a given time. By revealing basic structures of the form of rituals within narratives and the narrative requirements of ritual forms, the researcher's attention is drawn from the content towards their structural intersection. In this way, the inner dynamics of components otherwise perceived as separate come into view.

References

Amundsen, Arne B. *Svarteboken fra Borge.* Sarpsborg: Borgarsyssel Museum, 1987.
—. "Mellom inderlighet og fornuft." *Norges religionshistorie.* Eds. Arne B. Amundsen et al. Oslo: Universitetsforlaget, 2005. 243-294.
Bang, Anton Christian. *Norske Hexeformularer og Magiske Opskrifter.* Kristiania: Jacob Dybwad, 1901.
Boyer, Pascal. *The Naturalness of Religious Ideas. A Cognitive Theory of Religion.* Berkeley, CA: U of California P, 1994.
Bø, Olav, Ronald Grambo, Bjarne Hodne, and Ørnulf Hodne. *Norske Segner.* Oslo: Det Norske Samlaget, 1995.
Christiansen, Reidar Thoralf. *The Migratory Legends. A Proposed List of Types with a Systematic Catalogue of the Norwegian Variants.* Helsinki: Suomalainen Tiedeakatemia, 1958.
Daxelmüller, Christoph. *Zauberpraktiken. Eine Ideengeschichte der Magie.* Düsseldorf: Albatros/Patmos, 2005.
Eriksen, Anne. "Folkelig religiøsitet: forsøk til en avklaring." *Tradisjon* 23 (1993): 57-66.
Espeland, Velle. "Svartebøker frå Telemark." *Telemark Historie – Tidsskrift for Telemark Historielag* 24 (2003): 13-26.
Feilberg, Henning F. *Bjærgtagen. Studie over en gruppe træk fra nordisk alfetro.* København: Det Schønbergske Forlag, 1910.

Flatin, Kjetil A. *Tussar og trolldom*. Oslo: Norsk Folkeminnelag, 1930.
Garstein, Oskar. *Vinjeboka – den eldste svartebok fra norsk middelalder*. Oslo: Solum, 1993.
Grambo, Ronald. *Norske trollformler og magiske ritualer*. Oslo: Universitetsforlaget, 1979.
Gunnhejm, Christoffer. *Gamalt fraa Telemork. Segner og sogur*. Skien: Erik St. Nilssens, 1915.
Hartmann, Elisabeth. *Die Trollvorstellungen in den Sagen und Märchen der skandinavischen Völker*. Stuttgart: Kohlhammer, 1936.
Hodne, Ørnulf (1981). "Trolldomssaken mot Spå-Eilev. En undersøkelse av holdninger." *Norveg. Folkelivsgranskning* 24 (1981): 7-40.
—. *Trolldom i Norge. Hekser og trollmenn i folketro og lokaltradisjon*. Oslo: Cappelen, 2008.
Holbek, Bengt, and Iørn Piø. *Fabeldyr og Sagnfolk*. København: Politikens Forlag, 1967.
Honko, Lauri (1964). "Memorates and the Study of Folk Beliefs." *Journal of the Folklore Institute* 1 (1964): 5-19.
Hopkins, Jasper, ed. *Nicholas of Cusa on Learned Ignorance: A Translation and an Appraisal of De Docta Ignorantia*. Minneapolis: Arthur J Banning Press, 1985.
Iser, Wolfgang. *The Act of Reading. A Theory of Aesthetic Response*. London: Routledge & Kegan Paul, 1978.
Johannsen, Dirk. *Das Numinose als kulturwissenschaftliche Kategorie. Norwegische Sagenwelt in religionswissenschaftlicher Deutung*. Stuttgart: Kohlhammer, 2008.
Lawson, Thomas E., and Robert N. McCauley. *Bringing Ritual to Mind. Psychological Foundations of Ritual Forms*. Cambridge: Cambridge UP, 2002.
Lid, Nils. *Trolldom. Nordiske studiar*. Oslo: Cammermeyer, 1950.
Loupedalen, Knut. *Eventyr og Segnir fraa Telemarki*. Oslo: Cammermeyer, 1923.
Mathisen, Stein R. "North Norwegian Folk Legends about the Secret Knowledge of the Magic Experts." *Arv – Nordic Yearbook of Folklore* 48 (1993): 19-27.
—. "Den farlige kunnskapen. Makter, moral og viten i sagn om svarteboka." *Mellom sagn og virkelighet i nordnorsk tradisjon*. Eds. Marit

Anne Hauan and Ann Helene Bolstad Skjelbred. Tromsø: Vett og Viten, 1995.

Otto, Bernd-Christian. *Magie. Rezeptions- und diskursgeschichtliche Analysen von der Antike bis zur Neuzeit.* Berlin: Walter de Gruyter, 2011.

Qvisling, Jon Lauritz. *Mystiske fænomener i menneskelivet.* Kristiania: Aschehoug, 1909.

Raudvere, Catharina. "Trolldómr in Early Medieval Scandinavia." *The Athlone History of Witchcraft and Magic in Europe: Witchcraft and Magic in the Middles Ages.* Eds. Bengt Ankarloo and Stuart Clark. London: The Athlone Press, 2002.

Severi, Carlo. "Capturing Imagination: A Cognitive Approach to Cultural Complexity." *Journal of the Royal Anthropological Institute* 10.4 (2004): 815-838.

Skjelbred, Ann Helene Bolstad. "Troens grenser." *Tradisjon* 25 (1995): 63-70.

Slone, Jason. *Theological Incorrectness. Why People Believe What They Shouldn't.* Oxford: Oxford UP, 2004.

Solheim, Svale. *Norsk sætertradisjon.* Oslo: Aschehoug, 1952.

Stockhammer, Robert. *Die Wiederkehr der Magie und die Literatur 1880 – 1945.* Berlin: Akademie-Verlag, 2000.

Stokker, Kathleen. *Remedies and Rituals. Folk Medicine in Norway and the New Land.* St. Paul: Minnesota Historical Society Press, 2007.

Sørensen, Jesper. "Charisma, Tradition, and Ritual: A Cognitive Approach to Magical Agency." *Mind and Religion. Psychological and Cognitive Foundations of Religiosity.* Eds. Harvey Whitehouse and Robert N. McCauley. Walnut Creek: Altamira, 2005.

Whitehouse, Harvey. *Modes of Religiosity. A Cognitive Theory of Religious Transmission.* Walnut Creek: Altamira, 2004.

Whitehouse, Harvey, and Luther H. Martin, eds. *Theorizing Religions Past. Archeology, History, and Cognition.* Walnut Creek: Altamira, 2004.

Ritual, Narrative, and Identity in English Pageant Fictions of the Interwar Years

JAN RUPP

1. INTRODUCING PAGEANT FICTIONS

The beginning of the 20th century saw a large number of historical pageants in English towns and cities, which came to be a dominant form of public ritual at the time. Pageants were large-scale performances involving a huge amateur cast from the local community and tracing the town's or city's history through various prominent epochs of the wider, national story of Britain. Ordinary citizens would dress up as fur-clad ancient chieftains, Roman Britons or members of the Elizabethan aristocracy to dramatize a narrative of their origins and glorious progress thence. Pageants were a powerful means of (re-)constructing collective self-images with a view not only to the past but also, more importantly, to the present and future. In this way, historical pageants both highlighted and worked towards containing imperial and national change as well as the modern erosion of community.

This elusive sense of communal life and collective identification is also at the heart of later "pageant fictions," i.e., literary adaptations of the pageant genre especially in the interwar years. As I want to argue in this contribution, both early 20th-century pageantry and later pageant fictions are governed by a dynamic of ritual and narrative, but they hold very different potentials for collective identity respectively. The mass popular spectacles of early 20th-century public ritual relied heavily on narrative meaning-making for transforming notions of imperial Britishness into a more domestic Englishness (cf. Readman). Pageant fictions of the interwar years, for their part, bring to bear the distinctive repertoire of literary narrative, often to reconceive the conventional storytelling of historical pageantry. In doing so, they explore literary ways of representing community by drawing inspiration from ritual while enabling a higher degree of reflexivity than ritual action with regard to the identity constructed. There is a productive tension and cross-fertilization between ritual performances and literary representations, which makes it necessary to pay close attention to the different narrative, ritualistic and media-related properties of pageant script/performance on the one hand, and literary representation on the other.

Before I go into detail of what is ultimately a question of the relationship between ritual and literature as complementary but also competing forms of cultural expression, some further introductory remarks are in order. It is worth explaining more fully in what way early 20th-century historical pageants constituted a type of ritual, what their narrative structures and their implications for ideas of Britishness or Englishness were – and eventually, how these aspects were adapted and reworked in later pageant fictions of the interwar years. This contribution is interested in the distinctive engagement of ritual and narrative in literary versions of pageantry, but this requires a two-step argument which looks first at early 20th-century historical pageantry as an intertextual point of reference and then at its representation in 1930s pageant fictions.

Certainly, historical pageants were not rituals in the traditional sense of the word, which tends to make us think of either pre-modern cultural practices or primitive societies, or of more easily accepted modern-day rituals such as marriage, graduation ceremonies, or funerals. However, they displayed many of the features of what have been called "ritual-like activities" in recent ritual studies (cf. Bell 138ff.).[1] For one thing, pageants constituted a type of ritual because of their iterative character or relative "invariance" (150-53). Many pageants took place annually, and they displayed recurring patterns of telling local history always in connection with national history. This was seldom a straightforward or in any way "objective" representation

---

1 Bell's discussion of "ritual-like activities" highlights the significance of ritual as a cultural phenomenon up until today and argues for the ongoing usefulness of ritual as a critical term.

of history. Pageant scripts and performances were based on highly selective storytelling, capitalizing on grand narratives of heroism and national progress while leaving out or downplaying events which did not fit these agendas.

Moreover, pageants were rituals also with regard to their potential for transformation[2] and in terms of their level of "transcendence" (Michaels 5).[3] As part of their "sacral symbolism" (Bell 155-59), pageants employed not only historical dress and scenery. Importantly, they also projected popular cultural and historical narratives. Invoking pastoral ideas of England and Englishness or the iconic figure of the medieval Anglo-Saxon King Alfred served to transcend the more immediate performance and appeal to some larger goal emerging from this ritual action. Pageants frequently engaged in the power of ritual to inspire a sense of group identity and community.[4] In Edwardian England (1901-10), the transforming power and community-building effect of pageants worked towards shifting notions of British and English identity. Edwardian pageantry responded to a critical moment of imperial change and national self-understanding, which coincided with a more general feeling of anxiety concerning the loss of community and the transformation of life in modernity.

---

2   "Transformation" is often regarded as a key element of ritual per se (cf. Turner; van Gennep; Michaels 4f.).

3   All translations of German-language scholarship in this chapter are mine. Axel Michaels lists five key elements by which rituals are to be defined: "performance" or "embodiment," "formality," "framing," "transformation" or "efficacy," and "transcendence" (4-5). These elements constitute a "polythetic definition" (4) of ritual which gives the salient and most frequently shared features of rituals as a class of phenomena, but does not require that every ritual exhibit all these features at once. Catherine Bell's definition of ritual-like activities consists of a similar set of characteristics, listing "formalism," "traditionalism," "invariance," "rule-governance," "sacral symbolism," and "performance" (cf. 138ff.).

4   This is a basic function of ritual postulated early on in the study of ritual by scholars like Émile Durkheim. Durkheim, for whom ritual, like for many of his contemporaries, was closely connected to the sphere of religious practice, discusses this collectivizing impact of religious rites in *The Elementary Forms of the Religious Life* (cf. 43).

The narrative structures of the Edwardian pageant as well as their connection to the symbolic, transcendent, and identity-making aspects of group ritual were significantly reworked by literary versions of pageantry in the interwar years. I call these literary representations "pageant fictions" in order to point to their status as fictional literature, and to the formal range of literary narrative which they add to the pageant. Elements of literary narrative include additional levels of narrative mediation, specific modes of narrative "experientiality" conveying a broad range of experiences, and the non-pragmatic discourse of literature. Pageant fictions present critical and innovative versions of pageantry, while conversely drawing inspiration from ritual to extend literary themes and styles. Not least because narrative (or more generally aesthetic) aspects are foregrounded in pageant fictions as a matter of their "literariness," they sensitize us to the way in which historical pageants are characterized by narrative and aesthetic structures, too.

The representation of pageantry in writings of the interwar period signals a shift away from the avant-gardist and intellectual endeavour of high modernism to a more encompassing national culture. In this connection, writers covered new ground for the novel of consciousness, for example, by sounding out ways of representing the collective dimension of experiencing and perceiving, which ritual makes available. Likewise, 1930s pageant fictions rethink the historical narratives which in early 20th-century ritual culture served to relocate collective identity from the Empire to an insular, domestic Englishness. They underline the dynamic of imperial change and shifting notions of identity, but they also demonstrate that this connection needs to be specified in view of various stages of generic history through which the pageant can be traced. The connection between ritual and narrative plays out very differently in different cultural forms and media, and there are quite diverse potentials in terms of how and what kinds of Englishness are constructed. Broadly speaking, where early 20th-century pageantry capitalized on the power of ritual and mass spectacle to stir a large number of people into a common pursuit of group identity, pageant fictions take a more nuanced and internally self-reflexive approach, which can also reflect back, externally, on ritual culture.[5]

---

5 This is not to assume some false opposition or maintain a prerogative of literature by which pageant fictions would be defined, negatively, by the putative shortcomings of ritual. Pageant fictions often engage with ritual critically, but

In the two major analytical sections of this contribution, I will look more closely at the forms and functions of ritual and narrative in Edwardian pageantry (2) and 1930s pageant fictions (3) respectively. As a composite term, "pageant fictions" denotes literature and ritual as reciprocal and mutually enriching cultural forms of expression. At the same time, it is precisely because literature and ritual hold different media-specific potentials that this process of cross-fertilization becomes possible. This raises more general questions about the role of fictional literature in ritual culture, which I will take up in concluding my discussion (4).

2. Literal Re-enactment or Narrative Emplotment? Grand Narratives of Englishness and Britishness in Edwardian Pageantry

Around the turn of the 20th century, pageants emerged as a powerful form of public ritual not only in Britain or England, but across the Western world. Writing about "historical pageants in towns and cities of America from the end of the 19th century to the middle of the 20th," Catherine Bell speaks of "a veritable explosion of commemorative pageants in which people used costumes and elaborate scenery to dramatize historical events associated with their community" (161). These pageants, Bell explains, were a means for communities to both confront and resolve their differences, by creating "highly public images – the results of an intense community negotiation and heated disputes over interpretation and significance" (ibid.). Communities came together by retrieving "a particular sense of history and tradition," with pageants serving as "instruments for the very creation and dissemination of civic traditions" (ibid.). In this way, historical pageants were symptomatic of larger developments of growing urbanization, imperial change and the development of the nation state in the late 19th and early 20th centuries. Their telling of historical narratives testifies to the much-discussed nexus between "nation and narration" (cf. Bhabha), or to the as-

---

ritual as a topic in fiction also serves as a catalyst for extending literary modes of representation.

sumption that communities are constituted specifically as "narrative communities" (Müller-Funk 14) or as "imagined communities" (cf. Anderson) through narrative. However, pageants also highlight the role of cultural performance and ritual (indeed of ritual *and* narrative) in this process. Rather than only telling historical narratives, pageants staged and re-enacted history, combining verbal narrative with the multisensory medium of spectacle and performance.

In Britain, the "pageant vogue, or 'Pageantitis' as some Edwardians called it" (Yoshino, *Edwardian Pageant* 2), started with the Sherborne Pageant in 1905, produced by the playwright Louis Napoleon Parker with 900 volunteers to celebrate the 12th centenary of the Sherborne bishopric. This event was followed, to name a few, by the Warwick Pageant in 1906, the Oxford Pageant in 1907 and the York Pageant in 1909. Pageants were popular mass events not only in terms of the number of actors and volunteers they involved, but also with regard to the thousands of visitors who travelled around the country as part of a new form of local tourism. The six pageants organized by Parker alone involved "13,000 performers and half a million spectators" (3). Closely connected to the Edwardian period as they were, historical pageants in Britain continued to be a popular spectacle up to the middle of the 20th century, and especially in the crisis-ridden interwar years.

To some degree, of course, pageantry is one of the "ur-genres of English literature" (Esty, "Amnesia" 247) and has been linked to the Elizabethan age specifically, which, as an historical episode, is a prominent element in the Edwardian pageant's wide-ranging historical display. Other influences on the Edwardian pageant include 19th-century German folk festivals, the so-called "*Erinnerungsspiele*" (Withington, "Parker" 512) which celebrated local history by means of an amateur dramatic production. Louis Napoleon Parker was also an admirer of the new music drama of Richard Wagner. At the same time, despite all this intertextuality or "interrituality" (cf. Gladigow), the Edwardian historical pageant was regarded as a distinctively new form of public ritual by pageant-makers like Napoleon Parker, who claimed that "I invented a new form of dramatic art with the Sherborne Pageant" (qtd. in Yoshino, *Edwardian Pageant* 4). In his autobiography *Several of My Lives*, Parker underlined this innovative and differential character: "It is not a street procession./ It is not a gala./ It is not wayzegoose. [sic.]/ It is not a fête./ It is not a beanfeast./ It is not done on trollies./ It is not *tableaux-vivants*" (278). Robert Withington, a contemporary of Parker's and the author of the two-volume work *English Pageantry. An Historical Outline* (1918/1936), confirmed this view when he distinguished Parker's "modern 'community drama'" from older pageantry (cf. xviii-xix). As Withington argued, "the technique has changed, so far as the Parkerian pageant is concerned, becoming more that of the theatre" – despite certain other continuities and the fact that the "pageantic soul remains" (xvii). Withington's analysis pinpoints a characteristic convergence of theatre and ritual in the Edwardian pageant, which is in line with general tendencies of early 20th-century drama as described by theatre historians. As Erika Fischer-Lichte observes, Edwardian pageants brought together theatre and ritual, with rituals becoming theatricalized at the same time as theatre needed to open up to a degree of amateurism required by the all-embracing nature of group ritual (cf. 114). Amateurism was one of the central elements of Edwardian pageantry and its more democratic and socially inclusive outlook. The "newer 'folk play' or 'historical pageant,'" Withington explained, "is not limited to any class; [...] a pageant must, of necessity be a community affair" (*English Pageantry* xvii).

Another distinctive feature of the Edwardian pageant was its historical focus. According to Paul Readman, this was a "significant – and significantly new – cultural development" (168). As he explains, "pageant performances had of course taken place before the 1900s. But earlier forms of pageantry [...] had focused on the here and now, not on the past. While early 20th-century pageants had some aesthetic affinities with their predecessors, the emphasis on the past had not been seen before" (ibid.). This emphasis on the past in the Edwardian pageant concerned both English history and English local space. It testified to the "early twentieth-century currency of the idea that English national identity was importantly predicated on love of locality" (176). At the high point of Empire, this instigated a slightly paradoxical movement of the cultural imagination turning "inward" to the mother country, resulting in a "persistence and growth of insular ideas of English identity in the late nineteenth and early twentieth centuries" (189). These developments were reflected and influenced by the fact that "historical pageants celebrated the continuities of a locally grounded *English* nationhood with the empire left out" (186).

This shift from ideas of Britishness to Englishness might not have been as clear-cut as Readman suggests. In the first book-length study of the Edwardian historical pageant, Ayako Yoshino agrees with Readman's overall emphasis on "the Englishness as opposed to the Britishness of the nationalism appealed to in many pageant narratives," citing his argument that "Edwardian pageants assigned a 'distinctly peripheral' role to Imperial narratives" (*Edwardian Pageant* 125). But she still identifies a continuity with imperial identities in the pageant narratives, stressing "the allusion to imperial themes [... which] demonstrate that endorsements of imperial identity were part of the product" (ibid.). Moreover, Parker's seemingly self-contained and insular version of the English national story acquired an imperial dimension when the Parkerian pageant became a successful model outside of England as part of a "cultural imperialism." With regard to the history of Canadian theatre, Alan Filewod observes that the "pageant form [...] spread throughout the British Empire through the efforts of the British director Louis Napoleon Parker" (19). As Filewod explains, pageantry "circulated a romantic myth of Englishness through the Empire and into the United States," where it "expressed a myth of classical form" (ibid.). This social dimension of the pageant as a cultural export certainly did not sever ties with the Empire entirely. Focusing more on the text-internal dimension of pageant scripts and their narrative set-up, however, there is no doubt that pageant-makers like Napoleon Parker did strive for local English authenticity. In Parker's words, the Edwardian pageant was supposed to be "Drama covering all English history from 800 B.C. to the Great Rebellion; written by Englishmen, set to music by Englishmen, costumed and acted by English men and women" (qtd. in Yoshino, "Creator" 52). Elsewhere, Parker observed that

> Scenes in a Pageant convey a thrill no stage can provide when they are represented on the very ground where they took place in real life; especially when they are played, as often happens, by descendants of the historical protagonists, speaking a verbatim reproduction of the actual words used by them. (280)

It is true that Edwardian pageants sought historical verisimilitude and authenticity in terms of time, place and dramatic personnel. However, far from providing an objective or authentic account, they were heavily involved in narrative meaning-making. Joshua Esty observes that "[i]n a sense, the historical pageant tries, finally, to replace representation (symbolization, substitution, condensation) with literal re-enactment" ("Amnesia" 249). Nevertheless, it is worth distinguishing between the attempt to replace representation, on the part of pageant-makers like Napoleon Parker, and the eventual dramatic work which was a highly stylized representation all the same. Edwardian pageants did not simply "glean" identity from history, but configured the national past in such a way as to invest it with a more localized sense of Englishness to begin with.

It is important to differentiate between the kind of representation that pageant-makers professed to be striving for and the kind of national story they effectively constructed. Hayden White's notion of "narrative emplotment," i.e. his analysis of the extent to which historical representations tend to be superimposed with narrative and generic structures, is key to the study of the relationship between ritual and narrative in the Edwardian pageant, too. According to White, "[e]mplotment is the way by which a sequence of events fashioned into a story is gradually revealed to be a story of a particular kind" (7). In this way, the pageant's representation of history turns out to be all about symbolization, substitution, and condensation, and anything but a literal re-enactment or "verbatim reproduction," as Napoleon Parker suggested. Emplotment is a central mechanism by which pageants and the larger historical narratives which they staged were marked out as notable or "tellable" events (cf. Prince 28). It substantially constructed pageants as significant (media) events rather than reflecting their eventfulness or "tellability" as some kind of pre-existing quality.

As with many narratives, pageants fashioned the national past into a particular kind of story through the selection and combination of events, as well as through the degree of coherence they established between events. They did so according to narrative logic rather than to historical truth or facts, and actually produced very different versions of the nation's story. While Parker argued for covering "English history from 800 B.C." (see above), many pageants started at the time of Roman Britain, preferring a state of civilization, even though it was imposed by foreign Roman invaders, to the indigenous but more savage origins of the ancient Britons. Either way, the very choice of a beginning was important, as was the episode which the pageant ended with. If "the first episode suggested origin and was important in providing a point of reference for the narrative of progress that was often a feature of pageants" (Yoshino, *Edwardian Pageant* 73), the last episode, the Glorious Revolution of 1688 in many cases, demonstrated the climax of that narrative. Subsequent events, such as the Acts of Union with Scotland in 1707 and Ireland in 1801, or the history of the British Empire, were deliberately left out. In between beginning and ending, pageants ensured narrative continuity and coherence by glossing over historical caesurae such as the Norman Conquest, and through the "elision and watering down of discontinuity" (Readman 193). Instead, they capitalized on cultural narratives of heroism as part of a "preoccupation with 'great men'" (75), such as the Anglo-Saxon King Alfred, as representatives of the English nation at large. To a significant extent, it was only through these narrative manoeuvres fashioning the national past into a story of a particular kind, in White's sense, that the Edwardian pageant could hope for the sort of ritual transformation towards a more self-contained and circumscribed English identity that it sought to achieve.

The reason for this process of narrative meaning-making was not so much the past, however, but the present and future of turn-of-the-century Britain. Like many commemorative events, the Edwardian pageant demonstrated that cultural remembrance, despite its degree of retrospection, is essentially and paradoxically a forward-looking affair which responds to current problems of the present and future (cf. Bal et al.). The context in which the Edwardian pageant developed was "a time of growing social and political tension at home, and new challenges to Britain's international position" (Readman 155). For Erika Fischer-Lichte, the pageant movement both indicated and tried to contain a moment of crisis, precisely by harking back to a time when many modern anxieties, such as the fragmentation of society, individualism, or the loss of solidarity and cohesion in the wake of urbanization and industrialization had not taken hold yet (114). Another factor is the imminent danger of the First World War, or the much-discussed scenario of foreign invasion in turn-of-the-century literature more generally, as evidenced by an early representation of the pageant in fiction, the novel *Brother Copas* (1911) by Arthur Quiller-Couch. In it, one of the characters cites the threat of German invasion – "heaven knows how soon the Germans will be invading us?" (199) – as a motivation to leave class differences behind and shore up England's insular community in the spirit of the Edwardian pageant: "Lady Shaftesbury had won great popularity by insisting that, in a business so truly national, no class distinctions were to be drawn" (200).⁶ This quotation already touches on the ways in which the pageant movement was dealt with in literary representations, which will be discussed in the next section.

3. ENGLISH PAGEANT FICTIONS OF THE INTERWAR YEARS: CRITICAL REFLECTION AND LITERARY-RITUAL CROSS-FERTILIZATION IN THE MODERNIST NOVEL OF CONSCIOUSNESS AND IN DRAMATIC ADAPTATIONS

Resonating with the communitarian appeal in Quiller-Couch's *Brother Copas*, a similar sense of crisis and anxiety is also characteristic of English pageant fictions in the interwar period and specifically the 1930s when, somewhat belatedly, the pageant vogue attracted the interest of modernist writers. Among others, T.S. Eliot, E.M. Forster, John Cowper Powys and Virginia Woolf produced quite a diverse body of works, using the pageant as a dramatic form (Eliot, Forster), as a narrative device (Woolf, Powys), or even in combination with subgenres such as crime fiction, as in Victor L. Whitechurch's novel *Murder at the Pageant* (1930). As Yoshino rightly points out, fictional representations of the pageant, most of which were published during the 1930s and 1940s but include post-war novels such as A.S. Byatt's *The Virgin in the Garden* (1978), "sometimes give an insight into contemporary experience of these events or later changes in the pageant's image" and "can give clues to understanding the experience of the pageant by individual participants" (*Edwardian Pageant* 12). Indeed, many pageant fictions imaginatively reconstruct how pageants were received by contemporary audiences. Actually, their full potential or complete range of functions goes well beyond such a referential reading.⁷ With conveying ex-

---

6   For the currency of invasion narratives in turn-of-the-century English literature, see Frank.
7   On account of their fictional status, literary pageant texts involve no truth claim, but imaginatively assemble a possible set of (frequently conflicting) responses in order to put the pageant up for discussion, rather than seeking to establish what responses were articulated in historical actuality.

perientiality being a privilege and prime concern especially of narrative fiction (cf. Fludernik), pageant fictions retrieve and make available an often more diverse and multi-faceted range of experience than, for example, newspaper reports. In the non-pragmatic discourse of literature, pageant fictions often engage critically with the narrative manoeuvres of early 20th-century pageantry, its pursuit of collective identity, and the power of ritual. Importantly, they do so in a way not available to other texts and media, let alone to ritual performances, as I shall argue in more detail later on.

If fictional representations developed further the forms and functions of pageantry, engaging with ritual also served writers to further develop their themes and narrative styles. As a popular cultural form, pageantry seemed to achieve what had long been a modernist aspiration, i.e., bridging the gap between art and life. In turning to this folkloristic genre, writers like Forster and Woolf significantly extended their previous oeuvre. In *The Waves* (1931) and *The Years* (1937), Woolf had already shifted her concern with individual minds (as in *Mrs Dalloway* of 1924) to a more encompassing perspective on social life – a project which had failed, according to her own assessment.[8] Along these lines, placing a village pageant at the centre of her posthumously published novel *Between the Acts* (1941) seemed to hold a new promise, while also presenting an opportunity to reconfigure styles of psychological realism. The result is an often innovative configuration of ritual and narrative in the pageant fictions by Woolf and others, which can be appreciated by performing close narratological analyses.

Given the pageant's focus on collective identity and group ritual, many pageant fictions probe new ways of representing community and of capturing the collective processes of perception and experience involved. In John Cowper Powys's *A Glastonbury Romance* (1932), for example, internal focalization is presented in an extremely fluid and sometimes disorienting way. Powys chronicles the emergence of modern-day Glastonbury as a religious centre, which, in fictional terms, is boosted by the novel's monumental pageant, involving almost the entire fictional cast and providing a

---

8 As Woolf wrote on *The Years* in a letter to Stephen Spender on 7 April 1937, "[w]hat I meant I think was to give a picture of society as a whole; give characters from every side; turn them towards society, not private life; [...] Compose into one vast many-sided group at the end; [...] Of course I completely failed" (116).

mythology or "invented tradition" for Glastonbury's future as a centre of spiritual tourism.[9] Powys's voluminous novel uses narrative modes to represent multiple minds, but also to transcend them and render an overarching, collective level, at times diffusing the connection between identifiable characters and certain streams of consciousness. Techniques of multiple focalization are not unknown to modernist writers, but this way of using it to somehow reverse the inward turn of previous modernist fiction seems to be a specific influence or representation of the collective outlook of group ritual. Furthermore, Woolf experiments in *Between the Acts* with a type of "we-narrative"[10] alongside internal focalization, which is characteristically but also somewhat inconclusively introduced precisely at points where the novel's ritual action demands the emergence of a sense of togetherness, as I will discuss more closely below.

It is most plausible when Esty says of Powys's novel that "the most important formal feature of the novel [... is] its experiment in perspective" (*Shrinking Island* 68). As Esty suggests, "Powys seems eager to refine, and in some ways to outflank, the novel of consciousness" (68-69), to a point where "the details of an individual consciousness are far less important and interesting than its debt to a collective unconscious" (69). A similar argument could be made for Woolf's novel, though the larger claim this implies about the role of pageant fictions in the history of modernism requires a more systematic analysis that for reasons of space can only be hinted at here. However, for the purpose of this contribution it can be stated that writers like Woolf and Powys not only opened a new vista on the pageant

---

9 The connection of religious or spiritual renewal and pageantry in Powys's novel retrospectively elucidates a central aspect which already characterizes the pageant movement of the Edwardian period. As part of its various functions, early 20th-century pageantry responded to what Max Weber famously called the "disenchantment of the world," a process of rationalization and secularization in modernity in the course of which religious and mystic beliefs were relegated from public to private spheres. Against this background, Edwardian pageantry can be understood as an instance of "re-enchantment," reintroducing for spiritual and not least visual pleasure highly aestheticized displays of myth, magic, symbol, and ritual to the public realm (cf. Weber; Landy and Saler).

10 For the notion of "we-narrative," see chapter 6.1.1 of Fludernik's *Towards a 'Natural' Narratology*.

and on how it was experienced, but that in dealing with pageantry they also extended their writing. In developing new narrative forms, their pageant fictions performed an important function of literary genres "as 'answers' to cultural problems" (cf. van Gorp and Musarra-Schroeder ii), in this case the lack of a more communitarian literary form to respond to a context of "culture and crisis in Britain in the 1930s" (cf. Clark et al.). What seems crucial from the point of view of ritual is that this innovation in narrative was prompted or at least informed by Powys and others engaging with the pageant as a ritual form.

Like earlier Edwardian pageantry, literary representations of the interwar years can be seen to serve as both symptom and solution at a time of crisis (cf. Fischer-Lichte), which was both political and literary in nature. It was a political crisis because Woolf and others became "faced with the cultural isolation of the 1930s – [...] precipitated by [...] continental politics and imperial decline" (Esty, "Amnesia" 250). It was also a literary crisis insofar as "they began seeking [more] acceptable versions of national art" and "experimented with new forms, revising and abandoning [some of] their most successful practices of the 1920s" (246). Forster's abandonment of the novel after *A Passage to India* (1924) seems significant in this connection, while Woolf also engages very critically with the novel form in her writings of the 1930s.

In taking up the pageant-play, however, the way Woolf and her fellow writers made use of the genre was significantly different from Edwardian pageant-makers such as Napoleon Parker. They did display a new ritual consciousness, similar to the earlier pageant-makers, but were wary of advocating a return to ritual and domestic Englishness with quite the same confidence. Especially Woolf's representation of the pageant in *Between the Acts* is conspicuous for its scepticism against national sentiment as well as the power of ritual. As in her book-length essay *Three Guineas* (1938), Woolf is acutely wary of jingoist, paternalistic, and imperial overtones of collectivization, developing a pacifist and feminist alternative to the dominant models of nation and community of her time instead. In the process, pageantry clearly serves as a vehicle in searching for this new sense of community. In contrast to the slightly authoritarian or "authorial" figures of the Edwardian pageant-makers, however, the multiple, fragmented internal focalization of Woolf's village pageant can be seen to problematize its community-building impact and identity-forming power rather than simply asserting it.

The scale of Woolf's pageant is altogether smaller than the mass spectacles of the Edwardian period, but this helps her to scrutinize in miniature the workings of the pageant as a group ritual. The novel's action takes place in the small village of Pointz Hall, where the annual pageant is staged with the threat of war looming large and any sense of community becoming increasingly fragile even in a rural setting which is seemingly untainted by modern anxieties of social fragmentation. *"Dispersed are we ..."* (87), a crackling gramophone tune played during the play, provides the atmospheric undertones of the scene. In this situation, Woolf explores the remedial potential of the pageant in close dialogue with the genre's tradition, deriving specifically narrative ways of representing community, too.

Woolf partly adheres to tradition, in the characterization of her pageant master, for example, citing the idea that "strong leadership [...] was [...] a vital element of the modern pageant" (Yoshino, "Creator" 56): "'Bossy' they called her privately [...]. Her abrupt manner and stocky figure, her thick ankles and sturdy shoes; her rapid decisions barked out in guttural accents [...]. No one liked to be ordered about singly. But in little troops they appealed to her. Someone must lead" (58). However, the fact that this is a female character already goes some way towards suggesting that Woolf presents a different version of the male-oriented narrative of progress and "great men," which was often the backbone of the Edwardian pageant. Instead of the male-dominated "authorial narration" of figures like Louis Napoleon Parker, whose single-authored books of words contrast with the collaborative nature of the pageant performance, Woolf's fictional representation dethrones the grand narrative of Englishness, however localized, and foregrounds the experiential dimension of her village pageant by reconstructing multiple points of view. Eventually, the novel seems to be interested not so much in the pageant itself, but in the way it is perceived by the audience, focusing on the characters' thoughts and feelings "between the acts" rather than the pageant-play as such. During this process, with the narrative switching from mind to mind, it is frequently difficult to tell which character serves as an internal focalizer at a given moment. Woolf seems to purposefully blur the boundaries between various characters' thoughts in order to combine them into some collective perception of the events. At certain points, the novel moreover switches into a "we-narrative" with the community as a whole serving as a centre of consciousness:

> They stared at the view, as if something might happen in one of those fields to relieve them of the intolerable burden of remaining silent, doing nothing, in company. Their minds and bodies were close, yet not close enough. We aren't free, each of them felt separately, to feel or think separately, nor yet to fall asleep. We're too close; but not close enough. So they fidgeted. (60)

At points like these, Woolf's narrative overtly reflects, and dramatizes in narrative terms, the pageant's goal of collectivization and community. However, it is precisely Woolf's constant zooming in and out between narratorial accounts, internal focalization and passages of we-narrative that highlights the precarious nature of this endeavour. Symptomatically, the quotation above documents a highly ambivalent need for togetherness which is never fully realized, in fact, it is resisted as much as desired. As opposed to the Edwardian pageant which delivered a ready-made product for easy identification, Woolf focuses on the quest for group identity as a highly complex and fraught process, staging it on the level of form as a very matter of narrative representation.[11]

If these techniques of representing consciousness expand on Woolf's psychological realism from her earlier novels, her "feminization" of the pageant concerns not only aspects of narrative voice or discourse.[12] It is al-

---

11 Woolf's innovative treatment of narrative manifests itself with regard to both the modernist novel of consciousness and the "we-narrative" in her medley of styles. "We-narratives" are usually a type of homodiegetic narrative in which the narrator is part of a group of collective internal focalizers. Woolf uses various modes of representing speech and consciousness when it comes to the pronoun "we," but especially passages of interior monologue are very brief and never grow into a sustained first-person narrative that would self-confidently articulate group identity. Ever wary of the less benign tipping points of collectivization as well as acutely aware of the modern erosion of community, Woolf ultimately retains the heterodiegetic, figural narrative and its degree of narratorial control, as well as the degree of reflexivity between the levels of story and discourse respectively.

12 For the distinction between "story" and "discourse" in narratology, see Shen.

so visible in terms of ritual sequencing, i.e., in terms of the more story-oriented question of which historical episodes are selected and who the actors in them are. Again, in contrast to the Edwardian pageant's celebration of great English heroes, many of the protagonists in Woolf's pageant are girls and women, so that it "bears a distinctly feminine face" (Wiley 13). Additionally, these female characters are frequently anti-heroines, though not at their own cost, but, conspicuously, at the expense of the conventional grandeur they are supposed to represent. At the beginning of the novel's pageant-play, for example, "England is personified [...] as a girl who forgets her lines" (Yoshino, "Creator" 54):

While they looked apprehensively and some finished their sentences, a small girl, like a rosebud in pink, advanced; took her stand on a mat, behind a couch, hung with leaves, and piped:

Gentles and simples, I address you all ...

So it was the play then. Or was it the prologue?

Come hither for our festival (she continued)
This is a pageant, all may see
Drawn from our island history
   England am I ...

'She's England,' they whispered. 'It's begun.' 'The prologue,' they added, looking down at the programme.
'*England am I*,' she piped again; and stopped.
She had forgotten her lines. (*BTA* 70)

Arguably the most important change in Woolf's novel as in Eliot's and Forster's dramatic adaptations, however, is the fact that their historical displays do not end in the 17th century, but frequently continue up to the present. Where the Edwardian pageant glorifies the past, these accounts are parodied or replaced by alternative narratives in many pageant fictions, and are importantly juxtaposed with a critical look at the present. For example, rather than telling narratives of heroism, E.M. Forster's *The Abinger Pageant* (1934) satirically replaces stock protagonists such as King Alfred the Great with the worst of kings, i.e., with highly controversial figures such as the medieval King John. Furthermore, Forster invents a narratorial figure –

"This Woodman is the narrator" (385) – who leads the audience through the play and comments on the action. In the prologue, he gives a brief rundown of the action which mocks the pre-text of the historical pageant:

> And now the Britons are coming are coming down the paths I have cut, and you shall see the Romans come, then the bugle will sound and, like the falling leaves, the Romans will go back to Rome. Then the Saxons will come, and after them monks and the Coming of Christ. We will show you a great battle next – and then the Normans will come, and at the end of trouble there will be peace for a little – Domesday and its Book, and the settling of the land. (Ibid.)

As this passage shows, Forster's selection and presentation of historical events continuously debunks the conventional emplotment of the Edwardian pageant's grand narrative, moreover by foregrounding the rural space in which his pageant is staged, the fields of the Abinger parish. In his "Foreword to Visitors," Forster writes: "Our Pageant is not planned quite on ordinary pageant lines. It is rural rather than historical and tries to show the continuity of country life" (384). Consequently, Forster's pageant is a celebration of the English countryside and the pre-modern built environment – trees, flowers, place names, historical sites – rather than monarchs and great historical deeds. These items of nature and historic architecture now seem to vouchsafe English identity, and they are presented in a quite different, almost "non-narrative" way. Where Edwardian pageant-makers chronicle a story of progress, Forster presents lists or catalogues of place names and landmarks, which are interspersed with various historical episodes and further diffuse the smooth continuity of the Edwardian pageant's formula. Identity in Forster's play relies on the materiality of things of nature, as much as on the construction of narrative. The countryside provides an enduring reminder of "another England, green and eternal" (399), which is juxtaposed with the dystopian scenario of present-day England sketched by Forster's narrator in the epilogue: "Houses and bungalows, hotels, restaurants and flats, arterial roads, by-passes, petrol bumps and pylons – are these going to be England?" (Ibid.) As a commemorative event and public ritual, the Edwardian historical pageant was also motivated by the present and future, but Forster's treatment of narrative and ritual is deliberately different.

As in Forster's *Abinger Pageant*, which concludes with an episode entitled "Towards our own times," Woolf lets her pageant continue until the present time, and she, too, presents a very different set of episodes preceding it. Woolf's historical display is frequently a "literary" history. Instead of some historiographical narrative, she selects a number of dramatic texts from various epochs which come to represent the Restoration period, for example, and are performed as play-within-the-play in the novel's pageant. These literary texts contribute to charting an alternative version of the national story, alongside Woolf's privileging of female and ordinary characters in place of the male-dominated and often nationalistic narrative of the Edwardian pageant. Moreover, Woolf directly confronts present-day anxieties, which in the Edwardian pageant are ultimately bypassed and overcompensated for by glorifying the past. The last scene in Woolf's novel, tellingly entitled "The present time. Ourselves" (*BTA* 160), readily leaves the audience guessing: "'Ourselves ...' They turned to the programme. But what could she know about ourselves? The Elizabethans yes; the Victorians, perhaps; but ourselves, sitting here on a June day in 1939 – it was ridiculous. 'Myself' – it was impossible." (Ibid.) This quotation pinpoints the "cultural problem" of identity, which both Edwardian pageants and later pageant fictions responded to, but each with a very different configuration of ritual and narrative respectively. Where in the Edwardian pageant identity as a sense of self and nation emerged as a ready-made product from a rather circumscribed range of history, modernist writers like Woolf deliberately seemed to withhold narrative closure and present self-identification as an ongoing process. In doing so, they exposed readers and spectators to precisely the present-day reality which the historical pageant shunned away from – the loss of identity, the dispersal of community, the fragmentation of modern life.

Given the extent of mockery and criticism in 1930s pageant fictions, the question remains why Woolf, Forster and others did after all turn to the pageant. As has become clear in the examples above, part of the answer is that these writers rejected the pageant's nationalistic rhetoric, but not its communitarian appeal. This was in response to what appears as a dead end of late modernism, as writers "confronted the end of a socially alienating but aesthetically dazzling metropolitan life by exploring a more public and communal art" (Esty, "Amnesia" 246). In the circumstances, "the pageant-play seemed to offer a kind of spontaneous folk authenticity, not to mention a more participatory model for both the production and consumption of art" (250). This idea of a more public and communal art is dramatized in the final scene of Woolf's pageant, when the actors turn to the spectators and hold mirrors up to them. Symbolically breaking the fourth wall and involving the spectators as actors, this scene anticipates later 20th-century trends of drama pioneered by theatre practitioners like Jerzy Grotowski, who created an experimental theatre where the distinction between actor and role, between stage and audience and eventually between art and life collapses. This constitutes a convergence between ritual and theatre, as in the anthropological performance theories of Richard Schechner, where ritual and theatre are conceived as related modes of human expression and interaction (cf. Schechner).

Apart from looking ahead to these later developments of 20th-century drama, Woolf's evocation of a kind of ritual theatre also involves a highly suggestive "mirror scene," setting up a moment of self-recognition which immediately elicits uneasy feelings among the audience:

And the audience saw themselves, not whole by any means, but at any rate sitting still.
[...] It was now. Ourselves.
So that was her little game! To show us up, as we are, here and now. (*BTA* 166-167)

Symptomatically, there is a lingering sense of fragmentation in self-recognition and collectivization ("not whole by any means") in this quotation, though later on the villagers profess the value of group ritual: "O let us, the audience echoed, keep together. For there is joy, sweet joy, in company." (*BTA* 177) Eventually, however, the we-narrative is not sustained but reinstalled to its place within Woolf's medley of narrative modes as the pageant performance ends and the community disperse into their individual homes. The novel's pageant does engender a process of self-identification, but one that has hardly been completed, as Woolf's highly fragmentary narrative representation of collective consciousness shows.

At last, Woolf's novel ends with another evocation of communal theatre, or of the convergence of theatre and ritual located by theatre scholars like Erika Fischer-Lichte in the pageant movement. Having returned home, a young protagonist couple, estranged from themselves and from each other, is "[l]eft alone together for the first time that day" (*BTA* 197). As the evening invades, their marital silence and alienation become unbearable, thrown into relief by the day's events and the sense of community, however fragile, glimpsed in the village pageant. At this point, Woolf inserts another powerful reference to the theatre as the couple begins to act in the drama of their lives: "Then the curtain rose. They spoke." (*BTA* 197). These, the last two sentences of Woolf's narrative, suggest a continuation of the kind of ritual theatre that the pageant represents. They seem to resound with the gramophone's earlier final tune: "The gramophone was affirming in tones there was no denying, triumphant yet valedictory: *Dispersed are we; who have come together. But,* the gramophone asserted, *let us retain whatever made that harmony.*" (*BTA* 176-177). Regarding the dystopian atmosphere surrounding the novel's content, the context of its production and its posthumous publication after the author's self-chosen death, this is a suggestive concluding image of community drama in which the possibility of art and collective expression is envisioned as a lived-in practice.

4. CONCLUSION: PAGEANT FICTIONS AS A MEDIUM OF RITUAL CULTURE AND THEIR POTENTIAL FOR COLLECTIVE IDENTITY

Woolf's decision to end with an intermedial reference to ritual as social drama emphasizes once more the hybrid character of her pageant-novel, in which novel and pageant seem to operate in productive tension. This view is in line with Esty's suggestion of Powys's *A Glastonbury Romance* 'outflanking' the novel of consciousness (cf. Esty, *Shrinking Island* 69), or with Forster's abandonment of the novel form if interpreted in this sense.[13]

---

13 In a BBC interview of 1958, Forster answered the question of why he stopped writing novels as follows: "One of the reasons [...] is that the social aspect of the world changed so very much. I had been accustomed to write about the old vanished world with its homes and its family life and its comparative peace. All that went, and though I can think about it, I cannot put it into fiction form." In this light, the historicity and folk authenticity of the pageant seem to offer a viable alternative to the novel for Forster, even if he rejected much of the Edwardian model in his own pageant-plays.

Whatever Woolf's concluding vision of ritual theatre, though, it is tellingly open-ended, and balanced with a large number of other instances of ritual action in the text, which are treated with a marked degree of irony and reservation rather than straightforward endorsement. It does seem as if Woolf tentatively believes in pageantry as an element of national culture,[14] but it has to go through a process of fictional inspection first, as made possible through the non-pragmatic, multi-level and internally self-reflexive medium of the novel. The same goes for dramatic adaptations like Forster's *The Abinger Pageant*, which reworks ritual and collective English identity along similar lines. Pageant fictions are indeed an important medium of reflecting on ritual culture. In the end, one of the prime functions of pageant fictions consists in their potential as a tool for thinking about ritual and identity, just as dealing with ritual extends the repertory of fictional narrative representation.

Although different artistic forms are often placed in a constellation of rivalry, pageant fictions do not pit literature against ritual, but explore these as mutually illuminating and maybe even complementary forms of expression, which both respond to similar cultural problems or challenges. In doing so, they open up new perspectives on the pageant, while the pageant in turn serves Powys and others to adapt the novel of consciousness (as much as "outflanking" it) by including a collective dimension of perception and experience.

In order for this process of literary-ritual cross-fertilization to be possible, however, the example of pageant fictions also makes clear that literature and ritual hold very different potentials respectively. This invites discussion in some more general terms of the role of literature in early 20th-century ritual culture. If the Edwardian historical pageant and the later pageant fictions of the interwar years turn out to be very different moments in generic history, they may also account for a specific potential of literary representations of ritual compared to real-life ritual performances. As we have seen, pageants were taken up in a range of different forms and media

---

14 See Esty, *Shrinking Island* 253: "Although many readers continue to take the novel [*Between the Acts*] as a vexed recoil from group politics of any kind, a number of critics have recently observed that the novel's interest in national identity, though obviously ironized, is not fully rejected and indeed marks a kind of turn in Woolf's thinking."

– books of words, ritual performances, and eventually more literary dramatic texts and novels. Further material can be found in documentary text types, newspaper reports, ego-documents, souvenir books, and so forth, which I was not able to include here. All these forms and generic manifestations are governed by a dynamic of ritual and narrative, and at no point in generic history do we have a simple reproduction of history and identity. On the contrary, like literary texts, ritual scripts and pageant performances "explicitly model the world" and "do not attempt to reflect the real world accurately" (Bell 161).[15] Yet, if ritual performances go on to "reduce and simplify it ['the real world'] so as to create more or less coherent systems of categories that can then be projected [...] over the chaos of human experience" (ibid.), this does not necessarily hold true for literary representations of ritual. "Literary" rituals may also choose to "render experience coherently meaningful" (ibid.), like performances, but they may just as well stay with the complexity of meaning and, first and foremost, offer meaning and experience for critical inspection and reflection.

Eventually, because pageant fictions of the interwar period dealt with the nexus between ritual and narrative differently than Edwardian ritual scripts and performances, they also seem to hold different potentials for the making of identity and of Englishness, which is a central function of the pageant as such. Where the popular mass events of the Edwardian era overwhelmed spectators into ritual conformity, as many contemporary reports and historical studies suggest, later pageant fictions clearly made a more nuanced set of responses possible. Rather than falling in step with the patriotism of the Edwardian era, writers like Eliot, Forster and Woolf withheld narrative closure and rendered questions of historical representation and identity open to discussion. The pageant offered a possibility of integrating art and social life for these writers, but this seemed possible only after deconstructing the stock narratives of national heroism which were inscribed in the genre's memory.

---

15 Quite similar to literature, ritual is set apart from the everyday world, which enables it to critically intervene there, as Bruce Kapferer notes: "Ritual as a dynamic in virtuality that has no essential or necessary relation to the ordinary realities that surround it may, because of this fact, be greatly empowered as a force that can pragmatically intervene in ordinary realities" (35).

Woolf's narrative style in particular reconstructs a more multi-faceted picture of the pageant and its experience across "emic" and "etic" (or participant and observer) perspectives. It documents a variety of different points of view which, in the authorial narrations of books of words and their performances, tend to collapse in favour of synthesizing and emotionally-charged images of consensus. If Woolf's representation is anything to go by, what could be inferred from it regarding the function of literature and of literary representations of rituals? As Bell notes, ritual performances are liable to "both generate and integrate differences," but these are resolved in a "final performance depicting a synthetic consensus in very visible and memorable images of the hard-won communal cooperation" (161). On a related note, Alan Filewod has argued that "[p]ageants are regulatory readings that propose and stabilize ideologically determined communities, and, in that sense, they recruit the audience as complicit co-performers" (13). According to him, "pageants leave no room for critical negotiation, they offer a parade of icons that progressively accumulate as a narrative embodiment of the (presumably) consensual ideology shared by the audience" (ibid.). As cultural performances, pageants are indeed an effective way of disseminating norms and values, but their immense media-specific power in doing so by providing an all-encompassing, multi-sensory mass experience also tends to be a downside when it comes to the possibility for participants to decide for themselves whether to adopt these norms and values or not. As Bell notes with regard to the fascist spectacles of the 1930s, cultural performances are susceptible to manipulation and misuse precisely because of their collectivizing impact: "The sheer size of these spectacles, with hundreds of thousands marching, singing, and waving flags, guaranteed that the event overwhelmed and swept along the majority of those in attendance" (162).

On balance, this view is probably too deterministic or sceptical when it comes to the agency of participants and the possibility to dissent. What is more, Bell describes a special kind of large-scale mass spectacle rather than ritual per se. As recent studies on ritual reflexivity (or reflexivity in rituals) have shown, rituals do not necessarily impose meaning from the top down, but continuously evolve in a self-reflexive, bottom-up process (cf. Stausberg). Still, there is a case to be made for a difference in degree, because literary representations of ritual make a wider range of experience available and thus allow for a greater degree of reflexivity, too. Literary rituals do not mirror the real world or reproduce a real-life ritual, but open up a space from which one might not only re-live but also reconfigure ritual and collective identity in a more nuanced way than is possible in performances of ritual. In this light, pageant fictions offer important insights into early 20th-century ritual culture as well as into debates over the making of national identity in the interwar period, and encourage further discussion of the complex literary mimesis and formal-aesthetic rhetoric of ritual by which they proceed.

REFERENCES

Anderson, Benedict. *Imagined Communities. Reflections on the Origin and Spread of Nationalism*. Rev. ed. London: Verso, 1991 [1983].
Bal, Mieke, Jonathan Crewe, and Leo Spitzer, eds. *Acts of Memory. Cultural Recall in the Present*. Hanover, NH: UP of New England, 1999.
Bell, Catherine M. *Ritual. Perspectives and Dimensions*. New York: Oxford UP, 1997.
Bhabha, Homi, ed. *Nation and Narration*. London: Routledge, 1990.
Clark, John, Margot Heinemann, David Margolies, and Carole Snee, eds. *Culture and Crisis in Britain in the 1930s*. London: Lawrence & Wishart, 1979.
Durkheim, Émile. *The Elementary Forms of the Religious Life*. Transl. Joseph Ward Swain. London: George Allen & Unwin Ltd, 1915.
Esty, Joshua D. "Amnesia in the Fields: Late Modernism, Late Imperialism, and the English Pageant-Play." *ELH* 69.1 (2002): 245-276.
—. *A Shrinking Island. Modernism and National Culture in England*. Princeton, NJ: Princeton UP, 2004.
Filewod, Alan. *Performing Canada. The Nation Enacted in the Imagined Theatre*. Kamloops, BC: The University College of the Cariboo, 2002.
Fischer-Lichte, Erika. "Massenspektakel der Zwischenkriegszeit als Krisensymptome und Krisenbewältigung." *Krisis! Krisenszenarien, Diagnosen und Diskursstrategien*. Eds. Henning Grunwald and Manfred Pfister. München: Fink, 2007. 114-142.
Fludernik, Monika. *Towards a 'Natural' Narratology*. London: Routledge, 1996.

Forster, Edward Morgan. *The Abinger Pageant* (1934). *Abinger Harvest*. London: Edward Arnold, 1946. 383-400.

—. "EM Forster, in Cambridge, Reflects on His Life and Work." *BBC Television Service*. 21 December 1958. http://www.bbc.co.uk/archive/writers/12202.shtml (21.08.2012).

Frank, Michael C. "Reverse Imperialism: Invasion Narratives in English Turn-of-the-Century Fiction." *Stories of Empire. Narrative Strategies for the Legitimation of an Imperial World Order*. Eds. Christa Knellwolf King and Margarete Rubik. Trier: WVT, 2009. 69-91.

Gennep, Arnold van. *The Rites of Passage*. Transl. Monika B. Vizedom. London: Routledge, 1960 [1909].

Gladigow, Burkhard. "Typische Ritensequenzen und die Ordnung der Rituale." *Zoroastrian Rituals in Context*. Ed. Michael Stausberg. Leiden: Brill, 2004. 57-76.

Gorp, Hendrik van, and Ulla Musarra-Schroeder. "Introduction: Literary Genres and Cultural Memory." *Genres as Repositories of Cultural Memory*. Eds. Hendrik van Gorp and Ulla Musarra-Schroeder. Amsterdam, Atlanta, GA: Rodopi. I-ix.

Kapferer, Bruce. "Ritual Dynamics and Virtual Practice: Beyond Representation and Meaning." *Social Analysis* 48.2 (Summer 2004): 35-54.

Landy, Joshua, and Michael Saler, eds. *The Re-Enchantment of the World: Secular Magic in a Rational Age*. Stanford: Stanford UP, 2009.

Michaels, Axel. "Zur Dynamik von Ritualkomplexen." *Forum Ritualdynamik* 3 (2003): 1-12.

Müller-Funk, Wolfgang. *Die Kultur und ihre Narrative. Eine Einführung*. 2002. Wien, New York: Springer, 2008.

Parker, Louis Napoleon. *Several of My Lives*. London: Chapman and Hall, 1928.

Prince, Gerald. *A Dictionary of Narratology*. Rev. ed. Lincoln, NB: U of Nebraska P, 2003 [1987].

Quiller-Couch, Arthur. *Brother Copas*. Leipzig: Tauchnitz, 1911.

Readman, Paul. "The Place of the Past in English Culture c.1890-1914." *Past and Present* 186 (2005): 147-200.

Schechner, Richard. *The Future of Ritual: Writings on Culture and Performance*. London: Routledge, 1995.

Shen, Dan. "Story-Discourse Distinction." *Routledge Encyclopaedia of Narrative Theory*. Eds. David Herman, Manfred Jahn, and Marie-Laure Ryan. London, New York: Routledge. 566-568.
Stausberg, Michael. "Reflexivity." *Theorizing Rituals: Issues, Topics, Approaches, Concepts*. Eds. Jens Kreinath, Jan Snoek, and Michael Stausberg. Leiden: Brill, 2006. 627-646.
Turner, Victor. *The Ritual Process: Structure and Anti-Structure*. Chicago, IL: Aldine Publ, 1973.
Weber, Max. *The Protestant Ethic and the Spirit of Capitalism*. Transl. Talcott Parsons. New York: Scribner, 1958 [1905].
White, Hayden. *Metahistory. The Historical Imagination in Nineteenth-Century Europe*. Baltimore, MD, London: Johns Hopkins UP, 1973.
Wiley, Catherine. "Making History Unrepeatable in Virginia Woolf's Between the Acts." *Clio* 25.1 (1995): 3-20.
Withington, Robert. *English Pageantry. An Historical Outline*. 2 Vols. Cambridge: Harvard UP, 1918-20.
—. "Louis Napoleon Parker." *New England Quarterly* 12.3 (1939): 510-520.
Woolf, Virginia. *Between the Acts*. Oxford: Oxford UP, 2008 [1941].
—. *The Letters of Virginia Woolf*. Vol. 6. Eds. Nigel Nicholson and Joanne Trautmann. New York: Harcourt, 1980.
Yoshino, Ayako: "Between the Acts and Louis Napoleon Parker – the Creator of the Modern English Pageant." *Critical Survey* 15.2 (2003): 49-60.
—. *The Edwardian Historical Pageant. Local History and Consumerism*. Tokyo: Waseda UP, 2010.

Ritual and Narrative in the Intercultural British Novel at the Turn of the 21st Century

SCARLETT MEYER

1. INTRODUCTION

The connection between ritual and narration in literature and its function for the creation of community and identity may well be one of the features that literatures of all cultures share. However, during the 20th century, ritual and narrative take different forms and functions. In the Edwardian era, ritual pageants served to enhance English identity by enacting and stressing national heroism with later pageant fictions by writers like Virginia Woolf questioning the grand narrative of Englishness in the face of war and economic crises (cf. Rupp, this volume). Where in the first half of the 20th century pageants and pageant fictions were concerned with representations of national history and the role of the Empire, a large part of literature after the Second World War has been concerned with the consequences of postcolonialism. Immigration and ensuing multiculturalism call for negotiations of individual and collective identity tied to cultural diversity rather than national homogeneity: different cultures are part of one community, even one family, one individual. Often, the cultural heritage of the parental immigrant generation clashes with the culture of the country immigrated into. The connection between narration and ritual is important in this context. How cultural identity is negotiated within families with a migration background can well be explored by looking at the way the different family members embrace, reject or combine rituals from the competing cultures. The development of young second generation immigrants is the main concern of the intercultural *bildungsroman* – a genre that offers insights into the relationship of ritual and narrative in the context of the British intercultural novel. The focus lies on the protagonists' struggle to find their own position between the parents' culture and the surrounding, British, culture. Since rituals serve as "the master-keys to understanding cultures, [...] as powerful mechanisms for construction of the self and the other, of personal and collective identities" (Kreinath et al. xv), exploring the specific rituals that are described in the texts and the characters' experience of these rituals is a major task in the analysis of identity formation in these novels.

The genre of the *bildungsroman* is interesting not only because it depicts rituals as part of the protagonists' story. There is a more fundamental way in which ritual becomes an important feature for understanding the narrative, and this overlap of *bildungsroman* and ritual, more specifically rite of passage, lies in their structure. The sequentiality of events in the story – though it might not follow strict chronological order on the level of discourse – enables us to distinguish between beginning, middle and ending, thus permitting to draw parallels to Arnold van Gennep's threefold model of a rite of passage as separation, transition and incorporation (cf. 11). There seems to be an analogy between the narrative structure of the *bildungsroman* and the structure of the rite of passage (cf. Elsbree).

This chapter will analyse Meera Syal's *Life Isn't All Ha Ha Hee Hee* (1999) and Andrea Levy's *Fruit of the Lemon* (1999) as examples of the intercultural British *bildungsroman* in which ritual and narrative are closely linked and in which the representation of rituals, the characters' perception of rituals and their rites of passage function as means of creating cultural identity. While in Syal's novel the protagonist Chila undergoes a rite of passage that can be traced in specific rituals throughout the story, Levy makes less use of concrete representations of rituals; instead, the narrative structure of her *bildungsroman* at large can be read as a rite of passage in which the events function as stages of development comparable to the phases of ritual passage. In both novels, the characters' struggle of coming to terms with both the parental and the English culture also problematizes the relationship between those who regard themselves as white, "true-born Englishmen" and the immigrants, who are perceived as "other." The interrelation between narrative and ritual therefore also functions as a way of (de)constructing Englishness.

2. RITUAL AND IDENTITY IN THE INTERCULTURAL BRITISH NOVEL

Analysing the interrelation between narrative, ritual and identity in the intercultural British *bildungsroman*, van Gennep's model of rites of passage, as explicated in his well-known monograph *Les Rites de Passage* (1908), is particularly promising and has been applied to the study of literature by Langdon Elsbree. It resembles the structure of the *bildungsroman*, where a crisis of identity prompts a character to reflect on his or her own self-image and thus instigates character development and increasing reflexivity. Though van Gennep's ritual theory and in-depth classification of rites is a complex system, the most important facet of his research pertaining to the study of the *bildungsroman* is his tripartite model designating the different phases of rites of passage, which are crucial points in the identity formation process. These phases include "preliminal rites (rites of separation), liminal rites (rites of transition) and postliminal rites (rites of incorporation)" (van Gennep 11). Bridging the gap between anthropology and literary studies, Elsbree uses van Gennep's model to trace analogies between narrative and ritual in his ground-breaking study *Ritual Passages and Narrative Structures* (1991), seeing a "homology between rites of passage and narrative structures [which] depends on their biogenetic origins and co-existence as primary activities of the brain" (Elsbree 1).

The structural analogies between narrative structure and rites of passage become clear when van Gennep's model is applied to the development of the protagonist in the *bildungsroman*. During the course of the novel, the protagonist moves from an old sense of self, where there is little reflection on the character's position within the cultural world he or she inhabits (preliminal phase), to a new, more reflective sense of self, where the character is aware of his or her position and able to reflect on the process of identity formation that has taken place so far (postliminal phase). The transition from one to the other is triggered by a crisis (liminal phase), where the old self is called into question and has to be transformed and adapted. This crisis, or liminal phase, lies at the heart of the *bildungsroman*, and the protagonist, suspended between differing life designs and values, has to find a way to navigate through these conflicting worldviews before being able to assert his or her own position. "The tests endured and the roles assumed by the hero or heroine presuppose the betwixtness and betweenness of transitional passage" (Elsbree 21).

A central characteristic of the protagonists in the *bildungsroman* is their self-awareness in their social and cultural context and their increasing ability to reflect on their identity as a narrative construct which is subject to change. This aspect of self-reflection links the story, i.e. the sequence of events, to the level of narrative discourse, i.e. how the story is narrated. The perspectivation of the story is of fundamental importance for the analysis of the characters' experience and reflective processes. Elsbree more or less equates stories and rituals without taking into account the complexity of the process of narration and mediation and the insights these distinctive features of literature allow. However, it is important to consider in how far the characters' perception of rituals contributes to the analysis of their rite of passage: if they fulfil their ritual tasks without question, they are likely to be in a preliminal phase, whereas a reflection on their role in the culture and its rituals can only be expected at a later stage of the rite of passage.

In second-generation immigrant novels, the protagonists' choice of rejecting or embracing cultural rituals in their in-between position is related to the concept of Englishness as it is influenced by immigration and cultural integration. As Jan Rupp points out, the concepts of imperialistic Britishness and domestic Englishness were of major importance in the construction of a national identity in Britain in the early 20th century (cf. Rupp, this volume). At the turn of the 21st century, however, the contemporary intercultural novel rejects the imperialistic notion of Britishness in favour of a domestic but heterogeneous Englishness: the "children" of the former Empire come from the formerly colonial countries to the "motherland" and demand integration. The "grandchildren," i.e. second generation immigrants, already are at home in England and bring their heterogeneous cultural make-up into the discourse of Englishness. Thus, both Syal's and Levy's novels call the concept of "white" Englishness into question. Their protagonists are English citizens but do not fit into the white English assumptions about what is English and what is not. Much of the potential for conflict in *Life Isn't All Ha Ha Hee Hee* and *Fruit of the Lemon* derives from the white English characters' lacking awareness of England as a multi-ethnic society (cf. Frank 32). The central question regarding the representations of "non-English" rituals and their relation to Englishness is: how do the particular rituals, which are cultural indexes of the parental home countries, shape and challenge the notion of Englishness in a postcolonial context? In Syal's novel, Englishness becomes an issue as rituals which are placed in a different cultural setting call the concept of national identity as a static and inflexible ideology into question. In *Fruit of the Lemon*, the question of what is or is not considered English propels a major part of the plot and causes the protagonist's loss of a stable identity. Especially in the context of second-generation immigrant experiences, "Englishness" is in constant flux and cannot be pinned down to "Shakespeare, Queen Victoria, Industrial Revolution, gardening, that sort of thing" as Julian Barnes expresses it in his novel *England, England* (39), but has to take into account the plural character of present-day England. The protagonists' experiences of culturally different rituals, whether they embrace, reject or combine them, are important markers of how Englishness is negotiated in the intercultural novel.

3. Rituals, Rites of Passage and Female Emancipation in Meera Syal's *Life Isn't All Ha Ha Hee Hee*

Meera Syal's novel *Life Isn't All Ha Ha Hee Hee* is a *bildungsroman* with not one but three female protagonists, who all undergo change and experience personal growth in their formation of cultural identity. "Syal traces their uneasy passage between what is culturally expected – marriage, happiness-ever-after and children, and the flaws in this 'ideal'" (Wisker 25). The parental cultural heritage and the ensuing family expectations are at odds with the surrounding Western culture. Chila is the protagonist on whom the rituals of her parents' Indian culture have the greatest impact – not least because she is the bride in the wedding ceremony that opens the novel.

The narrative opens with the representation of the wedding – a ritual which is narrated from several different perspectives, including Chila's. This allows the reader to see how the characters perceive the same event – the ceremony – in very different ways; the centre of orientation shifts constantly from one participant to the next. With Chila's point of view, the reader experiences the significance of the distinct parts of the ritual and the effect they have on her. That she as the silently acquiescing bride in an arranged marriage becomes the focalizer problematizes the power relations in the ritual: it is her point of view which is chosen as the most important one when she has no power and influence in the ritual as such. During the ceremony, Chila questions the arranged marriage for the first time. In contrast to her acceptance of the decision that she is to become Deepak's wife, which is prevalent in her account of the events leading up to the wedding, she now feels uneasy and oppressed by her traditional bridal clothing, which hinders her physically to enjoy her own wedding:

She could not look up even if she wanted, weighed down by an embroidered dupatta encrusted with fake pearls and gold-plated balls. The heavy lengha prevented her from taking more than baby steps behind her almost-husband to whom she was tied, literally, her scarf to his turban. She would have liked to wear a floaty thing, all gossamer and light, and skip around the flames like a sprite [...]. She wanted to celebrate. But instead she was mummified in red and gold silk (Syal 13-14).

Here, Chila's life as the married woman she is about to become is already anticipated. She is represented as the obedient wife, tied to her husband, Deepak. The ritual structure and procedure that has her walk behind him communicates the husband's superiority over his wife and expresses the collective's expectations of her being the compliant wife following her husband's lead. Likewise, the heavy garment she wears symbolizes the traditional Indian role she is about to take on, and she longs for something less oppressive, "a floaty thing, all gossamer and light," which can be seen to represent the freedom of the less restrictive Western culture in which she grew up and which she perceives as more liberal, especially with regards to the role of women. Her gradual development from dutiful and submissive wife to independent single mother is already foreshadowed by means of focalization and the mediation of her experience of the wedding ceremony.

The ritual constituents of the ceremony such as traditional clothing are ways to re-establish communities – for example a community of married women into which the bride Chila now enters. Thus weighed down and restricted in its ability to move freely, "her body would only walk the walk of everyone's mothers on all their weddings, meekly, shyly, reluctantly towards matrimony" (Syal 14). The sense of community rituals can provide is mentioned repeatedly throughout the chapter, most explicitly at the end of the wedding day, when the heterodiegetic narrator captures the general mood of the majority of the wedding guests: "A perfect day, because rituals had been observed, old footsteps retraced, threads running unbroken, families joined, futures secured" (26).[1] Still, while the community of guests seems to judge the wedding's positive effect on the community unanimously as a homogeneous crowd, the individual participants' experiences during the performance of their different roles in these rituals cannot be ignored.

In the novel, role-playing is a major topic, and it gains extraordinary momentum in the performance of rituals – not least due to the traditional clothing, which basically functions as a costume for the person wearing it. That the performative aspect is crucial to the success of a ritual seems most evident with Pandit Kumar, the religious authority functioning as a priest, who bears the responsibility and power to proclaim Deepak and Chila husband and wife. When the ritual reaches this central point of transition, he, significantly, becomes the focalizer, and his performative role as well as his own understanding of it is highlighted.

Pandit Kumar was pregnant with his own importance at this solemn point, emphasized by his impressive belly, which strained the seams of his beige and gold-trimmed shalwar kameez. He often thought of Elvis Presley at this juncture in the wedding ceremony [...]. He had the stage [...] and he had a god-given duty to put on a good show (17).

The word choice in this passage underlines the transitional phase of the ritual, "pregnant" describing a physical stage of liminality, also relevant for the development of Chila's character, "solemn point" and "juncture" highlighting the impact this moment has on the lives of bride and groom. Pandit Kumar as a priest-like figure is a "ritual specialist" (Kreinath et al. xiii). His performative skills are crucial at this transitional moment – there are refer-

---

[1] This passage which illuminates the guests' perception of the wedding day can also be read as an ironic narrative comment on the function of rituals to secure a collective identity and an unchanging cultural world – the novel illuminates that the performance of a ritual is no guarantee that "threads run [...] unbroken" and "futures [are] secured" (Syal 26).

ences to "Elvis Presley," the "stage," and a "good show" – illustrating that without the aspect of performance, the ritual cannot be successfully carried out.

This is further emphasized by the behaviour of the other participants in the ritual. The distinction between participants in, and witnesses of, rituals is tricky since onlookers are always also partakers; the ritual performance needs an audience for which it is performed (cf. Braungart 106). The doli, the rite of separation detaching Chila from her family, closes the wedding day in a "tragic performance" (Syal 26), as the English guests perceive it. The wedding guests join in a chorus of moaning and wailing at Chila's departure with Deepak (22-23), and Chila herself performs the role of the mourning bride because the ritual requires her to cry:

They weren't real tears, you know. […] I knew everybody was watching to see how upset I was, because apparently, a girl who doesn't cry at her doli is considered a hard-hearted bitch […]. Nowadays, with seventeen video cameras following your every move, you can't be too careful (27-28).

Here, one of the central themes of the novel shines through: the tension between individual and collective. At the doli, Chila does her best to fulfil the collective's expectations and ritual conventions of how she should behave. Her individual feelings at the time of the performance move to the background. This experience can be linked to performative theories of rituals, where simulation of feelings and attitudes in order to meet the convention is said to be part of the performativity of rituals; the separation of any private feelings the participants in the ritual may have from their sense of duty toward a collective, public moral can even result in hypocrisy (cf. Tambiah 232). Chila's development manifests itself in her increasing denial to feign consent with the collective's expectations and to perform the conventional role of the submissive, acquiescent wife, in rituals as well as in everyday life.

The rituals in the novel only seem to condense and exaggerate performative characteristics of life which are already there, however subtle. At first, Chila tries to fit in with the people she interacts with – her efforts to perform a convincing role become particularly obvious when she practices facial expressions and gestures in front of a mirror in order to be able to pretend being a cheerful part of the community (cf. Syal 113). Later in the novel, her need to perform the roles expected of her decreases; she becomes more self-reliant. The rituals, therefore, only epitomize the role-play people engage in daily in their different responsibilities and functions (cf. Braungart 106) and can serve as indicators of Chila's emancipation, which takes her from obedient housewife to self-confident single mother.

An important stage for her rite of passage and quest for independence is her pregnancy, which fulfils the function of the liminal, transitional phase. Here, Chila becomes more reflective on her role in her marriage and on the rituals involving the prenatal period, which is interesting as pregnancy itself is naturally a liminal condition and, according to van Gennep, "a transitional period" (41). Deepak impregnates Chila after kissing her friend Tania – an act of infidelity that Chila witnesses and which instigates a process of separation: she gradually distances herself from her husband and her traditional role. Seeing Deepak kiss Tania, Chila realizes in a moment of epiphany that her life is a construct and charade, and she herself only an actress, performing happiness in order to keep the marriage intact (cf. Syal 183). Her becoming aware of the futility of acting as the compliant wife is the first step towards independence.

The first part of the novel ends here and the second one starts, significantly entitled "Spring," indicating new life and growth. Her bodily experience of pregnancy and the development of her courage to strive for more freedom despite the collective's expectations go hand in hand. Chila becomes aware of her unhappy marriage, the oppressiveness of the wife's traditional role and the censorious rituals regarding pregnancy. Clothing is used here again as a means of depicting women in their roles. A pregnant woman seems to be considered "impure and dangerous" (van Gennep 41) and within the traditional Indian community has to be made look "normal" to hide the "swelling of shame" (Syal 197). Reinforcing her slight feeling of oppression during the wedding, Chila now reflects on the dupatta as a symbol of the subjugation of women, "feeling her dupatta heavy on her shoulders, yoke of ages, transparent as air, heavier than iron, a woman's modesty symbolized by a scrap of silk" (202). However, Chila has not yet gained enough independence to break away from her husband completely: "If Chila ventured out too far, her fear dragged her back [...]. He was still with her. They were still married. They were soon to be parents" (271). Nevertheless, the use of the adverbials of time, "still" and "soon," emphasizes the transience of her married life. Deepak and Chila are in their marriage in a similarly liminal state as Chila is in her pregnancy.

With the birth of her son, Chila can finally overcome the need to keep playing the part. The relevance of her first childbirth as a moment of fundamental change is mirrored by the change of narrative structure. An entire chapter is devoted to the process of birth; the narrative mode differs significantly from other chapters in that its effect of immediacy is unprecedented in the novel and is achieved by the unfiltered, disrupted account of the birthing woman during labour. There are no quotation marks indicating direct speech; there is no distinction between speech and thought during the delivery of her baby. The heightened intensity of the liminal moment of childbirth is also underlined by the absence of a narrative use of past tense: there is only present experience. In addition, although much of Chila's utterances are directed at Sunita, the narrative omits Sunita's part of the dialogue – there is only the account of Chila's thoughts and utterances, resulting in an unusually strong focus on Chila. At this intense moment of pain and struggle, her breaking free from Deepak and the expectation of holding up her marriage finally comes about in an exclamation whose force is graphically underscored by the use of capital letters: "Ohoh-TELLHIMTOPISSOFFNOWGETHIMOUTOFHEREohoh" (287).

At the end of the novel, Chila reflects on her newly found position as a single mother amid a crowd of married couples attending the funeral service for Tania's father: "She felt light as air, solitary. It was so strange to be standing with the old ones, aged couples holding hands, taking part in the old ways, and feel so new and unfamiliar. It wasn't so bad, to be here alone" (333). Her feeling of lightness contrasts distinctly with her former metaphor of herself wearing a yoke. She is still part of the community, still a participant in a traditional ritual, but able to negotiate these old parts of her life and her new role in an act of incorporation; using van Gennep's terminology, this funeral serves as a postliminal rite for Chila. She plans a trip to India, indicating that she engages in a conscious process of coming to terms with her ethnic background: instead of an unquestioned affiliation with a traditional role (like at the beginning of the novel, in the preliminal phase), there are now, at the end of the novel, signs of a more reflective identity (cf. Frank 173). The narrative frame that opens and closes the novel consists of two rituals, wedding and funeral, and Chila's development can be deduced by the way she reflects on her position within these rituals.

However, as the structural frame of the narrative the rituals do not only serve the function of indicating Chila's character development; they are also important reference points for the negotiation of Englishness as it is transformed by rituals from immigrant cultures.

In both the nuptial and the burial ritual, the heterodiegetic narrator, who can use all participants and observers of the ritual process as a focalizer, presents the wedding parade and the funeral at least partly from the point of view of the – presumably white – English onlookers. This narrative technique results in the effect of a zooming in on, and in the end out of, the life of the second generation of immigrants with the three female protagonists Chila, Sunita and Tania. The Indian ritual elements of the wedding parade and funeral are first described from the perspective of those who are unfamiliar with them. Interestingly, the English spectators try to understand the things they see in terms of their own cultural rituals, which creates an unmistakable tension. Thus, the "old man" (Syal 10) – who is not given a name by the narrator, rendering him anonymous, prototypical – sees the horse-drawn carriage with the groom on it and immediately associates it with a Christmas tree (cf. ibid.).

Similarly, the gathering at the funeral of Tania's father is witnessed by the Keegans – an English couple who has their first appearance at this late stage of the novel. Mrs Keegan is offended by the behaviour she observes, as she judgmentally compares it to the Christian rituals of burial and mourning, which she prefers. She assigns higher value to her own tradition of burial than to cremation of the body, ignoring the fact that cremation is just as customary a Christian ritual as burial. The culture Mrs Keegan identifies with "chose to remember, they kept the body and didn't fry it and send it off into the air up a chimney" (331). Mrs Keegan's disrespectful tone of voice (or thought) continues when admonishing the loud mourning she witnesses: "And the way they wailed! As if they weren't drawing enough attention, dressing up in white clothes like they were off to a wedding" (ibid.). The reader knows that the "wailing" is an integral part of the Indian rites of separation in ritual passages, as it already appears at the beginning of the novel during Chila's wedding. The fact that Mrs Keegan deems the white clothing of the "ethnic" group inappropriate shows that she lacks cultural background knowledge and assumes that white is the colour of joy rather than grief in all societies. Different cultural concepts of funeral are clearly at odds in Mrs Keegan's reproachful comment. Mr Keegan as focalizer forms a counter-example to his wife's disapproval. He is willing to let go of his own traditions and be inspired by other and unfamiliar rituals: "True, they made a lot of noise. It was upsetting sometimes, the dramatics, the flinging themselves around. But he wondered if it wasn't better that way, to let it all out and not be ashamed" (ibid.).

Mrs Keegan's perception of a ritual that is not her own as well as the old man's estranged observation of the wedding parade show that they feel alienated by the non-white ethnic rituals they witness. Their latent racism probably makes many readers uncomfortable. However, these characters serve an important function: they hold up the mirror to readers who may feel alienated by the non-English words strewn into the narrative and make them aware of their own dormant prejudices and ideas of "white" Englishness. The performance of rituals needs an audience, and those who see but may not understand are part of that audience. The shift in the point of view – from alienated white onlookers to non-white ritual participants and back – underscores the different perceptions of what it means to be English. The fact that the story of second-generation immigrants and their experience of England and heterogeneous, hybrid Englishness is narrated through their own critical eyes already serves to render the assumed homogenous national idea problematic.

4. NEGOTIATING CULTURAL IDENTITY THROUGH RITES OF PASSAGE: ANDREA LEVY, *FRUIT OF THE LEMON*

In *Fruit of the Lemon*, the connection between ritual and narrative relates to the negotiation of race and identity. Unlike Syal's novel, it contains only few concrete rituals. Instead, it offers new insights into the relationship between ritual and narrative in terms of their structure since the plot pattern resembles a rite of passage for the protagonist. Faith Jackson, daughter of Jamaican immigrants to England, experiences a series of racist incidents that convey the impression that Faith is not accepted as thoroughly English, which considerably shakes her sense of identity. Only after a journey to Jamaica and the discovery of her cultural roots is Faith able to unite both her Jamaican background and her personal life in England. Faith's rite of passage, which is a struggle between being English and being Jamaican, consists of preliminal, liminal and postliminal phases but these phases are not determined by specific rituals. Rather, the events in the story which lead Faith to question and reflect on her cultural identity function as rites of separation and incorporation. The structural analogy between *bildungsroman* and a rite of passage is dominant here.

The tripartite narrative macrostructure of *Fruit of the Lemon* – England, Jamaica, England – calls for a pre-post comparison (cf. Frank 114) and invites a direct transfer of van Gennep's model of the rite of passage. Then, England would be the starting and end point, the preliminal and postliminal phase, while Faith's stay in Jamaica would represent the liminal phase. However, a close analysis of the novel shows that van Gennep's three-part model does not fully coincide with the character's development over the three structural parts of the novel. Rather, I will suggest that there are in fact two rites of passage coinciding with the two journeys Faith undertakes. The tripartite England-Jamaica-England structure should be split up into journey A (departure from England – journey – arrival in Jamaica) and journey B (departure from Jamaica – journey – arrival in England). Both are necessary for Faith's identity formation as she travels through different cultural and geographical spaces and learns about her cultural heritage (cf. Frank 197).

The twofold passage Faith masters (there and back again) is both a spatial and a psychological one, and both journeys are equally important for her process of identity formation as she learns to appreciate her hybrid cultural background, which includes her Jamaican heritage as well as her upbringing in England. This goes well with van Gennep's theory of ritual as he also states that "a rite of spatial passage [can] become a rite of spiritual passage" (22). The aspect of a journey as a quest for knowledge is already evident in Faith's middle name Columbine. This name, chosen by her mother in remembrance of her beloved goat, is also – as Mark Stein points out – the female form of Christopher Columbus' name, who undertook a journey to Jamaica as well: "Faith's travels are [...] a voyage of discovery" (68).

Faith's experiences in England are characterized by an increasing alienation from her fellow Englishmen and -women which is due to their latent racism: the racist assaults she has to suffer function as rites of separation and lead to her departure. Until Faith notices how prejudiced people are against her because of her black skin, she thinks of herself as downright

English, "born and bred in Haringey" (Levy 31). That she feels at home in the country where she was raised may be explained by Marc Augé's statement that "the actual place of birth is a constituent of individual identity" (43); the fact that she has dark skin and might therefore be considered as "other" does not even occur to her. For everybody else in the novel, however, including her family and those that foster racist prejudices against her, Faith's skin colour seems to play an important role in her belonging to the black, and not the white, community. She herself is supremely unconcerned about her being black, even oblivious of its significance. In a climactic series of racial assaults, however, Faith's sense of self is shaken as the white English people she encounters regard her not as entirely English because of her black skin and make her feel that she does not belong: she is repeatedly marked as "not from here." Speaking with Augé, they see Faith as an "exotic other defined in relation to a supposedly identical 'we'" (16) – a "we white English" in this case. The BBC, who reject her job application because of her skin colour, and the English village, where she visits and is questioned about her migration background, stand pars pro toto for the latent racism in England. She is forced to distance herself from her self-image as downright English and to take a critical view on the culture she thought to be part of.

Faith's preliminal phase is unmistakably over when the chain of racist affronts finds its climax in the physical assault on a black woman Simon and Faith witness. This attack and her friends' denial that it was racially motivated serves as the final rite of separation, severing the ties between Faith and her feeling English. It is then that she experiences a "crisis of identity, in which she confronts, maybe for the first time, that there is no room for her in the discourses of Englishness" (Medovarski 251). When she retreats to the confinement of her room, she sees herself as a black woman who could easily have been the victim of the attack she witnessed. Roger Bromley has remarked that in the central text passage pertaining to Faith's identity as only black the narrative situation changes slightly (cf. 135): Faith's autodiegetic narration incorporates a sentence that resembles heterodiegetic narration as she views herself in the mirror as if with the eyes of a stranger: "A black girl lying on a bed" (Levy 160). At this moment of the narrative, Faith is separated not only from the English community she formerly believed to be part of but also from the black community she never thought to be part of: "I covered the mirror with a bath towel. I didn't want to be black anymore" (ibid.). The rite of separation is complete; it triggers Faith's deteriorating sense of self, her identity crisis and liminal phase. Now, a transition is necessary for Faith to find a way of incorporating her experiences into a new identity that comes to terms with both her being English and her being black. During Faith's crisis, she is already mentally removed from her former English sense of self: her journey away from England and her self-image as an Englishwoman has psychologically already begun before a physical journey follows it.

In terms of a rite of passage, Faith's first trip functions as a liminal phase for the protagonist's identity formation. Faith's crossing from England to Jamaica is a liminal process comparable to Chila's pregnancy in *Life Isn't All Ha Ha Hee Hee*. In van Gennep's model, the passage of territorial border zones or thresholds is "structurally identical with the intermediate period of a ritual passage" (Thomassen 24), i.e. the liminal phase. Regarding the liminality of the border zone, airports and planes are of particular significance as, in Augé's terminology, non-places (cf. 64). In Augé's definition of place and non-place, "a place can be defined as relational, historical and concerned with identity, [while] a space which cannot be defined as relational, or historical, or concerned with identity will be a non-place" (63). In the non-place of the airport or aircraft, the absence of a specific cultural identity allows for heightened awareness of the culturally determined selves of those passing through.

Accordingly, Faith's impression of the lively Kingston airport in Jamaica underscores that she is in the liminal phase of her first rite of passage and not at all sure about her own cultural belonging: "I felt out of place [...] Culture shock is how the feeling is described. A name made up by someone with a stiff upper lip who wanted to deny the feelings of panic and terror." (Levy 169). She does not feel any sense of belonging to the Jamaican community she observes, but neither does she fully identify with the English anymore: in her reflection, the "stiff upper lip" as an "almost stereotypical characteristic of the British" (Gui 85) comes off as something negative, and her "English woollen jumper sticking to [her] body" (Levy 169) does not serve her well and seems to be something she would rather be rid of – as in Syal's novel, clothing becomes a symbol of cultural identity. Faith's aunt Coral points out the significance of her journey in terms of her identity formation: "'You can't leave England and come all that way without losing some bit of you'" (185).

Faith overcomes this liminal stage of her identity formation surprisingly soon: changing her clothing in order to adjust to the hot Jamaican weather is a rite of incorporation for her – supported by her aunt's remark that she truly looks like a Jamaican woman now. However, just as she had assumed to be English in England without considering her parents' origin and culture, she now feels Jamaican in Jamaica without taking her personal history as an English citizen into account. Her assumption that she is now part of the Jamaican community is premature – her rite of passage is not complete yet. In fact, she has to undergo another process of separation and liminal experience before she is able to arrive at a reflective stage of her identity formation in which she becomes aware and affirmative of her diverse cultural background.

Her second rite of passage starts with Faith's experience of being an outsider of the Jamaican community. The wedding ceremony she witnesses (which in van Gennep's model concludes with a secure, postliminal phase for the spouses) serves as a rite of separation in Faith's process of negotiating her cultural identity because she feels rejected by the Jamaican community just as she felt unwanted in England. At the beginning of the narrative representation of the ritual wedding, Faith still feels that she is actually a part of the community. With the other guests at the wedding not noticing Faith at first, she is happy to be "blending in" (Levy 293). Since she does not draw any curiosity, she applauds herself for looking Jamaican in her outward appearance. However much Faith feels to be inconspicuous and blending in, though, she is in fact not dressed like a Jamaican. This becomes clear when she enters the church wearing pants: her choice of clothing immediately gives her away as a non-member of the crowd, as a person who does not know the appropriate dress code for a Jamaican wedding. "Everyone stared. Little girls hid their laugh behind their hands, men shook their heads and old women sucked their teeth. I walked down the centre aisle to my aunt with the congregation's gaze following me like I was the bride" (295). Faith's pants receive as much resentment as a bridal gown would earn admiration. Instead of being a proper participant in the ritual, i.e. in the cultural community, she remains an outsider. Only after that experience of her own otherness is she able to refrain from acting as if she is either only English or only Jamaican. She now can integrate Jamaican culture into her English background in a fruitful way and find a way of negotiating both parts of her personal history, merging them into one. This rite of incorporation correlates with her return to England.

Faith's arrival in London is a final rite of incorporation for her, as she feels like a Jamaican immigrant on the one hand and like a London citizen on the other, having again travelled across borders and through a liminal phase. Now, her rite of passage is complete and her cultural identity confirms her diverse cultural background. To illustrate her hybrid self, the narrative makes use of a cyclic pattern. Her own experience of arrival echoes that of her parents when they immigrated, but it is not the same. Faith recounts her thoughts at the sight of England as follows:

At first I thought it may be a welcome home for me. [...] a welcome for me having travelled so far and England needing me. [...] But I knew I couldn't be right and I wasn't. [...] I knew this was England, November the fifth. There are always fireworks on November the fifth. It was Guy Fawkes' night and I was coming home. (Levy 339)

The choice of words in this passage is striking, as it directly quotes the description of her parents' immigrant experience as portrayed by Faith's mother: "Your dad thought [the fireworks] might have been a welcome for us, having come so far and England needing us. But I didn't think he could be right. And he wasn't" (8). Her using the same phrases to describe her arrival in England indicates that Faith is able to understand her parents' feeling upon coming to England. "The iteration synopsises the complete narrative process, it is a repetition with a difference, opening up alterity and heterogeneity" (Bromley 139). Faith is not an immigrant; she is familiar with English culture and can therefore make sense of the fireworks. She relives her parents' experience of arrival and novelty while at the same time using her English cultural knowledge to orient herself in a familiar world – an act of synthesis (cf. Frank 198) which indicates how she incorporates two cultural backgrounds into one hybrid identity and overcomes liminality. She is back "home," now equipped with the knowledge of her Jamaican family, which helps her redefine her own status in England as the daughter of immigrants – not in denial but affirmative of her cultural heritage.

Faith's twofold rite of passage serves as a way to trigger and foster identity formation, which again stresses the analogy of rite of passage and *bildungsroman*. The ritual passage through the English and Jamaican cultural spaces determines the way Faith constructs her sense of self in terms of a narrative of migration. *Fruit of the Lemon* opens with a racist insult addressed at Faith by her classmates in primary school: "'Your mum and dad came on a banana boat'" (3). By the end of the novel, Faith has overcome the shock of the truth of this statement and can now conceive her parents' past immigration experience as a part of her own story and identity. The novel closes with the slightly varied opening sentence: "I was coming to tell everyone ... My mum and dad came to England on a banana boat" (339). Regarding this frame of the entire narrative, the child Faith "struggles to keep her parents' immigrant status a secret [...] [and] can now reclaim the indisputable fact of her parents' arrival as a starting point for a different narrative" (Medovarski 273) in adulthood. Whereas her identity shifts back and forth between English and Jamaican in the first and second part of the novel, she finally finds a way of fusing these two notions of national identity into one, mirroring the historical interrelation between England and Jamaica as being linked by colonialism instead of being two entirely disparate and closed cultural spheres. Thus, *Fruit of the Lemon* addresses the difficulty of identifying Englishness especially with regard to national identity being shaped by colonialism and immigration. The characters in the novel illustrate that there is a reciprocal influence, of England on Jamaica and vice versa, which defies any chance of a notion of an autonomous and uniform national identity.

5. CONCLUSION

Second-generation immigrant novels employing the structure of the *bildungsroman* and rite of passage to trace their protagonists' development of, and reflection on multicultural identity can serve to illuminate the intersection between narrative and ritual. Moreover, the rituals depicted in the texts serve as important markers for the general process of personal growth and set the over-arching theme of "rite of passage" mise en abyme. They also function as cultural signifiers, and the diverging perception of these culturally specific rituals by people of different cultural belonging provides a basis for studying the way in which collective identity concepts such as "Englishness" are called into question in the two novels. The connection between ritual and narration can lie on the level of the plot, when specific rituals change the lives of the characters, but it can also lie on the level of discourse. In this case, the structure of a rite of passage becomes the scaffolding for the narrative. In either way, rituals in narrative can have a confirming, a problematizing or a subverting function for the negotiation of cultural identities – both for the collective and the individual.

References

Augé, Marc. *Non-Places: An Introduction to Supermodernity.* transl. John Howe. London and New York: Verso, 1995 [1992].
Barnes, Julian. *England, England.* London: Jonathan Cape, 1998.
Braungart, Wolfgang. *Ritual und Literatur.* Tübingen: Max Niemeyer, 1996.
Bromley, Roger. *Narratives for a New Belonging: Diasporic Cultural Fictions.* Edinburgh: Edinburgh UP, 2000.
Elsbree, Langdon. *Ritual Passages and Narrative Structures.* New York et al.: Peter Lang, 1991.
Frank, Tobias. *Identitätsbildung in ausgewählten Romanen der Black British Literature: Genre, Gender und Ethnizität.* ELCH 44. Eds. Ansgar Nünning and Vera Nünning. Trier: WVT, 2010.
Gennep, Arnold van. *The Rites of Passage,* transl. Monika B. Vizedom and Gabrielle L. Caffee. London: Routledge and Kegan Paul, 1960 [1909].
Gui, Weihsin. "Post-Heritage Narratives: Migrancy and Travelling Theory in V.S. Naipaul's The Enigma of Arrival and Andrea Levy's Fruit of the Lemon." *The Journal of Commonwealth Literature* 47.1 (2012): 73-89.
Kreinath, Jens, Jan Snoek and Michael Strausberg. "Ritual Studies, Ritual Theory, Theorizing Rituals – an Introductory Essay." *Theorizing Rituals: Issues, Topics, Approaches, Concepts.* Eds. Jens Kreinath, Jan Snoek and Michael Strausberg. Leiden and Boston: Brill, 2006.
Levy, Andrea. *Fruit of the Lemon.* London: Headline Review, 2004 [1999].
Medovarski, Andrea Katherine. "Un/settled Migrations: Rethinking Nation through the Second Generation in Black Canadian and Black British Women's Writing." Diss. York U, Toronto, 2007.
Stein, Mark. *Black British Literature: Novels of Transformation.* Columbus: Ohio State UP, 2004.

Syal, Meera. *Life Isn't All Ha Ha Hee Hee*. London: Black Swan, 2000 [1999].

Tambiah, Stanley J. "Eine performative Theorie des Rituals." *Ritualtheorien: Ein einführendes Handbuch*. Eds. Andréa Belliger and David J. Krieger. Wiesbaden: Verlag für Sozialwissenschaften, ³2006. 225-248.

Thomassen, Björn. "Revisiting Liminality: The Danger of Empty Spaces." *Liminal Landscapes: Travel, Experience and Spaces in-between*. Eds. Hazel Andrews and Les Roberts. London and New York: Routledge, 2012. 21-35.

Wisker, Gina. "Negotiating Passages: Asian and Black Women's Writing in Britain." *Hecate* 30.1 (2004): 10-29.

How to Commemorate a Fallen Soldier: Ritual and Narrative in the Bundeswehr

STEFANIE HAMMER

1. INTRODUCTION

On the 2nd of June in 2011, the German Secretary of Defence, Thomas de Maizière, stepped up to the pulpit of Heilig Kreuz Kirche in Detmold to remember a fallen soldier from the German military, the Bundeswehr, in a speech. His words carried forward a commemoration service that had begun with a sermon held by a priest, followed by prayers and the singing of hymns. When Mr de Maizière approached the podium, a commentator for the German Parliamentary television channel, broadcasting the service live, noted: "The religious service ends here. The worldly [weltlich] part of the service begins." Meanwhile the setting remained the same: de Maizière spoke in front of the same coffin covered by the German national flag and from behind the same pulpit in the same church as the military chaplain had before him.

What this short account exemplifies is the way preliminary interpretations influence our understanding of events. As interpretative schemas, these *frames*[1] help us to "organize our experiences" (Goffman 11), providing an answer to the question: "[W]hat is it that's going on here?" (8). Concerning the scene described, at least three such framings can be identified,

---

1 Instead of frame, one may also refer to the "'background,' 'setting,' 'context'" (Berger xiii).

of which only one will concern us here. First of all, there is the commentator's remark. With his words, he designates the end of the religious and the beginning of the civil service, indicating that both spheres are to be experienced differently. The TV audience he addresses is thus asked to perceive this service through the frames of religion, followed by politics.[2]

Secondly, those present at the service are ignorant of the commentator's remark. To the participants "[the] ritual provides a frame. The marked off time or place alerts a special kind of expectancy, just as the oft-repeated 'Once upon a time' creates a mood receptive to fantastic tales" (Douglas 62).[3] Their experience is structured by the expectation of a distinctive form of ritual which is meant to remember the dead.

Thirdly, as analysts from various disciplines, we bring our own frames to the event, which also "limit [our] experience, shut in desired themes or shut out intruding ones" (Douglas 63). We may therefore study the observable formalized activity as a ritual and thus as a unique opportunity for a community to reassure itself of its self-understanding, while we might also criticize the involvement of politicians as "symbolic politics" and thus as meaningless decorum. In addition, we could also consider the speeches as examples of stories[4] which "provide models of the world" (Bruner, *Making Stories* 25). In consequence, each interpretative scheme will focus on different aspects, understanding the event in a distinctive way.

Now, it is not the aim of this contribution to prove any of these interpretations wrong. Instead, the chapter will begin by reproducing each of the particular analytical interpretative schemas. In the first section, the framing of ritual in political science as *symbolic politics* will thus be contrasted with the more affirmative framing of ritual in *ritual studies* (2.1). Such a combined effort seems especially profitable for the field of political science. It

---

2 For an analysis of the particular relation of church and state in these services see Hammer and Herold.

3 As will be pointed out later, the audience consists of a rather heterogeneous group of people. Family members, military personnel, as well as politicians might perceive this event through rather different frames. While this may be true, it does not change the general argument here.

4 The possible differentiation between story and narrative is debatable. For the argument of this chapter it plays no central role, so both terms are used synonymously.

is here that symbolic measures, such as ritual and narrative, suffer from the dominant interpretation as an emotionally charged and thus irrational staging of politics that is set in opposition to rational political argumentation.[5] Concerning the subject-matter of narrative, political theorists have also been criticized for their reluctance to clearly define what they mean by narrative, "apparently taking the meaning as self-evident" (Whitebrook 129). The chapter at hand thus wants to do just the opposite, examining the most valuable findings of the study of narrative in *narratology* (2.2). I will then return to the example of the commemoration services of the German Bundeswehr (3). Finally, some conclusions based on a newly combined and therefore interdisciplinary framework will be drawn (4).

2. RITUAL STUDIES AND NARRATOLOGY

2.1 Ritual

Substantiating the basic idea of ritual as an eminent object of study, Roy Rappaport, himself one of ritual studies' most influential representatives, argues that ritual needs to be acknowledged as "the social act basic to humanity" (31). From this it follows that ritual is "as old as humanity. Perhaps it is even older" (Grimes, *Beginnings* xxiv). The study of ritual itself was initiated through the engagement with religious ritual, first aiming to uncritically preserve ritual knowledge in the form of religious manuals that spelled out "what is to be done and said" (ibid.). This admittedly short glimpse into the *Beginnings in Ritual Studies* (1995) is intended to clarify the strong theoretical binding between ritual and religion that may also be solidified by an etymological analysis, the Latin term *ritus* referring solely to religious actions (Dücker 14).

What distinguishes today's analysts from former priests is their interest in the *interpretation* of ritual activity.[6] Since the 1970s, the term ritual has

---

5   This one-sided argumentation is particularly strong in the German context. See, for example, Dörner, *Politainment*; Meyer, *Die Inszenierung des Scheins*; *Politik als Theater*.
6   For a detailed historical overview over the development of ritual studies see Grimes, *Beginnings in Ritual Studies*.

thus been acknowledged as a fundamental analytical tool "in defining the issues basic to culture, society and religion" (Bell 3). Even though ritual and religion are no longer considered as inherently connected, some analysts still treat religious ritual as the "classical" example and therefore as the point of reference to determine whether a formal activity qualifies as ritual or not (Grimes, "Ritual Studies" 422).[7]

It was Sigmund Freud who took the first step in secularizing the term when equating the compulsive behaviour of his patients with rituals, thereby opening the term for a variety of new meanings (Althoff 12). Today's inflated use of the term ritual, describing routines, ceremonies and festivals, as well as the fundamental debate on whether the term needs to be discarded altogether, is a consequence of this continuous terminological broadening (Michaels, "Inflation der Rituale?"). This dispute may only be settled through a delimiting definition, something which the term ritual still lacks. Instead, various authors have developed their own characterization of what ritual stands for.[8]

Accordingly, the list of proposed definitions is rather long, but may be systematized by making use of Burckhard Dücker's proposal to differentiate between three categories: *formal*, *substantial* and *functional* approaches to ritual. *Formal* definitions concentrate on the way rituals are carried out, while *substantial* approaches focus on the (mainly religious) content of ritual. *Functional* approaches instead examine the functions rituals fulfil for certain groups (Dücker 209).

Meanwhile, Barbara Stollberg-Rilinger reminds us that "definitions are not actually truths, but merely tools used to distinguish and arrange phenomena" ("Much Ado" 8). It is in line with her argument that this chapter applies Axel Michaels' definition of ritual, recognizing it as a useful tool for the particular analysis of the commemoration services. Michaels' definition fits Dücker's category of a formal approach. It pays particular attention to the extent to which rituals may be allowed to change before losing their capacity to stabilize and give orientation (Michaels, "Inflation der Rit-

---

7   For an analysis of the multidimensional relation between ritual and religion see Rappaport.
8   See Bellinger, *Ritualtheorien* for a collection of influential primary texts by some of the most prominent authors in ritual studies, e.g. Mary Douglas, Clifford Geertz, Ronald Grimes, and Victor W. Turner.

uale").[9] In his definition, Michaels first enumerates the qualities that determine whether an activity is to be recognized as a ritual or not, namely *performance, form, framing, transformation* and *transcendence* ("Dynamik von Ritualkomplexen" 4f.). Thus, when an activity is recognizable thanks to a certain formality; when it involves particular agents and is framed in space or time so that one can know when and where this action takes place; and when the activity also transforms an item by oftentimes elevating it beyond the immanent world, we may refer to it as a ritual. In an attempt to further differentiate between ritual and routine, Michaels attributes the usage of cultural symbols to rituals only. It is these symbols which mark something as different in the Durkheimian sense, as sacred (34).[10]

In accordance with a variety of other definitions, Michaels illustrates that rituals first and foremost constitute a distinctive form of action (3). Catherine Bell interprets this rare but consequential commonality in ritual studies as an "initial bifurcation of thought and action" (6). The dichotomy subsequently takes on many different variations, as for example the normative setting apart of thoughtful theoretical analysts from mindless ritual actors (21). In accordance, Bell also cites Edward Shils' idea that "'beliefs could exist without rituals; rituals, however, could not exist without beliefs'" (20) in order to expose this dichotomy as a hierarchy.

The consequential framing of ritual as activity, set apart from thinking, also draws from one of the earliest functional interpretations of ritual in Émile Durkheim's *The Elementary Forms of Religious Life*. Identifying the universal elements of religion, ritual and belief, Durkheim argues: "Between these two classes of facts, there is all the difference which separates thought from action" (Durkheim as cited in Bell 20). Barbara Stollberg-Rilinger follows this tendency to contrast thought with action even further back, considering it one of the principal motifs in the Enlightenment period ("Knien vor Gott" 523).

---

9   Gert Althoff also discusses changes in rituals and emphasizes the impact of precedence (Althoff 198).

10 Note that Michaels does not talk about the repetitive nature of rituals, a quality that is oftentimes attributed to ritual activity first. Rituals constitute formal activities, and it is due to their formality that they can be easily recognized when repeated. Repetition and formality are therefore two qualities which are inherently linked (Stollberg-Rilinger, "Much Ado" 11).

Taking the opposition between activity and thinking at face value, some analysts refer to ritual activity as meaningless.[11] This position is particularly strong among political scientists who examine rituals in their field. Having alluded to the one-sided interpretation of rituals as meaningless decorum in the introduction, we may now return to this understanding. Murray Edelman, the most prominent representative of this position, heavily criticizes *The Symbolic Uses of Politics*. Referring to elections as "ritual acts" which "give people a chance to express discontents and enthusiasms, to enjoy a sense of involvement" (3), Edelman further argues that

> [r]itual is motor activity that involves its participants symbolically in a common enterprise, calling their attention to their relatedness and joint interests in a compelling way. It thereby both promotes conformity and evokes satisfaction and joy in conformity (16).

As Bell's interpretation suggested, it is in clear opposition to rational thinking that Edelman uses the term ritual here, even though he is aware that "without such [symbolic] device no polity can survive" (3). Edelman indeed writes from the position of a critical ritual observer when he wants to reveal the difference between political participation and politics as "a spectator sport" to the presumably mindless mass of participants (5). He argues that "real" politics, set in contrast to the ritual events people believe to be political, is what takes place behind closed doors, "a cool and successful effort to get money from others or power over them" (1). The presumably rational political process hence differs largely from *The Myth of the State* (Cassirer) that "large masses of men need to believe about the state to reassure themselves" (Edelman 2).[12]

---

11 Frits Staal famously summarized this idea in an article titled "The Meaninglessness of Ritual," noting that "[r]itual, then, is primarily activity. It is an activity governed by explicit rules. The important thing is what you do, not what you think, believe or say" (4).

12 The way Edelman describes the two-dimensionality of the political process is intended as an analogy to a theatre performance, with its visible stage and hidden back, including also the idea of a preliminary staging process that Bell and Althoff describe as "ritualization" (Althoff, *Die Macht der Rituale*; Bell, *Ritual Theory Ritual Practice*.) Modern day politics may then be likened to the Aristo-

In his critical account, Edelman ignores an eminent functional aspect of symbolism: the issue of political identification and integration by the means of symbolic communication.[13] This is mainly due to his singular interpretation of rituals as a means of stability and conformity in the hands of the political elite. Trying to balance this one-sided belief David I. Kertzer states that "[p]olitical power always requires visibility" (13). Thus:

> True, kings use ritual to shore up their authority, but revolutionaries use ritual to overthrow monarchs. The political elite employ ritual to legitimate their authority, but rebels battle back with rites of delegitimation. Ritual may be vital to reaction, but it is also the life blood of revolution (2).

In addition, Kertzer emphasizes the eminent role of participation in such societies in which it is impossible for the individual to personally know even a small part of the political community. Hence, "[t]hrough participation in the rites, the citizen of the modern state identifies with larger political forces that can only be seen in symbolic form" (ibid.).

In line with Kertzer's argument Barbara Stollberg-Rilinger wonders whether we are "deceiving ourselves" by believing that modern political communities "should not rest on images, symbols, and rituals that emotionally overpower people, but solely on words, good reasons, and rational procedures" ("Much Ado" 18ff.). Rather, political communities have been and still are constituted on the basis of *imagined* ties (Anderson, *Imagined Communities*). These ties draw from common traditions of the past, projecting them onto the present and thereby constructing a meaningful future (Kertzer 9f.). When successful in pursuing such a coherent message, these imagined ties construct a political identity that ensures a sense of *peoplehood* (cf. R. Smith).[14] In ritual studies the understanding of this singular, in-

---

telian theatre that disburdens its audience from conflicting emotions by means of a cathartic effect. It appears that Edelman envisions a "political performance" more epic in nature, raising the awareness of the audience to real conflicts of its own.

13 For an affirmative understanding of symbolic politics see Dörner, *Politischer Mythos*, and Göhler, "Politische Symbole."

14 This is essentially the view of the modernist school of thought in the study of nationalism, summarized by Rogers M. Smith in the following way: "No politi-

tegrative power of ritual has slowly replaced the image of ritual as merely an activity still dominant in the 1960s (Dücker 184).[15] In political science some analysts have yet to take this step.

In conclusion, ritual activity may be understood as a means to provide room for a society to (re)assure itself about its self-understanding, its common-sense that is represented in the symbols that are a constitutive element of rituals. It is here that "rituals generate the social and reduce differences" (Dücker 36). This collective act, finally, creates the image of the collective as a transcendent collective being *sui generis* – the society as Emile Durkheim imagined it (Esser 403).[16]

Considering that rituals are such a powerful tool, the question about how rituals are constructed becomes important. It is a particularly urgent question when considering political rituals. Illuminating the process of how rituals are made, Gert Althoff proposes to consider two sides to a ritual: the public side, which ritual studies most often concentrates on, as well as the hidden side, where *ritual designers* reflect on the meaning of a particular ritual.[17] Designing a ritual involves the strategic use of symbols. A state performing the role of a ritual designer is thus putting its symbolic capital to use (see Bourdieu).

Whether symbolic politics resembles an elitist "pseudo politics" (Meyer, *Inszenierung des Scheins* 55) or is rather aiming for the symbolic integration of pluralistic societies is an empirical question. A valid answer can only be found when analysts conduct their studies with an open mind.

---

cal people are natural or primordial. All are the products of long, conflict-ridden histories, and all must be understood as human creations, formed by participants in preexisting forms of peoplehood" (32). For an overview over the different answers to Ernest Renan's famous question "What is the nation?" see A. Smith, *Nationalism* 4.

15 On the integrative power of ritual in postmodern societies, see also Wulf and Zirfas.
16 Catherine Bell accentuates that the recognition of the functionality of rituals is a second common element in ritual studies (see Bell 20).
17 Studies that concentrate on the making of ritual are rare. The publications of Bell, and Althoff, must be considered the exception. See also the section on ritual design in the six-volume series *Ritual Dynamics and the Science of Ritual* (Ahn).

Meanwhile, an analysis that approaches its subject in a biased way, such as Edelman does, is itself ritualized since it frames the object of study so as to "limit experience, shut in desired themes or shut out intruding ones" (Douglas 63) as has been previously argued.

When considering the "intransitive" power of symbolic action such as ritual (see Göhler, "Macht"), political theory is also interested in narrative. It is recognized as a constitutive element of political myths, together with ritual performances and iconic condensations (Dörner, *Politischer Mythos* 76; Müller-Funk 103; Münkler, *Die Deutschen* 15). Rituals, as well as iconic condensations, aim for permanence, projecting the idea of *la longue durée* that conceals the constructive nature of myths (Münkler, *Die Deutschen* 22; A. Smith, "The Genealogy of Nations" 101). Narrative, in contrast, is believed to be open to alternation, preventing political myths from becoming dogmatic. Nonetheless, apart from this contrasting of formal ritual activity with open narrative, ritual studies shows only little concern for the distinct functioning of narrative.

2.2 Narrative

The study of narrative is based on a paradox. As "homo narrans" (Müller-Funk 19), we "make sense of the world and of our lives with a process of 'emplotting' or 'storyfication'" (Ryan, "On the Theoretical Foundations" 8). Hence, narrative refers to a basic human strategy similar to ritual activity.[18] Nevertheless, the term narrative in itself is inherently academic in nature (Ryan, "Toward a Definition" 32).

The study of narrative as a singular object of analysis is a rather recent development.[19] Following the "narrative turn in the humanities" (see Kreiswirth) *The Traveling Concept of Narrative* caught the attention of an ever larger number of rather different analysts, such as historians and social scientists, as well as lawyers and even medical scientists (see Hyvärinen, Korhonen, and Mykkänen). As a result of this interdisciplinary prominence, the meaning of the term narrative has been broadened and partly "diluted"

---

18 Bruner cites Victor Turner's persuasive account in which Turner holds that narrative begins in the context of communal rites (Bruner, *Making Stories* 95).

19 For an account of the development of narrative studies, see the articles by David Herman and Monika Fludernik.

(Ryan, "On the Theoretical Foundations" 3). The challenge for narrative theory or narratology now is to coin a definition that is independent from a particular medium, such as literature, in order to remain open to the diverse research in the field. Notwithstanding, the proposed definition also needs to be distinctive enough to delimit a singular research object. Emphasizing this, Marie-Laure Ryan underlines once more that:

> Assessing the narrative status of a text is not a cognitive question that we must consciously answer for proper understanding, but a theoretical question that enables narratologists to delimit the object of their discipline, to isolate the feature to their inquiry, and to stem the recent inflation of the term narrative ("Toward a Definition" 33).

Adopting the model of structuralist Gérard Genette, Porter Abbott proposes the following definition:

> Simply put, narrative is *the representation of an event or a series of events.* 'Events' is the key word here, though some people prefer the word 'action.' Without an event or an action, you may have a 'description,' an 'exposition,' an 'argument,' a 'lyric,' some combination of these or something else altogether, but you won't have a narrative (*Cambridge Introduction* 12).

In linguistic terms, narrative therefore constitutes the signifier while the communicated meaning of the event equals the signified (Ryan, "On the Theoretical Foundations" 4).

Concerning the nature of events that are conveyed, narratologists agree that narrative is rather concerned with the unexpected, with "some breach in the expected state of things – Aristotle's peripeteia" (Bruner, *Making Stories* 17). It is in these moments of contingency that storytelling provides the means to bring order back to chaos (Whitebrook 87). It is this ability "to construct reality" (see Bruner, "Narrative Construction") that indeed determines the eminence of narrative in the political context, the focus of this chapter:

> Hence narratives of peoplehood work essentially as persuasive historical stories that prompt people to embrace the valorized identities, play stirring roles, and have the fulfilling experiences that political leaders strive to evoke for them, whether through

arguments, rhetoric, symbols, or 'stories' of a more obvious and familiar sort (R. Smith 45).

Nonetheless, narrative should not singlehandedly be considered as a strategy to achieve stability and unity. Rather, political competitions fought by means of contesting stories instead of force may just as well end in "fragmentation" (Whitebrook 87).[20]

Narrative thus shares with ritual the status of a powerful instrument in constructing political identification. It is therefore equally important to pay attention to story making as a "technique" (Whitebrook 11) since "[w]e know in our bones that stories are *made*, not *found* in the world. But we can't resist doubting it" (Bruner, *Making Stories* 22). *Narration* as "the production of narrative" (Abbott, "Narration" 339) involves several elements: the *addresser*, the *addressee*, as well as the *message* (Duyfhuizen 377). The *message* captures both, the *story* and the *discourse*, and thus the events as well as the events as represented (Abbott, *Cambridge Introduction* 13). The difference between story and discourse is then determined by the perspective a narrative takes on the events it represents (Bruner, *Making Stories* 23; Whitebrook 133).

Following Seymour Chatman's communication model of narrative, the eminent narrative agents, addresser and addressee, can be further differentiated (see Chatman). The *addresser* hence consists of multiple identities: the real author, the implied author, as well as the narrator (Duyfhuizen 377). In the context of narrative theory, the actual author, as "the person who created a text" (Jannidis 33), is less important than the implied author and the narrator, the agent transmitting the narrative (Phelan/Booth 388).[21] The *addressee* comprises the audience of a text and hence "any receiver of a text, be it a reader, a viewer, or a listener" (Rabinowitz 29) and, more specifically, the narratee, "the audience to whom the narrator is addressing the narration" (30). Differentiation between these diverse agents may be especially helpful when considering political narrative. Here, the (real and implied) author and narrator very often will not be identical and the narratee may just as well vary from the multiple recipients of the text.

---

20 For an account of what constitutes a successful political story, see R. Smith 34ff.
21 Concerning "the death of the author," see the two influential essays by Roland Barthes and Michel Foucault.

The production, processing and reception of text by the various agents are independent processes that are highly affected by the *genre* under which a narrative is placed (Kearns 201). Categorization hence is a meaningful matter for the understanding and constructing of narrative. In order to ensure a successful communicative act between narrator and narratee, the perception of narrative as belonging to the same genre is essential. The application of codes, conventions and genre marks supports this transmission of narrative discourse (204). Also "the immediate context may cause a reader to pay more conscious attention to the conventions of genre" (ibid.). A narrative "told" in the wrong context may thus very well distract from the narrative discourse. This is particularly true of stories being told in the political context. It is here that telling a story within the wrong context may lead to unintended consequences. Imagine an election campaign. In order to raise a powerful base, a viable candidate must employ a narrative that reaches the largest possible voters' coalition. Nonetheless, the narrative may need particular framing to cater to such a heterogeneous audience. For example, when giving a speech to young voters, a politician might want to dress "appropriately" and the set-up on the stage will be different from other occasions. Meanwhile the general narrative, "I'm the right guy for the job," remains the same.[22]

What initially differentiates narrative from ritual is that narrative is considered as intrinsically bound to meaning, whereas ritual is oftentimes conceived of as meaningless activity, as has been argued previously. Nonetheless, ritual may also provide the "focus" or "frame" for narrative (Douglas 62). In line with Mary Douglas, David Kertzer argues that

> [s]uccessful ritual [...] creates an emotional state that makes the message uncontestable because it is framed in such a way as to be seen as inherent in the way things are. It presents a picture of the world that is so emotionally compelling that it is beyond debate. (101)

This assumption is highly relevant for the particular empirical example to be examined next. The speeches held at the commemoration services can

---

22 Election campaigns are the most obvious example for this. See Hammer, "The Role of Narrative" for an analysis of the success story of the Obama campaign in 2008.

now be identified as narrative performances (see Bauman). For this type of narrative, the ritual frame functions as an important link between past, present and future performance, establishing an "intertextual field" (420) that limits the various interpretations of narrative to the intended meaning.

3. THE COMMEMORATION SERVICES OF THE BUNDESWEHR

On the 29th of May in 2003, a soldier from the Bundeswehr was killed. He would be the first of 34 German soldiers who died in Afghanistan between the years 2003 and 2011, serving in the NATO mission ISAF.[23] Remembering these men, fifteen commemoration services were organized by the Bundeswehr, under the supervision of four different Secretaries of Defence. Along the way, the character of these services shifted from internal military events, committed to the commemoration of a specific group, the Bundeswehr, to political events which pay tribute to the sacrifice of fellow citizens. Accordingly, different locations were chosen, first military grounds and later on local churches. In addition, a changing audience was addressed, ranging from family members to comrades and the greater public. The narrative performance of each Secretary of Defence reflected these adaptations. Their perspective, as narrators, ranged from that of a representative of the military to the position of a political representative. The most significant alternation, nevertheless, can be detected in the different manner of speaking about the dead soldiers. While the first soldiers were remembered as *victims* of cruel attacks, the later soldiers' deaths were commemorated as *sacrifices* for the freedom and peace of their countrymen. To achieve this metamorphosis from military victims to political sacrifices, the legitimate cause for which these men gave their lives needed to be addressed in the speeches. Answering the question why the soldiers had died indeed provided the political community with an opportunity to reassure itself about its self-understanding. The ritual framework was equally indis-

---

23 Before the deployment to Afghanistan, only two German soldiers were killed in action. One soldier was killed in 1993 as part of the UNTAC mission in Cambodia, another during the UNIMOG mission to Georgia in 2001 (see Kümmel and Leonard).

pensable in executing this transformational rite de passage (see van Gennep).

To begin with, the rules and standards of the Bundeswehr (Zentrale Dienstvorschrift) contain a separate chapter on the actions to be taken in the case of a death of a member of the military which dates back to the year 1991. This chapter names the responsible persons to contact and the ceremonial measures to be taken, given the consent of the family members. The setting includes covering the coffin with the German flag and placing a combat helmet on the coffin's front-end. The coffin is also to be guarded by several soldiers in dress uniform. In addition, the song "I had a comrade" ["Ich hatte einen Kameraden"] is to be played at the end of the ceremony.[24]

The stated actions were all taken in the fifteen examined services, eleven of which took place in churches and four at airport bases. Photos of the deceased soldiers in uniform, as well as medals awarded to them, were additionally put on display. The services then took the following course of events: a formal declaration to the press preceded each event, announcing the place and time of the service and naming those officials who would be present. The tasks of all those present were clearly designated by a protocol. While the two military chaplains, one Protestant and one Catholic, would speak some comforting words, blessing the dead and leading people in prayer, a small number of soldiers, mainly comrades, would guard the coffins.[25] Functioning as witnesses, the family members, a large number of military personnel and politicians remained rather passive. They would only move when signalled to do so. The respective Secretaries of Defence were present at each service, but only spoke at twelve of the fifteen occasions.[26] At the end of the services, the national anthem would be played. Then the coffins would be carried outside to the cars waiting. Finally, the song "I had a comrade" would be played by a single trumpet player when the coffins reached the hearses.

---

24 For a historical account of the meaning of the song, see Zimmermann.
25 On the changing role of the military chaplaincy in Germany see Dörfler-Dierken, "The changing role."
26 See appendix for a complete list of all the speeches. All citations from the speeches are based on my own translations. The speeches are available in the archives of the Ministry of Defence.

At first sight, the services that took place at the military base differ only marginally from those services held in local churches. A closer look at the protocol nonetheless reveals that the religious and political segments alternated during the airport services. For example: at the service on May 23rd in 2007, a military chaplain spoke, followed by the Secretary of Defence, Franz Josef Jung. Subsequently a musical piece was played and only then did the chaplain lead in prayer.[27] In the churches, the program was clearly divided into one religious and one political part. While the chaplains spoke and led in prayer in the first half of the service, this religious segment was separated from the political speeches by a musical piece. Only then did the Secretary of State, as well as a local political representative, speak, followed by the national anthem and the moving of the coffins. This division between religious and political elements at the later services was intended to mirror and maintain the institutional separation of church and state.[28]

Nonetheless, while those responsible for the protocol concentrate on the formal sequencing of the events, they neglect the common symbolic dimension present during all of the fifteen services. These common symbols were: the flag covering the coffin, the combat helmet, the awarded medals, as well as the uniforms of the guarding soldiers, together with the pictures of the dead, in uniform as well. All but one of these symbols characterize the service as fundamentally military. The flag that is placed on each coffin is ostensibly not a military, but a political sign. It signifies the political community of which the soldier was also part. Indeed, the flag functions here as a symbolic link between the military, the political and the civil sphere. It may therefore be interpreted as a projection of the self-understanding of the Bundeswehr: as a parliamentary military [Parlamentsarmee], together with its soldiers who are conceived of as "citizens in uniform" (Bundeswehr 10).

---

27 This program is based on Thomas Elßner's protocol of the commemoration service at the airport in Cologne on 23rd of May 2007 (89).

28 At a conference on the subject of the commemoration rituals of the Bundeswehr on the 23rd of January 2012 in Bonn, an animated discussion concerning the question of whether military chaplains may sing along to the national anthem demonstrated that the military chaplaincy itself is very much interested in safeguarding its independence from the political and military elements of the services.

The coffin, helmets, the medals, the guards and the flag were still visible when the commemoration ritual moved into the church. In addition, a third category of symbols was now notably present. In the church, the coffins with the flag were placed in the altar room, under the cross. All those speaking, including the Secretary of Defence, now spoke from behind the pulpit. And while those four services held on military ground brought together mainly military personnel, the services in the church were attended by a more diverse group of people. Together with local citizens, who were now allowed into the churches, numerous, even high-ranking, political representatives came as well. Chancellor Angela Merkel, for example, attended each one of the four services organized by Secretary of Defence Karl Theodor zu Guttenberg and even spoke herself on one occasion.

The speeches from the Secretaries of Defence reflect an awareness of the different possible framings of the ritual as military, political and civil events. Especially when analysing the addressed audiences, this becomes clear. In the beginning of the speeches, those directly present at the services are named, first the family members, followed by political representatives in hierarchical order. These attendees must thus be recognized as the narratees. Nevertheless, as narrators, the Secretaries also reached out to a wider audience. Their multiple affiliations as Commanders of the armed forces, as well as members of the federal cabinet, but also as citizens made it possible for them to address a variety of recipients. Secretary of Defence zu Guttenberg reflected this idea of multiple membership in one of his speeches when saying that:

Nothing in the world makes one more speechless than death. And nothing would be more inappropriate for the private man Karl Theodor zu Guttenberg than finding words to address the deaths of the four fallen soldiers. Words which do not comfort, but words which must be found since I am personally responsible, as Secretary of Defence, as a member of the government and as a parliamentarian, for your grief (zu Guttenberg 04/24/2010).[29]

Another example can be found in a speech by Franz Josef Jung: "Today we bid farewell. We bid farewell from the son, the brother, the friend and the

---

29 All quotations from the speeches are translations based on the official protocols of the Ministry of Defence.

comrade" (Jung 07/02/2009). Nonetheless, not all of the Secretaries made use of this variety of affiliations in their speeches. Consider for example a quote by Peter Struck, who was the first Secretary of State to speak at a commemoration service for a soldier who died in Afghanistan. At the service, Struck clearly spoke from the position of the Commander of the Armed Forces when saying: "This stroke of fate hit *us* all hard. The *members of the armed forces* mourn their comrades" (Struck 06/10/2003). His addressed audience, the narratee, is then reduced to members of the Bundeswehr, indeed the only group of people present at the airport area in Cologne apart from the soldiers' family members.

The first services thus provided room for the Bundeswehr to revive its feeling of commitment, with members of the German military present and the Commander of the Armed Forces speaking. However, in order to make use of such rituals as moments of political peoplehood, the inclusion of the general public was necessary. Its participation was made possible by broadcasting the services on TV so that a broader audience could be "present." Nevertheless, the speakers also had to acknowledge this "implied reader" in their speeches. An exemplary citation from a speech by zu Guttenberg demonstrates what is meant by this: "They lost their lives when they were on duty and because they were on duty in the name of their fatherland, the federal German Republic, because they bravely served in our name and for us, in Afghanistan" (zu Guttenberg 04/09/2010). The "us" then signifies a political community that is made aware of its presence at the ritual only through these words. Indeed through Guttenberg's pronouncement it is (re)constructed. In commemorating "their dead," the "imagined" community comes alive, as another citation by Karl Theodor zu Guttenberg further emphasizes:

We carry the memory of many encounters, of the time spent together, a smile and some gentle touch – and this may not only mean an actual touch, but also a touch of the soul. The appreciation of his brave and courageous commitment is a part of this because he who lives in the memory of his loved ones lives on and is not dead. Gone and dead are only those who are forgotten. (zu Guttenberg 10/15/2010)

In order to achieve this common bond between the present family members, the military affiliates and the broader public, the narrator must also talk about the life of the soldier who died in a way that is relatable to those people in the (actual and virtual) audience who may have never met this person. The narrative discourse thus changes. In the earlier speeches, the speakers singularly treat the professional life of the deceased and leave out any biographical details, such as the day and place of birth. Their speeches thus echo the tone of a job description when they speak about the soldier. As an example, consider this citation:

Mischa Meier joined the 261st division of the Bundeswehr in Lebach in 1999 and was trained to become a paratrooper. Later he was promoted to the position of group leader of the 263rd division. His career was a success. Only four weeks ago he received his appointment as a professional soldier ('Berufssoldat'). He was a fun-loving and happy person and he was an enthusiastic soldier. (Jung 09/01/2008)

The following quotation from one of the later speeches stands in stark contrast to this:

Georg Kurat was born on the 5th of March 1989 in Munich. In one week he would have turned 22. Having finished school, he completed his training as a mechanic. On the 1st of July in 2009 he joined the 112th division of the Bundeswehr in Regen. Georg Kurat worked hard to advance in his career. He decided to become a professional soldier because he wanted to help. Last year in October, he joined the mission abroad together with his comrades. He believed in the commitment to enable the people of Afghanistan to live a life of peace and freedom. His most urgent wish to move into an apartment with his partner after his return will now remain unfulfilled. His friends and his comrades, his parents describe Georg Kurat as a passionate sportsman, as a motivated young man, who met the people around him with an open heart. We miss him. (zu Guttenberg 02/25/2011)

Here the speaker Karl Theodor zu Guttenberg replicates the picture of a fellow man and not that of a comrade. Referring to significant stages in the life of the dead, e.g. his day of birth and his educational record, his speech is phrased in a fashion more common to civil funerals. The virtuous manner in which he describes the professional ethos of the dead soldier, his "wanting to help" to "enable the people of Afghanistan to live a life of peace and freedom" is a part of this.

Pertaining to the transformational aspect in the rituals, a further aspect in the narrative performance is decisive. In 2008, at the second funeral service to take place in a church, Secretary of Defence Franz Josef Jung uttered the following consequential words: "I bow before you with great thankfulness and appreciation for the dead who fell for our country in a mission for peace. May Patrick Behlke and Roman Schmidt rest in peace" (Jung 10/24/2008). Following his remark, the term "fallen soldier" was to be permanently used for soldiers who died in battle.

Nevertheless, the usage of the term "fallen soldier" is rather ambiguous. In the German context the term "Gefallener" is historically linked to the haunting crimes of the national socialist rule and has therefore been "disavowed" (Münkler, *Die Deutschen* 19). Furthermore, in international law to fall as a soldier means that a combatant dies in a war. Now, according to the German government, the Federal Republic of Germany is fighting a "non-international, armed conflict" in Afghanistan and not a war (Bundesregierung 11). Nonetheless, the term also carries another symbolic meaning in reference to which it is being used at the services.[30] Categorizing those soldiers who died from an extraneous cause ("durch Fremdeinwirkung") as fallen establishes a symbolical link between this singular group of past, present and future soldiers. Recognizing a soldier as "fallen" sets him apart and hereby sacralizes him (Mol 5). An "internal hierarchy" (see Münkler, "Semantische Frontbereinigung") is thus instituted between those dead that are recognized as *sacrifices*, while others represent profane *victims* (Münkler, "Militärisches Totengedenken" 30). The term sacrifice carries various meanings: etymologically, the German term "Opfer," which fails to voice the difference between sacrifice and victim, refers to a gift (see Münkler and Fischer). The Latin "sacrificium," on the other hand, draws from the words "sacer," holy, and "facere," to make (Carter 2). Furthermore, while we *passively* fall victim *to* something, we *actively* sacrifice our lives *for* something.

Through ritual the community in whose name the sacrifice was made must now come together and bear witness to this selfless act. It is in this sense that the commemoration rituals examined here constitute *a rite of passage* (see van Gennep). In the same speech in which Secretary of Defence Franz Josef Jung used the term "fallen soldier" for the first time, he also raised the following question: "why do we send our soldiers on the dif-

---

30 For a critical analysis of the term "fallen soldier" see Dörfler-Dierken, "Identitätspolitik der Bundeswehr."

ficult mission to Afghanistan? Why do we send them into harm's way? You, the family members, the comrades, but also the citizens of our country deserve an answer" (Jung 10/24/2008). He went on to provide the following answer: "Our commitment in Afghanistan is necessary in the interest of the security of our country" (ibid.). The deixis used in this citation is of great interest. Considering the first sentences, a communicative act is constructed between a third-person plural, "*we* send *our* soldiers," and a second person plural, "*you*, the family members, the comrades, but also the citizens of our country." Thus, *we* have to answer *your* question. In this context, the "we" can only refer to the members of the German parliament, who command the German military to act by means of a legislative action.

As political representatives, parliamentarians indeed answer to the questions of those represented at the ceremony, including the soldiers and their family members. With the final inclusive phrase "the citizens of *our* country," the speaker hence comes full circle as he now addresses every single member of the community. By referring to the representatives and the represented, the speaker, Secretary of Defence Jung, thus constructs an imaginary communication between the different members of the political community, which in addition serves as a moment to re-identify as a meaningful whole. Continuing his speech, Jung purposefully reminds the political community of the spirit of its founding document:

This spirit is described in the preamble of our basic law [Grundgesetz] which states, I quote: 'Acknowledging its responsibility before God and all humans, animated by the will to serve as an equal member in a united Europe to bring peace to the world'. (Jung 10/24/2008)

Secretary of Defence Thomas de Maizière follows a similar strategy when voicing his answer to the question for which cause the soldier gave his life:

He was a soldier – with all his might and with his whole heart. He was brave and he was courageous. He had taken an oath to loyally serve the Federal Republic of Germany and to defend its justice and peace. No one but soldiers take this oath and we ask of no one but soldiers to take it. He was willing to give everything: to give his own life. (De Maizière 06/10/2011)

Again, the picture of the "brave" soldier is linked to that of the virtuous citizen who fulfils the promise he gave to his country. The professional aspect of being a soldier is completely absent here. Thus, instead of grouping soldiers together with other occupations that involve a high risk, such as police- or firemen, the death of a soldier is set apart from such victims. His sacrifice is the result of a soldier's singular commitment.

Finally, through these services, the political community is also given a future task: to commemorate their dead. A promise is therefore delivered: "They gave their lives. We will not forget them. We will honor them in our memory" (De Maizière 06/03/2011). This duty is voiced in each of the speeches. It gains credibility when it is made in the name of the broader public and in a church, with the narrator speaking from behind the pulpit and in front of the altar, in the presence of symbols which represent a force that transcends the political community. It is this symbolic cosmos that Secretary of Defence zu Guttenberg makes visible when he says:

And so I ask everyone here in this church, but also in the rest of the country: Maintain the given meaning of the lost lives of these four soldiers. The meaning which is summarized in the oath they took as soldiers, but which is also present in the oath of the political representatives responsible for them. May God be with them and may God be with us. (zu Guttenberg 04/24/2010)

4. Conclusion

The preliminary interpretative schemas we bring to the analysis of a particular empirical example frame our experience of "what it is that is going on." As political scientists we tend to be sceptical of symbolic actions in the political sphere, searching for the "real" power politics we have grown accustomed to seeing. As professional analysts of ritual, we focus on formalized activity that we value as an integrative measure for a group that is assembling in the presence of its sacred symbols. Finally, as narratologists, we listen to the stories being told to bring back order into a world that has been disrupted by some sudden event.

The chosen example of the commemoration services of the Bundeswehr can be interpreted through all of these frames. It can be framed as an example of decorative symbolism that leads the attention away from the true political arena, where the actual actions are taken that lead to the deployment of a military and thus to the killing of soldiers. The services can also be recognized as mourning rituals which follow the formal structure of such events, commemorating the dead in the presence of family members and friends. And indeed, the stories being told at the events do try to make sense of a sudden rupture in the lives of the families left behind, the death of a loved one.

All of these frames constitute unique ways to see these particular events. Nonetheless, it is also possible to broaden each frame and thereby construct an interdisciplinary schema that is able to teach us more about this particular experience. Using the insights of ritual studies and narratology, as political scientists we might begin to consider these events as meaningful opportunities that may stabilize or disintegrate a community through symbolic measures which are urgently needed in times of crisis. The death of a fellow man constitutes such a state of emergency. The death of a soldier in a post-heroic society may not be legitimated without such symbolism (see Münkler, *Die neuen Kriege*). Accordingly, the services administered by the German Bundeswehr may not represent historical artefacts, but the symbolic complementation of the rational decision-making process taking place elsewhere.

Apart from this, the combined effort to consider ritual and narrative as inherently linked is also profitable in the context of ritual studies and narratology. As the example of the speeches made by the various Secretaries of Defence proves, paying closer attention to the framing of a narrative through a certain kind of ritual opens up new meaningful interpretations of the stories told. In addition, considering narrative as an independent component of ritual, with its own rules and meanings, increases our chances of understanding the formal activity at hand as meaningful.

Appendix

Fallen soldiers in the Bundeswehr 2003 – 2011

Number of fallen soldiers	Day and place of service	Speech by Secretary of Defence
2003		
1	No record of an official service available	-
4	06/10/2003 Cologne Airport	Peter Struck
2005		
2	06/29/2005 Cologne Airport	-
1	11/16/2005 Cologne Airport	-
2007		
3	05/23/2007 Cologne Airport	Franz Josef Jung
2008		
1	09/01/2008 Church in Zweibrücken	Franz Josef Jung
2	10/24/2008 Church in Zweibrücken	Franz Josef Jung
2009		
1	05/07/2009 Church in Bad Saulgau	Franz Josef Jung
3	07/02/2009 Church in Bad Salzungen	Franz Josef Jung
1	10/12/2009 Church in Fulda	Franz Josef Jung
2010		
3	04/09/2010 Church in Selsingen	Karl Theodor zu Guttenberg Angela Merkel
4	04/24/2010 Church in Ingolstadt	Karl Theodor zu Guttenberg
1	10/15/2010 Church in Selsingen	Karl Theodor zu Guttenberg
2011		
3	02/25/2011 Church in Regen	Karl Theodor zu Guttenberg
3	06/03/2011 Church in Hannover	Thomas de Maizière
1	06/10/2011 Church in Detmold	Thomas de Maizière
34 in total		

Speeches by German Secretaries of Defence

Struck, Peter, 06/10/2003, Köln/Wahn. Available upon request at the German Ministry of Defence.
Jung, Franz Josef, 05/23/2007, Köln/Wahn. Available at: www.bmvg.de (last access: 07/19/2012).
Jung, Franz Josef, 09/01/2008, Zweibrücken. Available upon request at the German Ministry of Defence.
Jung, Franz Josef, 10/24/2008, Zweibrücken. Available upon request at the German Ministry of Defence.
Jung, Franz Josef, 05/07/2009, Bad Saulgau. Available upon request at the German Ministry of Defence.
Jung, Franz Josef, 07/02/2009, Bad Salzungen. Available at: www.bmvg.de (last access: 07/19/2012).
Jung, Franz Josef, 10/12/2009, Fulda. Available at: www.bmvg.de (last access: 07/19/2012).
zu Guttenberg, Karl Theodor, 04/09/2010, Selsingen. Available upon request at the German Ministry of Defence.
zu Guttenberg, Karl Theodor, 04/24/2010, Ingolstadt. Available upon request at the German Ministry of Defence.
zu Guttenberg, Karl Theodor, 10/15/2010, Selsingen. Available upon request at the German Ministry of Defence.
zu Guttenberg, Karl Theodor, 02/25/2011, Regen. Available at: www.bmvg.de (last access: 07/19/2012).
De Maizière, Thomas, 06/03/2011, Hannover. Available at: www.bmvg.de (last access 07/19/2012).
De Maizière, Thomas, 06/10/2011, Detmold. Available at: www.bmvg.de (last access 07/19/2012).

REFERENCES

Abbott, Porter. *A Cambridge Introduction to Narrative*. Cambridge: Cambridge UP, 2003.
—. "Narration." *Routledge Encyclopedia of Narrative Theory*. Eds. David Herman, Manfred Jahn and Marie-Laure Ryan. London/New York: Routledge, 2005. 339-344.

Ahn, Gregor, ed. *Ritual Design*. Section IV of *Reflexivity, Media and Visuality*. Vol. VI, *Ritual Dynamics and the Science of Ritual*. Wiesbaden: Harrassowitz Verlag, 2010.

Althoff, Gert. *Die Macht der Rituale. Symbolik und Herrschaft im Mittelalter*. Darmstadt: Wissenschaftliche Buchgesellschaft, 2003.

Anderson, Benedict. *Imagined Communities: Reflections on the Origin and Spread of Nationalism*. London: Verso, 2003.

Bauman, Richard. "Performance." *Routledge Encyclopedia of Narrative Theory*. Eds. David Herman, Manfred Jahn and Marie-Laure Ryan. London/New York: Routledge, 2005. 419-421.

Bell, Catherine. *Ritual Theory, Ritual Practice*. New York: Oxford UP, 1992.

Bellinger, Andrèa and David J. Krieger, eds. *Ritualtheorien. Ein einführendes Handbuch*. 4th ed. Wiesbaden: VS Verlag, 2008.

Berger, Bennett M. Foreword. *Frame-Analysis: An Essay on the Organization of Experience*. By Erving Goffman. Boston: Northeastern UP, 1986. xi-xviii.

Bourdieu, Pierre. *Praktische Vernunft. Zur Theorie des Handelns*. Frankfurt: Suhrkamp, 1985.

Bruner, Jerome. "The Narrative Construction of Reality." *Critical Inquiry* 18 (1991): 1-21.

—. *Making Stories: Law, Literature, Life*. Cambridge: Harvard UP, 2002.

Bundesregierung. *Fragen- und Antwortenkatalog zu Afghanistan. Stand 2011*. <http://www.bundesregierung.de/Content/DE/Artikel/Afghanistan/FragenAntworten/2010-06-08-faq-afghanistan.html>.

Bundeswehr. *ZDv 10/1 Innere Führung. Selbstverständnis der Bundeswehr*. 2008.

Carter, Jeffrey. *Understanding Religious Sacrifice: A Reader*. London: Continuum, 2003.

Cassirer, Ernst. *The Myth of the State*. New Haven: Yale UP, 1946.

Chatman, Seymour. *Story and Discourse: Narrative Structure in Fiction and Film*. Ithaca, NY: Cornell UP, 1978.

Dörfler-Dierken, Angelika. "Identitätspolitik der Bundeswehr." *Identität, Selbstverständnis, Berufsbild: Implikationen der neuen Einsatzrealität für die Bundeswehr*. Eds. Angelika Dörfler-Dierken and Gerhard

Kümmel. Schriftenreihe des Sozialwissenschaftlichen Instituts der Bundeswehr 10. Wiesbaden: VS-Verlag, 2010. 137-160.

—. "The Changing Role of Protestant Military Chaplaincy in Germany: From Raising Military Morale to Praying for Peace." *Religion, State and Society* 39.1 (2011): 79-91.

Dörner, Andreas. *Politischer Mythos und symbolische Politik: Sinnstiftung durch symbolische Politik am Beispiel des Hermannsmythos.* Opladen: Westdeutscher Verlag, 1995.

—. *Politainment. Politik in der medialen Erlebnisgesellschaft.* Frankfurt a.M.: Suhrkamp, 2010.

Dörner, Andreas and Ludgera Vogt, eds. *Wahlkämpfe. Betrachtungen über ein demokratisches Ritual.* Frankfurt a.M.: Suhrkamp, 2002.

Douglas, Mary. *Purity and Danger: An Analysis of the Concepts of Pollution and Taboo.* London: Routledge, 1966.

Dücker, Bernhard. *Rituale. Formen – Funktionen – Geschichte. Eine Einführung in die Ritualwissenschaft.* Stuttgart: Metzler, 2007.

Durkheim, Emile. *The Elementary Forms of Religious Life.* Oxford: Oxford UP, 2001 [1912].

Duyfhuizen, Bernhard. "Narrative Transmission." *Routledge Encyclopedia of Narrative Theory.* Eds. David Herman, Manfred Jahn and Marie-Laure Ryan. London/New York: Routledge, 2005. 377.

Edelman, Murray. *The Symbolic Uses of Politics.* Urbana and Chicago, IL: U of Illinois P, 1985.

Elßner, Thomas. "Der Tod kennt keine Uniform." *Bedingt erinnerungsbereit. Soldatengedenken in der Bundesrepublik.* Eds. Manfred Hettling and Jörg Echternkamp. Göttingen: Vandenhoeck & Ruprecht, 2008. 85-96.

Esser, Harmut. *Soziologie. Allgemeine Grundlagen.* Frankfurt a. M.: Campus, 1996.

Fludernik, Monika. "Histories of Narrative Theory (II): From Structuralism to the Present." *A Companion to Narrative Theory.* Eds. James Phelan and Peter J. Rabinowitz. Malden, MA: Blackwell, 2005. 36-59.

Göhler, Gerhard. "Rationalität und Symbolizität der Politik." *Politische Theorie – heute.* Eds. Michael Th. Greven and Rainer Schmalz-Bruns. Baden-Baden: Nomos, 1999. 255-274.

—. "Politische Symbole – symbolische Politik." *Politik und Bedeutung: Studien zu den kulturellen Grundlagen politischen Handelns und politi-*

scher Institutionen. Eds. Werner Rossade, Birgit Sauer and Dietmar Schirmer. Wiesbaden: Westdeutscher Verlag, 2002. 27-42.

—. "Macht." *Politische Theorie: 25 umkämpfte Begriffe zur Einführung*. Eds. Gerhard Göhler, Matthias Iser and Ina Kerner. Wiesbaden: VS Verlag, 2011. 224-240.

Goffman, Erving. *Frame-Analysis: An Essay on the Organization of Experience*. Boston: Northeastern UP, 1986.

Grimes, Ronald R. "Ritual Studies." *The Encyclopedia of Religion*. Ed. Mircea Eliade. Vol. 11. New York: MacMillan, 1987. 422-425.

—. *Beginnings in Ritual Studies*. Columbia, SC: U of South Carolina P, 1995.

Hammer, Stefanie. "The Role of Narrative in Political Campaigning: An Analysis of Speeches by Barack Obama." *National Identities* 12.3 (2010): 269-290.

Hammer, Stefanie and Maik Herold. "Zivilreligion in Deutschland? Transzendenz und Gemeinsinnsstiftung in den Trauerritualen der Bundeswehr." *Politik und Religion im vereinigten Deutschland. Beiträge zu Problemen von Säkularisierung und kulturellem Pluralismus*. Eds. Gert Pickel and Oliver Hildalgo. Wiesbaden: VS-Verlag, 2012. 99-128.

Herman, David. "Histories of Narrative Theory (I): A Genealogy of Early Developments." *A Companion to Narrative Theory*. Eds. James Phelan and Peter J. Rabinowitz. Malden, MA: Blackwell, 2005. 19-35.

Hyvärinen, Matti, Anu Korhonen and Juri Mykkänen, eds. *The Traveling Concept of Narrative*. Helsinki: Collegium, 2006.

Jannidis, Fotis. "Author." *Routledge Encyclopedia of Narrative Theory*. Eds. David Herman, Manfred Jahn and Marie-Laure Ryan. London/New York: Routledge, 2005. 33-34.

Kearns, Michael. "Genre Theory in Narrative Studies." *Routledge Encyclopedia of Narrative Theory*. Eds. David Herman, Manfred Jahn and Marie-Laure Ryan. London/New York: Routledge, 2005. 201-205.

Kertzer, David I. *Ritual, Politics and Power*. New Haven, CT: Yale UP, 1988.

Kreiswirth, Martin. "Narrative Turn in Humanities." *Routledge Encyclopedia of Narrative Theory*. Eds. David Herman, Manfred Jahn and Marie-Laure Ryan. London/New York: Routledge, 2005. 377-382.

Kümmel, Gerhard and Nina Leonhard. "Death, the Military and Society. Casualties and Civil-Military Relations in Germany." SOWI Arbeitspapier 140. Strausberg, 2005.

Meyer, Thomas. *Die Inszenierung des Scheins. Voraussetzungen und Folgen symbolischer Politik.* Frankfurt a.M.: Suhrkamp, 1992.

—. *Politik als Theater: die neue Macht der Darstellungskunst.* Berlin: Aufbau-Verlag, 1998.

Michaels, Axel. "Inflation der Rituale?" *Humanismus aktuell* 7.13 (2003): 25-36.

—. "Dynamik von Ritualkomplexen." *Forum Ritualdynamik* 3 (2003): 1-12.

Mol, Hans. *Identity and the Sacred.* New York: The Free Press, 1976.

Müller-Funk, Wolfgang. *Die Kultur und ihre Narrative.* Wien: Springer, 2008.

Münkler, Herfried. *Die neuen Kriege.* Reinbek: Rowohlt, 2002.

—. "Militärisches Totengedenken in der postheroischen Gesellschaft." *Bedingt erinnerungsbereit. Soldatengedenken in der Bundesrepublik.* Eds. Manfred Hettling and Jörg Echternkamp. Göttingen: Vandenhoeck & Ruprecht, 2008. 22-30.

—. *Die Deutschen und ihre Mythen.* Berlin: Rowohlt, 2009.

—. "Semantische Frontbereinigung. Politologe kommentiert zu Guttenbergs neuen Umgang mit dem Kriegsbegriff." Interview with the *Deutschlandradio*, 04/09/2010.

Münkler, Herfried and Karsten Fischer. "'Nothing to Kill or Die for...' – Überlegungen zu einer politischen Theorie des Opfers." *Leviathan* 28.3 (2000): 343-363.

Phelan, James and Wayne C. Booth. "Narrator." *Routledge Encyclopedia of Narrative Theory.* Eds. David Herman, Manfred Jahn and Marie-Laure Ryan. London/New York: Routledge, 2005. 388-392.

Rabinowitz, Peter J. "Audience." *Routledge Encyclopedia of Narrative Theory.* Eds. David Herman, Manfred Jahn and Marie-Laure Ryan. London/ New York: Routledge, 2005. 29-31.

Rappaport, Roy A. *Ritual and Religion in the Making of Humanity.* Cambridge: Cambridge UP, 1999.

Ryan, Marie-Laure. "On the Theoretical Foundations of Transmedial Narratology." *Narratology Beyond Literary Criticism.* Ed. Jan Christoph Meister. Berlin: De Gruyter, 2005. 1-23.

—. "Toward a Definition of Narrative." *The Cambridge Companion to Narrative*. Ed. David Herman. Cambridge: Cambridge UP, 2007. 22-38.

Smith, Anthony. *Nationalism: Theory, Ideology, History*. Cambridge: Polity, 2004.

—. "The Genealogy of Nations: An Ethno-Symbolic Approach." *When is the Nation? Towards an Understanding of Theories of Nationalism*. Eds. Atsuko Ichijo and Gordana Uzelac. London: Routledge, 2005. 94-122.

Smith, Rogers M. *Stories of Peoplehood: The Policies and Morals of Political Membership*. Cambridge: Cambridge UP, 2003.

Staal, Frits. "The Meaninglessness of Ritual." *Numen* 26.1 (1979): 2-22.

Stollberg-Rilinger, Barbara. "Knien vor Gott – Knien vor dem Kaiser. Zum Ritualwandel im Konfessionskonflikt." *Zeichen – Rituale – Werte. Internationales Kolloquium des Sonderforschungsbereichs 496 an der Westfälischen Wilhelms-Universität Münster*. Ed. Gert Althoff. Münster: Rhema, 2004. 501-534.

—. "Much Ado about Nothing? Rituals of Politics in Early Modern Europe and Today." *Bulletin of the German Historical Institute* 48 (2011): 9-24.

Van Gennep, Arnold. *The Rites of Passage*. London: Routledge, 1960.

Whitebrook, Maureen. *Identity, Narrative and Politics*. London: Routledge, 2001.

Wulf, Christoph and Jörg Zirfas. *Die Kultur des Rituals*. München: Fink, 2004.

Zimmermann, Harm-Peter. "Der gute Kamerad. Militärischer Totenkult in freiheitlicher Absicht." *Tod und Trauer. Todeswahrnehmung und Trauerriten in Nordeuropa*. Eds. Thorsten Fischer and Thomas Riis. Kiel: Ludwig, 2006. 248-260.

Notes on Contributors

Ahn, Gregor is Professor of Religious Studies at Heidelberg University. His main research focus is – beside Old Iranian history – on contemporary religions and theoretical approaches on the history of religions. He has also published various articles on ritual theory, especially ritual design.

Hammer, Stefanie, M.A., teaches political theory at the University of Erfurt. Her research concentrates on the multifaceted relationship between religion and politics. Recent publications include "Zivilreligion in Deutschland? Transzendenz und Gemeinsinnsstiftung in den Trauerritualen der Bundeswehr" (with Maik Herold, 2013) and *Variationen der Macht* (ed. with André Brodocz, 2013).

Johannsen, Dirk is Associate Professor in the Cultural History of Popular Religion at the Department of Culture Studies and Oriental Languages (IKOS), University of Oslo. His research interests include popular religion, the Scandinavian history of religions and cognitive cultural studies. Recent publications include "No Time to Philosophize. Norwegian Oral Tradition and the Cognitive Economics of Belief" (2011) and *Konstruktionsgeschichten. Narrationsbezogene Ansätze in der Religionsforschung* (ed. with Gabriela Brahier, 2013).

Meyer, Scarlett was a student assistant with the Heidelberg Collaborative Research Centre 619 "Ritual Dynamics" and recently graduated from Ruprecht-Karls-Universität Heidelberg with a teacher's degree in English and German literature and linguistics.

Nünning, Ansgar is Professor of English and American Literature and Cultural Studies at Justus-Liebig-University in Giessen. He is the founding and managing director of the "Giessener Graduiertenzentrum Kulturwissenschaften" (GGK), established in 2001, of the "International Graduate Centre for the Study of Culture" (GCSC), funded by the Excellence Initiative and inaugurated in 2006, and of the European PhD Network "Literary and Cultural Studies." He has published widely on English and American literature, cultures of memory, narratology, and literary and cultural theory, including 15 monographs and more than 200 scholarly articles in refereed journals and collections of essays. His narratological publications include *Cultural Ways of Worldmaking: Media and Narratives* (ed. with Vera Nünning and Birgit Neumann, 2010), *An Introduction to the Study of Narrative Fiction* (with Birgit Neumann, 2008), *Erzähltextanalyse und Gender Studies* (co-edited with Vera Nünning, 2004), two volumes on new approaches in postclassical narratology, including transgeneric, intermedial and interdisciplinary narrative theory (co-edited with Vera Nünning, 2002), two collections of articles on unreliable narration and multiperspectival narration (1998, 2000), as well as numerous articles on narratological approaches and concepts, e.g. unreliable narration, the implied author, multiperspectivity, description, and meta-narration, and an issue on "Recent Trends in Narratology" of the peer-reviewed journal *GRM: Germanisch-Romanische-Monatsschrift* (2013).

Nünning, Vera is Professor of English Philology at the English Department of Heidelberg University. She has published widely on English literature and culture from the 18th to the 21st century as well as on narrative and cultural theory. Recent publications include *Methoden der literatur- und kulturwissenschaftlichen Textanalyse* (ed. with Ansgar Nünning, 2010), *Cultural Ways of Worldmaking: Media and Narratives* (ed. with Ansgar Nünning and Birgit Neumann, 2010), and *New Approaches to Narrative: Cognition – Culture – History* (ed., 2013). She has been Fellow at the Marsilius-Kolleg at the University of Heidelberg as well as at the Johannes Gutenberg Research College at the University of Mainz.

Rupp, Jan is a postdoctoral research assistant at the English Department of Heidelberg University. He is currently working on literary representations of ritual in English modernism for his second book (habilitation). His publications include *Genre and Cultural Memory in Black British Literature* (2010) and *Medialisierung des Erzählens im englischsprachigen Roman der Gegenwart* (ed. with Ansgar Nünning, 2011).

Ryan, Marie-Laure is an independent scholar based in Colorado. She is the author of *Possible Worlds, Artificial Intelligence and Narrative Theory* (1991), *Narrative as Virtual Reality: Immersion and Interactivity in Literature and Electronic Media* (2001), and *Avatars of Story* (2006). She has also edited *Cyberspace Textuality: Computer Technology and Literary Theory* (1999), *Narrative Across Media: The Languages of Storytelling* (2004), *Intermediality and Storytelling* with Marina Grishakova (2010), and the *Routledge Encyclopedia of Narrative* with David Herman and Manfred Jahn (2005). Two more edited books are forthcoming in 2014: *Storyworlds Across Media*, co-edited with Jan-Noël Thon, and *The Johns Hopkins Guidebook to Digital Humanities*, co-edited with Lori Emerson and Ben Robertson. She has been Scholar in Residence at the University of Colorado, Boulder, and Johannes Gutenberg Fellow at the University of Mainz, Germany. Her website is at http://users.frii.com/mlryan/.

Schörner, Günther is Professor of Classical Archaeology at the University of Vienna, Austria. His research interests include rituals and their visualisation in the Roman Empire, material culture studies and culture contact studies. He is the author of *Votive im römischen Griechenland* (2003) and editor of *Romanisierung – Romanisation* (2005) and *Medien religiöser Kommunikation* (2008). He carries out fieldwork in Germany, Italy and Turkey.

Sommer, Roy is Professor of English at the University of Wuppertal, Germany, where he is a member of the interdisciplinary Center for Narrative Research and a co-editor of the Center's electronic journal, *DIEGESIS*. He also serves as the director of Wuppertal's Center for Graduate Studies. His research interests are multicultural and postcolonial fiction, comedy and narrative theory. Recent publications include a collection of essays, *Narratology in the Age of Cross-Disciplinary Narrative Research*, edited with Sandra Heinen (2009), and a book on the history and poetics of British comedy (*Von Shakespeare bis Monty Python*, 2012). His website is at www.storysharing.uni-wuppertal.de.

Vette, Joachim, Dr. theol., taught Old Testament studies for many years at the University of Heidelberg. He now leads the Ecumenical Institute for continuing education in Mannheim. His research interests include Old Testament narrative and the reception history of the Psalter.